Water AND THE Word

Baptism and the Education of
the Clergy in the Carolingian Empire

VOLUME I

PUBLICATIONS IN MEDIEVAL STUDIES

The Medieval Institute
University of Notre Dame

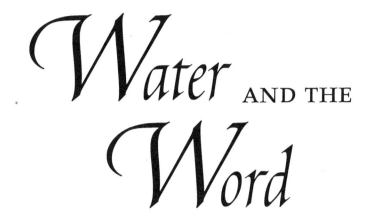

Water AND THE Word

Baptism and the Education of
the Clergy in the Carolingian Empire

VOLUME I

A Study of Texts and Manuscripts

S U S A N   A .   K E E F E

UNIVERSITY OF NOTRE DAME PRESS
Notre Dame, Indiana

Manufactured in the United States of America

A record of the Library of Congress Cataloging-in-Publication Data
is available upon request from the Library of Congress.

ISBN 0-268-01965-7

This book is printed on recycled paper.

Optimo magistro et
dilectissimo amico
Roger E. Reynolds

Contents

VOLUME I

VOLUME II

Acknowledgments

This study is a much-revised and expanded version of a doctoral dissertation submitted to the Centre for Medieval Studies of the University of Toronto in 1981. I owe this book's inspiration, guidance, and completion to my friends at Toronto. I wish to thank Professor Arnold Angenendt for my initial interest in baptism in the Carolingian period. To Father Leonard Boyle I will always be deeply grateful for introducing me to the world of manuscripts. His reverence for books and his instruction in paleography led to the choice of my dissertation, "Carolingian Baptismal Expositions: The Manuscript Evidence." Among all of the other friends at Toronto who taught, assisted, and encouraged me, Professor Roger Reynolds's untiring support as my thesis advisor and his continued generosity in helping prepare this book cannot be adequately described. The long hours he spent proofreading the manuscript information in this book, his supplying of microfilm of manuscripts and data on codices he collected in Europe, his alerting me to "new" manuscripts containing Carolingian texts, and his introducing me to European scholars from whom I have received invaluable assistance, are all but a slight indication of my immeasurable debt to him as a scholar and mentor. To him I dedicate this book.

Many other persons and institutions made this study possible. I wish to thank the Deutscher Akademischer Austauschdienst, the Mellon Foundation, and the Hill Monastic Manuscript Library for grants and fellowships to enable me to do the manuscript research and writing of this book. I am especially grateful to Dr. Julian Plante and all of the staff at the HMML. I lost a warm friend and a wise counselor with the death of Professor John Benton at Caltech. His lively interest in my research, assistance in proofreading my first article, and imaginative suggestions nourished my work as a Mellon Fellow at Caltech from 1981 to 1983. Also I am truly grateful to the members of the History Department at Harvard who showed so much interest in my work and supported me with their friendship and hospitality during 1987–88.

For the final stages of preparing this work for publication I am deeply grateful to the secretarial staff at the Duke Divinity School. My admiration and thanks go to Gail Chappell, Sarah Freedman, Carol Rush, and Danielle Spiwak for the long hours and care they spent entering the Latin texts into the word processor.

Abroad, my thanks go to many who assisted me personally in their libraries and granted me permission to photograph and edit the Carolingian baptismal instructions in this study. I received enormous assistance, like so many countless others, from Professor Bernhard Bischoff. If this study has value for those working with Carolingian manuscripts, it is largely due to his information. I will not forget his attention to me as a beginning graduate student and his ever-prompt replies to all my queries since that time. Also, my deep thanks go to Professor Horst Fuhrmann at the MGH for welcoming me there as a visiting scholar in 1979.

Finally, I wish to name those libraries whose manuscripts I was allowed to examine in person and which provided microfilm. The cooperation and generous spirit of their librarians and staff should be acknowledged, but I also want to express my enormous appreciation for the service they perform caring for and making accessible these treasures of our past: the Bibliothèque municipale of Albi; the Bibliothèque municipale of Angers; the Bibliothèque municipale of Arras; the Bibliothèque municipale of Autun; the Staatsbibliothek in Bamberg; the Biblioteca de la Universitat de Barcelona; the Archivo y Biblioteca Capitular de la Catedral in Barcelona; the Deutsche Staatsbibliothek in Berlin; the Burgerbibliothek of Bern; the Bibliothèque Royale Albert Ier in Brussels; the Bibliothèque municipale of Cambrai; the Pembroke College Library in Cambridge; the Erzbischöfliche Diözesan-bibliothek in Cologne; the Diözesanarchiv in Eichstätt; the Stiftsbibliothek of the Benediktinerabtei in Einsiedeln; the Real Biblioteca del Monasterio de San Lorenzo de El Escorial; the Stiftsbibliothek of the Benediktinerstift St. Georgenberg in Fiecht; the Biblioteca Medicea Laurenziana in Florence; the Biblioteca Riccardiana in Florence; the Universitätsbibliothek of Freiburg im Breisgau; the Stiftsbibliothek of the Zisterzienserstift in Heiligenkreuz; the Stiftsbibliothek of the Benediktinerstift in Lambach; the Bibliothèque municipale of Laon; the Bibliotheek der Rijksuniversiteit in Leiden; the British Library in London; the Biblioteca Comunale of Mantua; the Domstift Archiv und Bibliothek of Merseburg; the Biblioteca Ambrosiana in Milan; the Archivio della Badia di Montecassino; the Section Médecine of the Bibliothèque Interuniversitaire of Montpellier; the Museo del Duomo e Biblioteca Capitolare of Monza; the Bayerische Staatsbibliothek in Munich; the Biblioteca Nazionale Vittorio Emanuele III in Naples; the Hispanic Society of America in New York City; the Archives du Gard in Nîmes; the Archivio storico diocesano in Novara; the Bibliothèque municipale of Orléans; the Bodleian Library in Oxford; the Bibliothèque Nationale in Paris; the Institut de Recherche et d'Histoire des Textes in Paris; the Biblioteca Nazionale Centrale Vittorio Emanuele II in Rome; the Biblioteca Vallicelliana in Rome; the Bibliothèque municipale of Rouen; the Stiftsbibliothek of the Augustiner-Chorherrenstift in St. Florian; the Stiftsbibliothek St. Gallen in St. Gallen; the Stiftsbibliothek of the Benediktinerstift in St. Paul im Lavanttal; the Bibliothèque municipale of Sélestat; the Württembergische Landesbibliothek in Stuttgart; the Bibliothèque municipale of Tours; the

Bibliothèque municipale of Troyes; the Biblioteca Apostolica Vaticana; the Bibliothèque municipale of Vendôme; the Biblioteca Capitolare Eusebiana of Vercelli; the Bibliothèque municipale of Verdun; the Bibliothèque municipale of Vesoul; the Österreichische Nationalbibliothek in Vienna; the Herzog August Bibliothek in Wolfenbüttel; the Zentralbibliothek of the Kantons,- Stadt,- und Universitätsbibliothek in Zürich; and the Stiftsbibliothek of the Zisterzienserstift in Zwettl.

Abbreviations

BHL   *Bibliotheca Hagiographica Latina Antiquae et Mediae Aetatis*, ed. Socii Bollandiani (Subsidia Hagiographica, VI; 2 vols., Brussels, 1898–1901, and Supplement, ibid., XII, 1911).

BHM   *Bibliotheca Hieronymiana Manuscripta*, ed. B. Lambert.

CCCM   *Corpus Christianorum Continuatio Mediaevalis.*

CCSL   *Corpus Christianorum Series Latina.*

CLLA   *Codices latini liturgici antiquiores*, ed. K. Gamber

CPPM   *Clavis Patristica Pseudepigraphorum Medii Aevi*, by Ioh. Machielsen.

CSEL   *Corpus Scriptorum Ecclesiasticorum Latinorum.*

DACL   *Dictionnaire d'Archéologie Chrétienne et de Liturgie*, ed. F. Cabrol and H. Leclercq, 15 vols., 1907–53.

MGH   *Monumenta Germaniae Historica.*

   AA   *Auctores Antiquissimi.*

   Capit.   *Capitularia regum Francorum.*

   Conc.   *Concilia.*

   Epp.   *Epistolae.*

   LL.   *Leges.*

   Poet.   *Poetae latini aevi Carolini I.*

   SS.   *Scriptores.*

ms/(s)   manuscript(s).

PL   *Patrologia Latina*, ed. J.-P. Migne.

PLS   *Patrologia Latina Supplementum.*

RB   *Revue Bénédictine.*

ZRG Kan. Abt.   *Zeitschrift der Savigny-Stiftung für Rechtsgeschichte. Kanonistische Abteilung.*

Introduction

The Carolingians were fond of quoting a short saying they attributed to Augustine: "What is baptism? The bath of water with the word. Take away the water, it is not baptism. Take away the word, it is not baptism."[1] Its attribution to a well-known authority, its question-response form, its didactic purpose to define a word, its brevity and simplicity are characteristic of a unique genre of literature that arose in the Carolingian period: the Carolingian baptismal instruction. While expositions on baptism existed before the latter-eighth and ninth centuries, the texts which are the subject of this study belong in a distinct way to the Carolingian Reform. How and why they came into being can only be understood in the context of the Reform.

The Carolingian Reform is an enigma. The term "Reform" is itself controversial, but whether one substitutes "*Renovatio*," "Revival," "Renaissance," or "Achievement," what took place beginning around the mid eighth century is still the subject of investigation. In the broadest sense it has been called a program, educational in nature and religious in content, aimed at the thorough Christianization of all of society. The program was spelled out in a stream of royal and ecclesiastical reform legislation beginning with Karlmann, Pepin, and Archbishop Boniface in the eighth century and continuing through the ninth century.[2] Unsolved, however, is how the program, officially developed in capitularies, was carried out in individual programs of learning and study for the clergy and people, which might differ from diocese to diocese and monastery to monastery. The term "Carolingian Reform" must include both the aim of the reform legislation as a whole and the individual interpretation of that program wherever it was implemented.[3]

---

[1] Text 1, vol. II, pp. 155 f. (See *Augustini in Iohannis evangelium tractatus* cxxiv, *Tract.* XV, nr. 4; *CCSL* XXXVI, p. 152.)

[2] See Rosamond McKitterick, *The Frankish Church and the Carolingian Reforms, 789–895* (London, 1977), pp. xv–xx.

[3] John Contreni takes "program" to include everything the Carolingians did toward "shaping a fundamentally Christian society." His definition of the Carolingian Renaissance could also be applied to the Carolingian Reform as it is meant in this study: "The Carolingian Renaissance formed part of a program of religious renewal that Carolingian political and clerical leaders sponsored and encouraged in the hope that it would lead to the moral betterment of the Christian people. As a conscious effort to im-

The word "Reform" has been preferred in this study because it expresses the perception of the Carolingians themselves in what they were about. Karlmann issued his capitulary of 742 "that the law of God and ecclesiastical religion, which among past rulers fell into ruin, might be *recuperated*, and that the Christian people can attain salvation and not perish, deceived by false priests."[4] In his *Admonitio Generalis* of 789 Charlemagne urged pastors to "strive to lead the people of God to eternal life," and to that end announced to them that he would send out *missi*, who with them "might correct what needs to be corrected."[5] In the pages below, the consciousness of manuscript compilers and composers of baptismal instructions of the larger aim of their work, the reformation of the whole of society, will be seen.

The essence of the Reform was the Christianization of society through education. Education was a goal constantly reiterated in capitularies, which often themselves served as instructions on Christian norms of behavior, values, and beliefs. Education was the goal that prompted the enormous output at monastic and episcopal scriptoria of books for those who needed to learn so that they could teach. One of the greatest achievements of the Carolingian era was this literary productivity. While education ranged in meaning from the most basic instruction in the Christian faith to a thorough training in the liberal arts, this study is concerned with the effort to inform and enfold the grassroots level of society.

The education of the people of God began with baptism. Imagine, for a moment, the Latin West in the year 800. Charlemagne's empire stretched from Barcelona to the Elbe (dividing former West and East Germany), and from Denmark to below Rome almost to Naples. Within this vast realm coexisted a formidable diversity of languages, codes of law, local customs, and beliefs. The conversion of the Carolingian empire to Christianity was far from complete, however one measures conversion. Some areas had experienced centuries of the presence of the church, others were heathen, still others had been introduced to Christianity through missionaries but kept many of their pagan practices and ways of thinking. A final group were the people of newly con-

---

prove man through knowledge of the Scriptures, the renaissance emphasized study, books, script, and schools." "The Carolingian Renaissance," Essay III, pp. 62 and 59 in *Carolingian Learning, Masters and Manuscripts* (Hampshire, UK, 1992).

[4] "Quomodo lex Dei et aecclesiastica relegio (*sic*) recuperetur quae in diebus praeteritorum principium dissipata corruit, et qualiter populus christianus ad salutem animae pervenire possit et per falsos sacerdotes deceptus non pereat." *MGH Capit.* I, ed. A. Boretius (Hannover, 1883), p. 25. The same words were repeated and amplified by Pepin in his capitulary of 744; ibid., p. 29, nn. 1–2.

[5] "O pastores . . . ut vigili cura et sedula ammonitione populum Dei ad pascua vitae aeternae ducere studeatis. . . . Quapropter et nostros ad vos direximus missos, qui ex nostri nominis auctoritate una vobiscum corrigerent quae corrigenda essent." Ibid., p. 53.

quered areas who had been baptized forcibly and who were Christian in nothing more than name.

The rite of baptism played a crucial role in the Carolingian world with its great divide between the baptized and the unbaptized: the faithful and the infidels. Baptism established one's identity in society and membership in the church. The Franks perceived baptism as a realignment of allegiances. An exchange of lords took place. Pagan, heathen, or infant renounced the devil and idolatry and professed faith in the Triune God. The famous words of Bishop Remigius told by Gregory of Tours may be recalled, when Clovis, the first of the Frankish leaders to be baptized, finally stepped up to the cleansing pool: "Bow your head in meekness, Sicamber. Worship what you have burnt, burn what you have been wont to worship!"[6]

Charlemagne took advantage of baptism as an exchange of lords. The name acquired by baptism, "fidelis," was the name for a vassal. In one of the more infamous acts of Christian history, he forced-baptized the people he conquered in order that they would keep the fealty owed him by their act of submission. The *Royal Frankish Annals* under the years 775, 776, and 777 record:

> While the king spent the winter at the villa of Quierzy, he decided to attack the treacherous and treaty-breaking tribe of the Saxons and to persist in this war until they were either defeated and forced to accept the Christian religion or entirely exterminated. . . . In great terror all the Saxons came to the source of the River Lippe; converging there from every point they surrendered their land to the Franks, put up security, promised to become Christians, and submitted to the rule of the Lord King Charles and the Franks. The Lord King Charles with the Franks rebuilt the castle of Eresburg and another castle on the River Lippe. The Saxons came there with wives and children, a countless number, and were baptized. . . . The Lord King Charles for the first time held a general assembly at Paderborn. All the Franks gathered there and from every part of Saxony came the Saxons. . . . Many Saxons were baptized and according to their custom pledged to the king their whole freedom and property if they should change their minds again in that detestable manner of theirs and not keep the Christian faith and their fealty to the Lord King Charles.[7]

These vignettes of Clovis and Charlemagne are often recounted, but in each lies a larger story. The pivotal event that had changed Clovis's mind was the promise from the people under his command that they would willingly

[6]*Historiae francorum* II. 31. Transl. by Lewis Thorpe, *Gregory of Tours: History of the Franks* (Middlesex, England, 1974), p. 144.

[7]Transl. by B. W. Scholz, *Carolingian Chronicles* (Ann Arbor, 1972), pp. 51–56. For further examples from the years 780–796 see pp. 58, 62 f., 73–75. The author for these years of the *Royal Frankish Annals* is an unknown contemporary, probably a member of the royal court chapel (Scholz, pp. 5 f.).

give up their gods and be instructed by Bishop Remigius, a man, Gregory of Tours relates, of "immense learning and a great scholar more than anything else; but he was also famous for his holiness."[8] In the eyes of the Franks, baptism was associated with instruction from those who could impart knowledge and good moral example.

Charlemagne's military policy was, in fact, met with indignant protest from his own famed counselor and friend, Alcuin, because these heathen had no knowledge of the faith into which they were being baptized. In a letter of 796 addressed to Charlemagne and holy preachers, Alcuin praised God that through Charlemagne "many peoples far and wide have been led from the errors of impiety into the way of truth," but asked Charlemagne that he now send "pious preachers, virtuous in manner, learned in the knowledge of the sacred faith" to the "new people." Emphatically he went on,

> That also must be considered with the greatest diligence, that the office of preaching and the sacrament of baptism is done in order, lest the washing of sacred baptism profits nothing in the body, if knowledge of the catholic faith does not precede in the mind of one having use of reason. . . . For it is not possible for the body to receive the sacrament of baptism before the mind receives the truth of the faith . . .[9]

In a society as uncertainly Christian in many areas as that which Charlemagne ruled, baptism played a vital role as an opportunity for imparting at least a minimal knowledge of the Christian faith. This was not only true among the newly conquered heathen, but throughout the rural dioceses. In the Carolingian world, illiterate for the most part, baptism was perceived as entailing necessary instruction by well-taught priests. Whether those who came to the font were infants in the arms of sponsors or adult converts, the Carolingian reform of the whole of society began in a fundamental way with baptism.

---

[8]*Historiae francorum*, II. 31. Transl. by Thorpe, p. 144.

[9]*MGH Epp.* IV, *Ep.* 110, pp. 156–58: "Domino excellentissimo et in omni Christi honore devotissimo Carolo, regi Germaniae, Galliae atque Italiae, et sanctis verbi Dei praedicatoribus. . . . Gloria et laus Deo Patri et domino nostro Iesu Christo, quia in gratia Sancti Spiritus—per devotionem et ministerium sanctae fidei et bonae voluntatis vestrae—christianitatis regnum atque agnitionem veri Dei dilatavit, et plurimos longe lateque populos ab erroribus impietatis in viam veritatis deduxit. . . . Sed nunc praevideat sapientissima et Deo placabilis devotio vestra pios populo novello praedicatores; moribus honestos, scientia sacrae fidei edoctos et evangelicis praeceptis inbutos; sanctorum quoque apostolorum in praedicatione verbi Dei exemplis intentos. . . . Illud quoque maxima considerandum est diligentia, ut ordinate fiat praedicationis officium et baptismi sacramentum, ne nihil prosit sacri ablutio baptismi in corpore, si in anima ratione utenti catholicae fidei agnitio non praecesserit. . . . Non enim potest fieri, ut corpus baptismi accipiat sacramentum, nisi ante anima fidei susceperit veritatem."

Charlemagne apparently took Alcuin's words to heart. Sixteen years later he saw baptism as an opportunity for instruction when he sent a questionnaire to the archbishops of his realm asking how they and their suffragan bishops taught the priests and the people on baptism. At least, that was how the famous questionnaire was interpreted by Theodulf of Orléans, one of the suffragans who responded to it at the request of his archbishop:

> I am certain you know why Charlemagne has asked his questions on baptism. Not for his need to learn, but for his desire to teach; not to be taught something he himself did not know, but so that others might be roused from the sleep of an idle torpor to do the things that need to be done. For this is always dear to him: to exercise bishops in the search of the Holy Scriptures and prudent and sound doctrine, every cleric in discipline, philosophers in knowledge of things divine and human, monks in religion, all generally in sanctity: primates in counsel, judges in justice, knights in practice of arms, prelates in humility, subjects in obedience, all generally in prudence, justice, fortitude, temperance, and concord.[10]

Charlemagne was concerned, according to Theodulf, with the moral condition of his empire. The instruction necessary before baptism, the celebration itself, and, following entrance into the church, the weekly participation in the Liturgy of the Word and the Eucharist offered a way in which every man, woman, and child could become part of the virtuous society he envisioned. Thus, the Christian education of the people beginning with their baptism received the full support and involvement of the political leaders. Charlemagne's questionnaire will be taken up again in this study in relation to the Carolingian Reform. Education can unite minds and shape common beliefs and ways of doing things, but the Reform was primarily concerned with the Christianization of *every individual,* and not with political unity. The evidence for, and the consequences of, this fact will be shown in the texts and manuscripts of this study.

In order to achieve the transformation of the whole of society, attention necessarily was focused on the local priest, the sole contact between the people and the world of learning. The words that came out of the mouths of pastors Sunday after Sunday, year in and year out, in hundreds of villages and rural parishes across Carolingian Europe shaped the people's moral standards, their ethical behavior, their attitude toward death, their idea of justice and sin, their view of God.

With these pastors lay the task of the real conversion of Europe to Christianity—that very slow, gradual change, through education, away from age-old polytheism and animism. In order to teach, however, the educators themselves had to be taught. The closest it will be possible to come to knowing what the peasant or villager of the ninth century thought about his or her bap-

---

[10]Edited in vol. II, Text 16, p. 281.

tism and the Christian faith are the texts supplied to local priests for their own education.

Alcuin's letter to Charlemagne, just quoted, is also addressed to preachers, that is, priests. The letter, in fact, was a form of instruction for them. It includes a detailed reiteration of what should be the content of the instruction given the people before they are baptized, based on Augustine's *De caticizandis rudibus*.[11] By spelling out the program of instruction, the letter in itself was meant to teach.

Almost nothing is known about the local priest of Carolingian Europe— where he came from, what kind of training he had prior to his appointment, or his moral quality. Judging from some of the clerical reform legislation issued throughout the latter-eighth and ninth centuries, there was urgent need for their educational improvement. Priests had to be examined on such basics as whether they knew the words of the Lord's Prayer and the Creeds, whether they knew how to celebrate baptism and the mass, whether they even possessed a book of the Gospels. Other legislation, however, suggests they were qualified to read Latin, preach on the Gospels, explain the sacraments, and run schools.

It is highly unsatisfactory to rely on reform legislation alone in order to assess the quality of the Carolingian clergy, because of the didactic intent of the

---

[11]"Therefore, that order of teaching people of mature age diligently, I believe, must be observed, which St. Augustine ordained in his book which he entitled, 'On Catechizing Those New to the Faith.' First one must be instructed concerning the immortality of the soul and the future life and the recompense of good and evil people, and the eternity of the lot of both kinds; afterwards, for which sins and crimes one suffers eternal punishments with the devil and for what good things or good deeds one enjoys eternal glory with Christ. Then, the faith of the Holy Trinity most carefully must be taught, and the coming into the world of the Son of God, our Lord Jesus Christ, for the salvation of the human race must be set out. Then, as I said, the new mind must be fortified concerning the mystery of his passion, and the truth of the resurrection, and the glory of the ascension into heaven, and his future coming to judge all peoples, and the resurrection of our bodies and the eternity of punishments for the wicked and of rewards for the good. When one has been strengthened and prepared with this faith, one should be baptized." (Igitur ille ordo in docendo virum aetate perfectum, diligenter, ut arbitror, servandus est, quem beatus Augustinus ordinavit in libro, cui de catecizandis rudibus titulum praenotavit. Primo instruendus est homo de animae inmortalitate et de vita futura et de retributione bonorum malorumque et de aeternitate utriusque sortis. Postea: pro quibus peccatis et sceleribus poenas cum diabolo patiatur aeternas, et pro quibus bonis vel benefactis gloria cum Christo fruatur sempiterna. Deinde fides sanctae Trinitatis diligentissime docenda est, et adventus pro salute humani generis filii Dei domini nostri Iesu Christi in hunc mundum exponendus; et de mysterio passionis illius, et veritate resurrectionis et gloria ascensionis in caelos et futuro eius adventu ad iudicandas omnes gentes et de resurrectione corporum nostrorum et de aeternitate poenarum in malos et praemiorum in bonos, mox—ut praediximus—mens novella firmanda est. Et hac fide roboratus homo et praeparatus baptizandus est.) *MGH Epp.* IV, *Ep.* 110, pp. 158 ff.

written legislation, but until very recently there has been little else to go on. Now, other genres of literature are being studied systematically, such as penitential books, canon law collections, sermon collections, and liturgical expositions. These kinds of texts may reveal what the clergy in specific locations actually knew, when they are found in manuscripts intended to serve as schoolbooks or instructional readers for priests. Adequate attention has not been paid to the book as a whole in which Carolingian texts pertaining to the education of the clergy are preserved.

This study focuses on one genre of literature written for the education of the Carolingian clergy: Carolingian baptismal instructions. This literature has never been brought together and studied collectively in the context of the books in which it circulated. As a corpus, read in comparison to one another, the baptismal tracts tell how baptism was celebrated and interpreted across Carolingian Europe. At the same time, in their manuscript context, they are an important new source of information regarding the nature and the success of the Carolingian Reform to educate the clergy. With these texts, the way in which the ideals set out in the Carolingian capitularies took on reality is seen. It is one thing to require that all priests know how to baptize and to instruct the people in the faith; it is another to create books of instruction for the priests, duplicate and distribute them; yet it is still another to anticipate and insure their reception by individual clerics with vastly different levels of training in Latin, familiarity with the Roman rite, and desire or capability to change. The variety in the baptismal instructions that will be shown below is an attestation, in part, to the individual resources and wisdom with which bishops and their assistants met the challenge of the Reform.

This study has three major objectives. One is to describe the codices in which the baptismal instructions are found, in order to show with what other kinds of material the baptismal tracts are associated and where, how, and by whom these codices were intended to be used. Another is to bring together the baptismal texts and study them systematically. Why were there so many different baptismal commentaries? How do they differ, and what do they tell about the celebration and interpretation of baptism across the Carolingian empire? Finally, a third objective is to interpret the Carolingian Reform in light of the baptismal instructions and the manuscripts in which they were copied. Major questions about the Reform have not yet been answered, including who took on the responsibility of implementing the reform decrees; how they thought to do this effectively; and to what extent the goals set out in the reform legislation were achieved. The answers to these questions, as far as they can be had, lie in the kinds of manuscripts and texts which will be examined here.

Volume I is devoted to analysis and interpretation of the material in volume II. It is divided into three parts. The first is concerned with the manuscript context of the baptismal instructions. The baptismal instructions are an integral part of the books in which they were copied. Their differences cannot be appreciated unless one first finds out where, how, by whom, and for whom their manuscripts were written. These are daunting questions. It has only been possible to pose them for many manuscripts because of the work of Bernhard Bischoff. Literally thousands of medieval manuscripts have now been securely dated to the Carolingian period, and his identification of the specific scriptoria, even individual scribes and exact dates of many manuscripts have wrought a modern renaissance in Carolingian studies.[12]

Almost all the codices of the Carolingian baptismal instructions contain a great deal of other material as well. In manuscript catalogues these codices are variously labeled "miscellanies," "florilegia," or "collection volumes." They have rarely been appreciated as carefully designed books, each the work of a compiler with a particular purpose and probably a specific recipient in mind. Volume II contains descriptions of the manuscripts used in this study. When the entire contents of the books are known, the purpose and intended user of each codex often can become evident.

In Part II of volume I the baptismal expositions themselves are analyzed. They have never been studied as a corpus, in part because many are anonymous and never captured the attention of editors more interested in the works of celebrated authors. Before the era of Bernhard Bischoff, the dates of many manuscripts we now know to be Carolingian were uncertain; as a consequence, anonymous works had little value. Also, the baptismal instructions are not obvious sources of information for historians, liturgiologists, or theologians. They are didactic tracts concerned above all with defining the ceremonies and words of baptism. Finally, they have been ignored as a corpus because they were thought unoriginal and repetitive. Manuscript cataloguers rarely give them any attention, so it would be difficult for anyone surveying the contents of Carolingian manuscripts to recognize how extensive and variated the baptismal literature is.

Their seeming repetitiveness is one reason why the baptismal instructions need to be studied collectively. Only when compared closely do their differences emerge. Sixty-four Carolingian baptismal instructions are included in this study. Undoubtedly more will be found. While some of the texts could be seen as variations of others, the essential criterion for giving each of the texts a separate name is whether it shows the intentional work of an author or editor, even if he has not altered his model greatly. Chapters on baptism within much larger works (for example, the *De exordiis et incrementis* of Walafrid Strabo or the *De institutione laicali* of Jonas of Orléans) are not considered Car-

---

[12]A large percentage of the manuscripts employed here were dated and sometimes located by him in personal correspondence. He has catalogued over six thousand ninth-century manuscripts (see "Über den Plan eines paläographischen Gesamtkatalogs der festländischen Handschriften des neunten Jahrhunderts" in *Archivalische Zeitschrift* 59 [1963], p. 166). When this catalogue is published, systematic studies of many genres of Carolingian literature will be that much more possible.

olingian baptismal instructions in this study, unless a redactor deliberately extracted the chapters on baptism from a larger work to use independently in another context as a baptismal instruction, as in the case of the chapters on baptism in Isidore's *De ecclesiasticis officiis* and Hrabanus Maurus' *De institutione clericorum*.

Twenty-five of the sixty-four baptismal instructions studied here have never been edited. Even, however, among those that have, in most cases more manuscript witnesses have now been found. Only a few of them have received recent critical editions. Thus, a new or first edition of each of the baptismal instructions is provided in volume II.

The contents of individual baptismal commentaries and the words of liturgical *ordines* of baptism will sometimes be compared in minute detail. It is only by this means that one can see the care taken by the authors and redactors in their work. The task before scholars in Carolingian studies today is to explain the sensitivities of the Carolingians that prevented a homogeneous culture from forming. Differences did not melt in a Carolingian crucible. The baptismal instructions reveal that this diversity was rich and meaningful, sometimes due to long-held indigenous liturgical customs or to the particular needs of different areas.

In Part III of Volume I some conclusions about the Carolingian Reform are drawn. In its broadest context this study is about the Christianization of Europe—not the superficial conversion of conquered peoples, but the slow replacement of one mindset with another that came about through the education of the people under the care of pastors. The education of the clergy themselves was critical to the process. The baptismal instructions are able to contribute to our understanding of the Carolingian Reform because, for one, the subject of baptism was a major concern of the reformers, and the instructions were written in response to demands that priests know how to baptize correctly and explain the faith to their parishioners. What the instructions say about the celebration and interpretation of baptism is not uniform. A close inquiry as to why this is so changes how the goals of the Carolingian Reform must be understood. A second reason the baptismal tracts as a corpus offer new insight about the Reform is because they circulated in several different kinds of books. This fact reveals how the instruction of the clergy was a project that affected the entire archdiocese, including the metropolitan, the diocesan bishops, episcopal and monastic scriptoria, libraries, and schools and parish priests. In Part III, one conclusion is that it is now imperative to assess the Reform according to individual archdioceses and even dioceses.

PART I: THE MANUSCRIPTS

1

Collection Volumes: Baptismal Instructions as Part of a Larger Effort to Educate the Clergy

It was said that although the codices containing the baptismal treatises have been called florilegia, miscellanies, or collection volumes, each was the plan of a compiler or overseer with a particular purpose and probably a specific recipient in mind. A full grasp of the nature and the contents of these collection volumes is essential to the conclusions of this study. It is not intended that every reader will read the manuscript descriptions in detail.[1] Some may wish to, others will gain a concept of what a collection volume may entail, their variety, and the richness of some of them even by glancing over the descriptions. The purpose of this chapter and the following is to show for whom these books were compiled and where they were meant to be put to use. The first consideration must be the kinds of material other than baptismal found in them and the combination of material in any one volume.

First of all, if one reflects on the different genres of literature in these volumes,[2] it is a repertory particularly suitable to secular clergy, even if lay people, monks, and nuns might receive benefit from some of the texts. Most frequent are explanatory works on the mass, the Creeds, the Lord's Prayer, and the clerical grades; compositions of a catechetical nature on the faith and Christian doctrine; works of Isidore; *interrogationes sacerdotales*; and scriptural exegesis. High interest is also shown in disciplinary texts: royal capitularies and diocesan statutes; canons excerpted from church councils and papal letters; canon law collections; and penitentials. Another interest is pastoral and liturgical works: sermons and homiliaries; liturgical *ordines*; blessings and exorcisms; information for calculating the date of Easter; and liturgical calendars. Some interest is also shown in letter collections, grammatical works, glossaries, and orthography.

Over three-fourths of the material includes texts that every priest, according to clerical reform capitularies, was required to know and be able to explain. Two such capitularies outlining priestly requirements can be read in the descriptions of Sélestat, Bibl. mun. 132 (Sch, ff. 18v.–19v.) and Munich,

---

[1]Located in vol. II, pp. 1–124.
[2]See "A Topical Survey" in vol. II, pp. 125–148.

13

Clm 6325 (Mu3, ff. 132v.–33). The Sélestat capitulary would seem to necessi-
tate the priests' familiarity[3] with the following items: an exposition on the
faith; an exposition on the Lord's Prayer; an exposition on the Creed; a psalter
(perhaps with glosses); an exposition on the mass including an explanation of
the canon of the mass ("Te igitur") and other prayers; an evangeliary; a
homiliary; the entire office of baptism; a penitential; a computus; an exposition on baptism; the words of the offertory of the mass; and an exposition on
the clerical grades. The Munich capitulary requires all priests to learn (*discere*)
the faith of Athanasius and other texts on the faith; the Apostles' Creed; the
Lord's Prayer with an exposition; a full sacramentary with special masses of
commutation; exorcism formulas for catechumens and possessed; a commen-
dation of the soul;[4] a penitential; a computus; a Roman antiphonary for the
night office and mass; an evangeliary; a *liber comitis*; a homiliary for Sundays
and feasts (perhaps with an *ordo* of days requiring preaching); a monastic rule
and a canonical rule; a canonical *liber pastoralis*; a *liber officialis*; the pastoral letter of Pope Gelasius; and how to write charters and letters (perhaps requiring
a formulary for charters and letters).

These capitularies list liturgical books as well as expositions on the rites
and the prayers. In that of Munich, the priest must be able to compose letters
("scribere cartas et epistolas").[5] Other Carolingian capitularies required
priests to know and be able to preach on the eight principal vices;[6] read
and set an example from the *Pastoral Rule* of St. Gregory;[7, 8] and be able to
explain the renunciation of Satan in baptism.[9] Also, decrees since the time

---

[3]Expressions include, "Let them understand . . . let them know and be able to interpret . . . let them know by heart . . ." ("Intellegant . . . sciant et interpretari possint . . .
memoriter teneant.")

[4]See F. Paxton, *Christianizing Death* (Ithaca, 1990), pp. 130 f.

[5]See R. McKitterick, *The Carolingians and the Written Word* (Cambridge, English,
1989), p. 128, on local priests functioning as scribes or notaries in their area.

[6]Canon XIII of the Council of Rheims of 813: "Ventilata est ratio octo principalium
vitiorum ut unusquisque [sacerdos] diversitatem illorum sciret et ab illis domino
auxiliante se intellegeret custodire et aliis praedicare." (*MGH Conc.* 2, pars I, p. 255).
Cap. XV of the *Capitula Ecclesiastica* (ca. 810–13): "Ut unusquisque presbyter capitula
habeat de maioribus vel de minoribus vitiis per quae cognoscere valeat vel praedicare
subditis suis, ut caveant ab insidiis diaboli." (*MGH Capit.* I, p. 179).

[7]Canon X of the Council of Rheims of 813: "Lectae sunt sententiae libri pastoralis
beati Gregorii, ut pastores eclesiae [*sic*] intellegerent, quomodo ipsi vivere et qualiter
sibi subiectos deberent ammonere." (Ibid., p. 255).

[8](*non est.*)

[9]Cap. XVIII of the Council of Tours of 813: "Episcoporum sit magna sollicitudo
presbyteris suis tradere baptismi sacramentum et quid in eodem renuntiandum
quidve credendum sit. Renuntiatur ergo diabolo et operibus eius. Opera enim
diaboli opera carnis esse intelleguntur, quae sunt homicidia, fornicationes, adulteria,
ebrietates et multa alia his similia, quae nimirum diabolico instinctu prius
cogitatione mentis concipiuntur quam opere perpetrentur. Pompe vero eiusdem

of Boniface demanded that priests be examined before their ordination and annually by their bishop or bishop's representative,[10] which might explain the presence of some of the *interrogationes sacerdotales* in our manuscripts.

The capitularies do not say the items they list that priests must know should be put together in volumes, which every priest should possess. The contents of some of our manuscripts, however, are almost a blueprint of the items spelled out in the clerical reform capitularies. Albi, Bibl. mun. 38 bis (Al1), for example, consists of a canon law collection; an *interrogatio sacerdotalis*; two expositions on the clerical grades; a baptismal exposition; a penitential; five different expositions on the Creed; a calendar; and a computus. Albi, Bibl. mun. 43 (Al3) consists of a treatise on the Trinity; an *interrogatio sacerdotalis*; an exposition on the clerical grades; two expositions on baptism; an exposition on the Athanasian Creed; and a canon law collection. Laon, Bibl. mun. 288 (L) contains an exposition on the Lord's Prayer; an exposition on the Athanasian Creed; two expositions on the mass; two expositions on baptism; a collection of homilies; and an *interrogatio sacerdotalis*. Orléans, Bibl. mun. 116 (Or) contains an exposition on the Athanasian Creed; an exposition on the Lord's Prayer; three explanations of the faith; three expositions on baptism; two on the mass; a collection of prayers; a collection of homilies; two *interrogationes sacerdotales*; an exhortation on the eight principal vices; and a capitulary listing priestly requirements.[11]

If, then, the material of our collection volumes is preeminently suited for secular clergy, it must still be asked how any particular volume was intended to serve. The variety of material in any one manuscript indicates the purely educational intent of these codices. The fact that their compilers juxtaposed liturgical and didactic texts, combining in a single volume everything from a Creed commentary to a computus, shows that they were using the capitularies listing what a priest should know as a guideline for what reading material they should use to *educate* the clergy. They were not supplying the clergy with

---

sunt superbia, iactantia, elatio, vana gloria, fastus et alia quamplurima, quae ex his oriri videntur." (Ibid., pp. 288 f.)

[10]For example, from a council of 742: "Decrevimus quoque secundum sanctorum canones, ut unusquisque presbyter in parrochia habitans episcopo subiectus sit illi, in cuius parrochia habitet; et semper in quadragesima rationem et ordinem ministerii sui, sive de babtismo [sic] sive de fide catholica sive de precibus et ordine missarum, episcopo reddat et ostendat." (Ibid., p. 3, c. 3, and repeated ca. 769; see *MGH Capit.* I, p. 45, c. 8.) See also *MGH Capit.* I, pp. 109 f. E. Vykoukal, "Les examens du clergé paroissial a l'époque carolingienne," *Revue d'histoire ecclésiastique* 14 (1913), pp. 81–96, distinguishes many kinds of clerical examinations: before ordination, of foreigners, annually in Lent, at an episcopal visitation, by *missi*, at a synod, in writing; his example of the last is Charlemagne's baptismal questionnaire (Text 14).

[11]See their descriptions in vol. II. Some other examples are Lg, Mi2, and Mp2.

service books. These volumes were not meant to be carried in procession to
the font, brought into the confessional, or read from the pulpit. Rather, the
ordo of baptism, the penitential, or the collection of homilies in them were
meant for study. These texts were serving, in our manuscripts, to educate the
cleric about baptism, about penance, and about the meaning of the Scriptures.

The purpose of these books to provide study texts for clerics can be seen by
looking more closely at some of the material. Penitentials, for example, are
booklets which help direct the priest in the hearing of confession and assign-
ing of penance. Allen Frantzen distinguishes two types of manuscripts containing penitentials: first, small, handbook-sized pamphlets containing
nothing but the penitential. These probably were intended to be used by a
confessor. Second are manuscripts of larger size and scope containing three
or four penitentials. Frantzen calls these volumes "collection books," which
probably served as exemplars for copies that were actually used for hearing
confession in outlying churches. The fact that the penitentials in them are diverse—some quite old and foreign—he finds surprising, because regional
churches, he says, were anxious to enforce their own disciplinary standards.
He explains it as conservatism, an unwillingness to reject older material.[12]

Another explanation for their diversity, however, could be that they were
not intended for liturgical use, but to provide moral instruction for clerics. As
Frantzen himself points out, the penitentials are padded with moral instruction.[13] The *ordo confessionis* often preceding the penitential (in four of our codices) is actually a sort of moral sermon. In our manuscripts the penitentials are
usually supplemented with instruction and exhortations on penance from
canon law, sermons, and Scripture. In Milan, Bibl. Ambros. L 28 sup. (Mi2),
for example, the Penitential of Halitgar, a decree of Gregory I, an "inquisitio"
on penance attributed to Jerome, a sermon on the eight principal vices, the
preface to the penitential of Cummean, and an *ordo* for giving penance follow
one another.[14] Another example is Leningrad (now St. Petersburg), RNB Q. V.
I. no. 34 (Lg). Raymund Kottje has proposed that in its original form it was
used as a handbook for "Seelsorgspraxis."[15] It once contained a Roman *ordo*
for the scrutinies followed by Theodulf's baptismal exposition, followed by
three expositions on the mass, calendar material, the penitential of Halitgar, a
canon law collection, and a calendar for Corbie. Was this volume, however,
intended to be carried into the confessional? One would also have to argue
that the volume was carried during scrutiny masses for catechumens, since it

---

[12]A. Frantzen, "The Tradition of Penitentials in Anglo-Saxon England," *Anglo-
Saxon England* 11 (1983), pp. 26 f.

[13]Ibid., p. 25.

[14]For other examples of penitentials supplemented with penitential-related material, see Mp2 and Mu10.

[15]R. Kottje, *Die Bussbücher Halitgars von Cambrai und des Hrabanus Maurus*
(Berlin/New York, 1980), p. 34.

contains an *ordo* for the scrutinies. Yet it is extremely unlikely that the baptismal *ordo* was intended here as liturgical directive. Juxtaposed to Theodulf's baptismal commentary, it served to illustrate it. (The baptismal commentary of Jesse of Amiens includes an *ordo* of scrutinies as illustration, as will be shown.) Also, would a practical handbook that served the priest on active duty contain *three* expositions on the mass? Rather, this codex was intended to educate the priest on the requirements of his office.

Liturgical *ordines* are another kind of material in our manuscripts. Although they are what a priest uses to guide him through the celebration of the mass, baptism, penance, burial, or one of numerous other ecclesiastical rites, *ordines* were copied in our manuscripts for a different purpose. Five of our codices contain collections of Roman *ordines*.[16] None of them consists of purely liturgical directives. B2 possesses only one *ordo Romanus*, Al2 and P5 each contain four, Z1 has six, and S5 has eight. Most of their contents consist of liturgical commentary and instruction on the ecclesiastical offices from such authors as Isidore, Amalarius, Hrabanus Maurus, and Walafrid Strabo. Andrieu calls them didactic manuals, not meant to be carried into a church, but to be studied in a library.[17] He sees these compilations as a response to the needs of the time, when clerical reform capitularies insisted that priests be examined on their knowledge of their office. He believes the *ordines* were the core of the clerical instruction and that they were increasingly padded with commentaries and explanations revealing the meaning of the rites.[18]

Altogether, the number of different *ordines* in our codices is not very large. The most popular include the deposition of relics in a new church (in four codices); the dedication of a church (in three codices); the mass (in three codices); baptism (in three codices); and the Ember Days. The dedication of a church was weighted with symbolism and its rite offers valuable theological reflection for any cleric, even if no priest beneath the rank of a bishop could dedicate a church. The mass, baptism, and the Ember Days (special days of prayer and fasting four times a year) were the rites most necessary, in terms of the people's participation, for a priest himself to understand so as to be able to explain to them.[19]

Another kind of material in our codices is Carolingian legislation. It is even debatable whether the Carolingian capitularies, when they were first issued

---

[16]Albi, Bibl. mun. 42 (Al2); Bamberg, Staat. Bib. Lit. 131 (B2); Paris, BN lat. 1248 (P5); St. Gall, Stiftsbibl. Cod. sang. 446 (S5); and Zürich, Zentralbibl. Car. C. 102 (Z1).

[17]M. Andrieu, ed., *Les Ordines Romani du Haut Moyen Age*, vol. I (Louvain, 1931), p. 476.

[18]Ibid., p. 479, and on B2, see p. 482.

[19]Regarding the Ember Days, for example, the Diocesan Statute attributed to Waltcaud of Liège, listing things his priests must know, states: "Cap. XVII. Quomodo a presbiteris quattuor temporum ieiunia agantur vel denuntiantur in plebe et quomodo observentur." P. Brommer, ed., *Capitula Episcoporum* I (*MGH Capitula Episcoporum, Pars I*) (Hannover, 1984), p. 49.

in written form, ever were meant to be a public decree in themselves, or were simply a follow-up description of legislation enacted through oral decree.[20] If there is some evidence that the Carolingian capitularies had "a real legislative and dispositive function" (McKitterick's expression),[21] the vast majority of the royal or episcopal capitularies, in any case, are not preserved in exclusive volumes as exemplars, but in books like ours, scattered amid a variety of other kinds of texts, usually in an unofficial (unsubscribed) form, and often anonymous, incomplete, or obviously edited.[22]

Perhaps the reason Theodulf's first diocesan capitulary is found so frequently in our manuscripts is because it is rife with moral instruction. He sets forth the unselfish life priests should exemplify, gives a long description of the Christian virtues, and lists the eight principal vices and the works of mercy. Throughout the capitulary there are numerous quotations from Scripture.[23] It is possible that some of the clerical reform capitularies in collection volumes such as ours may have only been created for clerical instruction.

Taking yet another kind of material, sermon collections were included in our codices for the personal instruction of the priest and not with the primary intention to serve as a homiliary for part or all of the liturgical year. The sermons in our collection volumes seem to have been regarded as an excellent means to familiarize priests with the church Fathers, give them models of fine preaching, and exhort them to higher moral standards in small dosages of reading. The single word *sermo* before some homilies seems to have served to alert the cleric that here was good instruction, since no indication is given as to which day the sermon should be preached.[24] In El Escorial, Real Bibl. S. Lor. L. III. 8 (Es1), for example, a series of homilies, many on moral themes,[25] is preceded by Alcuin's *De virtutibus et vitiis* and followed by an *interrogatio* on the sins of Adam and the faith. The sermon material is thus a collection of moral instruction, not a collection corresponding to the liturgical year. In Laon, Bibl. mun. 288 (L), a collection of homilies partially identical to that in Es1 is clearly

---

[20]See R. McKitterick, *The Frankish Church*, pp. 18–43.

[21]Ibid., p. 25. See even more recently on this, Janet Nelson, "Literacy in Carolingian Government" in *The Uses of Literacy in Early Medieval Europe*, ed. by R. McKitterick (Cambridge, 1990), especially pp. 283–91.

[22]McKitterick's own hypothesis is that if the initial issuing of a capitulary had a legislative purpose, it was "eventually intended to serve a didactic purpose . . . and to supply a source of regulative and admonitory canons for reference and guidance, rather than have the force of statutory law." (*The Frankish Church*, p. 25)

[23]Theodulf's *Capitula I* has been edited by P. Brommer, *Capitula Episcoporum*, pp. 103–42. It is by far the most copied of all the Carolingian capitularies. Brommer lists forty-nine manuscripts, a third of them from the ninth century.

[24]See J. Contreni's remarks about Carolingian sermon literature and its use (citing H. Barre's conclusions) in "The Carolingian Renaissance," p. 70.

[25]See ff. 60v.–77: "Qualis [*sic*] sint christiani boni et quales mali;" "De diebus quadragesimis et de penitentia agenda."

intended as instruction for the cleric himself, because interjected in the middle of the collection is a questionnaire (*interrogatio*) on the creation of man and the sins of Adam.

Paris, BN lat. 10741 (P10) contains a collection of fifteen catechetical sermons falsely attributed to St. Boniface. The first four are on the Creed, the origin of the human condition, the vices and virtues and Ten Commandments, and the eight Beatitudes. In the fifth the author admonishes his audience to remember their baptismal vows, be merciful, kind, chaste, and peace-lovers, observe Sunday, come to church, give alms, pay their tithe, memorize the Lord's Prayer and the Creed, be good sponsors, remember that baptism and confirmation are given only once, and fast. The next eight sermons continue to exhort the faithful to lead moral lives by impressing them with the capital sins (especially idolatry), God's commandments, the works of mercy, the temptations of the devil, and the importance of observing fasting and sexual abstinence during Lent. Despite the appropriateness of these sermons for the people, this manuscript was not intended as a preaching manual. A canon law collection takes up three-quarters of the volume. Examples also abound of single sermons used to supplement other instruction, such as in Milan, Bibl. Ambros. L 28 sup. (Mi2), which contains a sermon on the eight principal vices in the midst of penitential texts, and in Munich, Clm 14508 (Mu9), which has a sermon on the Lord's Prayer immediately following an exposition on the Lord's Prayer.

Canon law collections, another kind of material in our codices, contain a vast amount more than acts of councils and papal decrees, including selected sentences of the fathers, *dicta* on numbers, liturgical commentaries, Isidorian instruction in question-response form, and other "para-canonical" material (Roger Reynolds's expression). Perhaps one reason for this is because every priest was supposed to possess a canon law collection. Thus, they were a prime vehicle for educating the clergy.[26]

Computational tables appear in some of our codices. They might seem to be evidence for the book's use as a practical manual, because one refers to them to find the date of Easter in a given year. Yet, in the above-mentioned capitularies a computus was a required item for all priests to understand (*intellegere*) or to learn (*discere*). They were copied in our manuscripts primarily to teach the cleric how to read timetables, as part of his general education. In almost every case a computus is adjacent to instruction related to time, such as "On the age of the moon" or "On the six days of creation," or a "*ratio paschalis.*"[27]

Another kind of material in our codices is the clerical questionnaire (*interrogatio sacerdotalis*). Assuming that a percentage of bishops actually conducted clerical examinations, *interrogationes sacerdotales* gave the interroga-

---

[26]On the contents of the *Collectio Sangermanensis*, for example, see Chapter 9, p. 139.

[27]See nr. 14 in vol. II, pp. 142 f.

tors, whether bishops, *missi*, or archdeacons, a list of questions to ask the priests. An examination in Paris, BN lat. 1012 (P4), for example, is entitled, "How priests must be examined according to canon law."[28] A series of questions is given as to their parentage, education, tonsure, place of birth, who recommended them for the priesthood, if they paid money for it, and so forth, followed by a series of specific questions on the Creed. Other *interrogationes* begin, "Tell me, why is a priest blessed?"[29] or, "Question. What is a canon?"[30] or, "Questions before anyone approaches sacred orders."[31] These formulas for clerical examinations would make very useful study guides for the cleric himself. Other *interrogationes sacerdotales* are little more than rephrasings of passages from Isidore on the church and its ministers, or of passages in the Bible, in question-response form. Such *interrogationes* were not intended even in origin to be formulas for actual clerical examinations.[32] They are simply instructions cast in the popular didactic form of a dialogue, in these cases between a cleric and his superior.

As to expositions on the clerical grades, or Ordinals of Christ, that are in the form of *interrogationes sacerdotales*, it was seen above that the Sélestat capitulary required priests to be examined on the clerical grades Christ fulfilled, and it is possible that these texts may sometimes have been copied in a manual for a bishop or his *missus*, to examine candidates for ordination. The Ordinals of Christ are brief tracts describing how Christ himself instituted all the minor and major orders when, for example, he washed feet (as subdeacons would do) or read from Isaiah (as lectors would do) or cast out demons (as exorcists would do). In our manuscripts they are either part of larger clerical *interrogationes*,[33] or, with their seven (or eight) clerical grades, they are copied beside other *dicta* on the number seven (or six or eight),[34] or they are part of an Isidorian instruction that attained near-canonical status in the ninth century.[35]

Finally, prayers and hymns are a distinct kind of material in our codices. Of eight manuscripts containing them, five were probably intended as schoolbooks. Sometimes the function of the prayers or hymns is very obvious. In Angers, Bibl. mun. 277 (An), for example, a "Hymn Before Eating"[36]

---

[28]"Qualiter requirendi sunt sacerdotes secundum canonum institutionem." See vol. II, p. 68, P4, ff. 27v.–29.

[29]"Dic mihi, pro quid est presbiter benedictus?" in Albi, Bibl. mun. 38 bis(Al1), f. 42.

[30]"Interrogatio. Quid est canon?" in Albi, Bibl. mun. 43 (Al3), f. 18.

[31]"Interrogationes antequam ad sacros ordines aliquis accedit" in Montpellier, Bibl. Interuniv. Méd. 387 (Mp2), f. 50.

[32]See the title in St. Gall, Stiftsbibl. Cod. sang. 40 (S1), p. 304: "Ioca episcopi ad sacerdotes."

[33]In Al1, ff. 40v.–41v.; Al3, f. 16v.; Au, ff. 113v.–114v.; and P5, ff. 67v.–68v.

[34]In Mu9, ff. 125v.–126; Mu10, f. 93; and W3, f. 135v.

[35]In S5, pp. 79–85; Sch, ff. 24–28; and V3, ff. 46v.–48.

[36]"Himnum ante cibum," ff. 23–31v.

was written down a center column with only two or three words to a line and ample space between the lines. On its wide left and right margins it has been heavily glossed. This was probably the work of some monastic scholar. The hymn is from the *Cathemerinon* of Prudentius (a collection of hymns for daily use).

These examples show that the manuscripts containing the baptismal instructions could not have been intended as manuals in the sense of vademecums which the priest would use when baptizing, preaching, or hearing confession. If a volume contains pastoral or liturgical texts (a penitential, sermon, baptismal *ordo*, or hymn), it also contains expositions and commentaries. Furthermore, a handbook assembling essential texts to help the priest through his daily duties would probably not contain more than one penitential or one canon law collection. Our manuscripts, however, often contain two or more of the same kind of text in a single volume. Or, on the opposite extreme, they do not give enough of the text to make it truly serviceable. Very often there are only excerpts or parts of liturgical *ordines*, calendars, or canon law collections, or only a few selected sermons instead of a homiliary sufficient to cover the liturgical year. Also, if their contents were intended to be applied to the people, it would seem that a greater effort would have been made to include prayers the people were expected to know in Old High German.[37]

Rather, the combination of didactic and non-didactic texts transformed the purpose of the latter. The compiler's primary intention was the education of the cleric. Material that in other kinds of codices may have been meant to conduct liturgy, enact law, or examine a priest here has the purpose of edification. The pedagogical intent of the codices raises the question whether the texts in our collection volumes need reflect the liturgy celebrated, or the crimes committed, or the canon law applied, in the areas where the volumes were compiled. A compiler far removed from Orléans and its specific problems conceivably might have copied Theodulf of Orléans's capitulary only for its moral instruction, and a penitential used long ago under the specific conditions of a community in Ireland conceivably might have been copied by a Carolingian scribe in northern Italy only for its exemplary use of Old Testament passages. The answer to this question will emerge in the course of this study, as the reason for the large number of different baptismal instructions in our codices comes to light. Now it must be sought more precisely by whom or where the codices were intended to be used.

---

[37]For the rare examples of Old High German in our volumes, see Mu3, ff. 1–7 (glosses on Isidore); Me, f. 16 (a baptismal renunciation and profession of faith); Al1, ff. 26v.–29v. (glosses on canons); and V3, ff. 2–3v. (an *ordo* of confession).

2

The Intended Recipients and Uses of the Volumes

A volume for the education of the clergy could be possessed by a schoolmaster or a bishop, a *missus* or a parish priest. It could serve as an exemplar or master-form for creating multiple copies, a reference book, or a study guide.

A great difficulty in labeling collection volumes is that it is not always known what was considered appropriate for a "schoolbook" or a "bishop's handbook." Even though the selection of material in each is always some-what different, our volumes fall under one of four kinds of books: (1) instruction-readers for priests, (2) bishops' pastoral manuals, (3) bishops' reference works, and (4) schoolbooks. These four types still leave it uncertain, in many cases, whether the manuscript was intended for a missionary priest, a rural parish priest, a cleric training to be a priest in an episcopal school, a cleric training for the secular clergy in a monastic school, a monk in a monastic school intending to serve as a monk-priest on lands owned by his monastery, a monk in a monastic school for whom the material was edifying but not essential, a bishop interested in preserving works of well-known authors, a bishop desiring to provide exemplars from which scribes in his scriptorium could select material and make schoolbooks or instruction-readers for priests.

The very exercise of trying to imagine for what use or for whom any one manuscript compiler intended his volume underscores how little is known about the education of the clergy in the Carolingian period. Did most parish priests receive education in episcopal schools? Did they obtain any schooling after they became pastors? Did clerics in episcopal or monastic schools study from their own books or take notes from a teacher's book? Should *schoolbook* mean what a student has copied, or what a teacher uses? Did the process of learning Isidore's *Origines* or a canon law collection involve copying it? Are some of our manuscripts the work of copyists who were students in schools?[1]

Despite the difficulty of labeling our volumes, being able to identify these four different destinations indicates that some of the baptismal instructions

---

[1] The model studies of the cathedral school of Laon by John Contreni and the scriptorium, library and school of Corbie by David Ganz, while they do not address the education of parochial clergy, provoke such questions in their descriptions of the manuscripts and methods of masters at these centers. For the few insights on students copying texts, see J. Contreni, "The Carolingian School: Letters from the Classroom," Essay XI in *Carolingian Learning, Masters and Manuscripts*, pp. 90 f.

reached the hands of parish priests, some were in bishops' manuals, some were studied in a schoolroom, and some were preserved in library exemplars. This is a beginning in detecting where and how the education of the clergy took place. Especially, the instruction-readers are evidence that the Reform reached the grassroots level of society.

The purpose of this chapter is to describe the features of each of the four types of books and to discuss the significance of the fact that the baptismal instructions are found in these four distinct types, and not only in one type.

(1) Instruction-Readers for Priests

Some of our manuscripts were intended to be placed in the hands of particular priests who were already ordained and charged with the care of souls of a local church. These are the manuscripts that in their contents correspond precisely to the items spelled out in clerical reform capitularies, a few of which were described in Chapter 1. That parish priests actually were given books in addition to those necessary to carry out their office may seem too optimistic an interpretation for an age in which a book took so much time and effort to create, but on the basis of our manuscript evidence it does seem possible to say that they received such books. Also, the manuscript evidence is supported by reform legislation. It seems priests could hardly be told that they would be examined on their knowledge of their office,[2] and even threatened with deposition,[3] unless there were books for them to improve their knowledge and to prepare for their examination.

Although there is precedent long before the Carolingian period for bishops seeing that their priests came to their office prepared[4] and for bishops making

---

[2]"Ut presbiteri non ordinentur prius quam examinentur" in Mu12, f. 139; "Volumus ut omnes sacerdotes nostri hoc ordine requirantur" in Sch, f. 18v; "Omnes ecclesiasticos de eorum eruditione et doctrina diligenter examinere . . ." in a capitulary of Charlemagne. (*MGH LL.* I, p. 106.)

[3]"Sacerdotes, qui rite non sapiunt adimplere ministerium suum nec discere iuxta praeceptum episcoporum suorum pro viribus satagunt vel contemptores canonum existunt, ab officio proprio sunt submovendi, quousque haec pleniter emendata habeant." (*MGH Capit.* I, p. 46, c. 15; A. Boretius believes this capitulary was promulgated by Charlemagne circa 769.)

[4]Canon XXVI of the Fourth Council of Toledo in 633: "De officiali libello parochitanis presbyteris dando. Quando presbyteres in parochias ordinantur, libellum officiale a sacerdote suo (id est episcopo) accipiant, ut ad ecclesias sibi deputatas instructi succedant, ne per ignorantiam etiam ipsis divinis sacramentis offendant: ita ut quando ad litanias vel ad concilium venerint, rationem episcopo suo reddant, qualiter susceptum officium celebrant vel baptizant." Quoted by M. Férotin, ed., *Le Liber Ordinum en usage dans l'église wisigothique et mozarabe d'Espagne du cinquième au onzième siècle* (Paris, 1904), p. xvii, who believes that the *libellum officiale* referred to is a strictly liturgical book, the *Mozarabic Rituale,*, containing a large number of offices and prayers for a priest (not a bishop) and not supplemented with commentaries or instruction.

diocesan visitations,[5] the instruction-readers for priests have no precedent before the Carolingian Reform. With their appearance bishops have gone an extra step in their concern that their priests be educated. It must be assumed that bishops commissioned these instruction-readers that so closely reflect the items spelled out in episcopal capitularies. These were not required liturgical books, but an additional helpful tool for a priest who it sometimes is apparent needed quite basic instruction. Some examples of instruction-readers below will show that their level of sophistication differed, but the contents of some are very elementary.

Did the bishop himself plan their contents or peruse them before giving them out? A book of any sort was a valuable possession, and it is likely that a priest was presented with it at a formal occasion such as his ordination or at an episcopal visitation. In this case the bishop had direct contact with the book and the man who received it. He must have known both the man and the appropriateness of the book given to him, whether he was less or more proficient in Latin, and whether he was to serve in a missionary area.

One thing that distinguishes instruction-readers from schoolbooks is their lack of non-essential items.[6] Whereas schoolbooks often contain miscellaneous pieces of a purely edifying nature and generally have a greater variety of material, instruction-readers tend to provide anything that would help a priest become more learned in his office, but usually have a more limited and economical selection of texts, and are devoid of the occasional practice-writing or miscellaneous *excerpta* typical of schoolbooks. Those of our manuscripts proposed as instruction-readers are listed in Table 1.[7] Their often very modest size (see Table 1 for their measurements) supports the idea that attempts were made to produce many of these books for personal ownership. Descriptions of all the codices classified as instruction-readers can be found in volume II. Here only a few illustrations will be given.

The unassuming-sized volume, Munich, Clm 6325 (Mu3) [205 x 130 mm. (approximately 8" x 5¼"), 142 folios with 18 lines to a page], contains the capitulary cited in Chapter 1 listing items every priest must learn. The other contents of the codex consist of a selection of these items: a book of the offices (Isidore's *De ecclesiasticis officiis* preceded by Old High German glosses related to the work), an exposition on the prayers of the mass (which includes an exposition on the Lord's Prayer), and an exposition on baptism. Thus, the

---

[5]Martin of Braga at the Second Council of Braga in 572 had declared that: "The bishops in every church should perambulate their dioceses and first examine their clergy, in what manner they observe the order of baptism and the mass, and how they observe any other rites; if their findings are satisfactory, thanks be to God; if not, they shall teach the ignorant." Translated by E. C. Whitaker, *Documents of the Baptismal Liturgy* (London, 1960), p. 227. See also Canon XI of the Council of Narbonne of 589 in José Vives, *Concilios Visigoticos e Hispano-Romanos* (Barcelona/Madrid, 1963), p. 148.

[6]Some examples already mentioned in Chapter 1 are Al3, Al1, L, and Or.

[7]See pp. 160–163.

capitulary serves as a reminder to the priest to learn well the book's contents. The Old High German (in a slightly later ninth-century hand) might have been added to increase the book's usefulness for educating a parish priest who was stationed in the missionary diocese of Freising, where the book was written.

Another unpretentious-sized codex, Vienna, ÖNB 1370 (Vi6) [180 x 130 mm. (approximately 7" x 5¼"), 120 folios with 18 lines to a page], following exorcism prayers and a baptismal instruction, contains material on how a cleric ought to live (taken from the Council of Aachen of 816, canons XV–XXXVI), the pastoral instruction regarded as the work of Arno of Salzburg, an excerpt from Gregory's *Pastoral Rule*, an exposition on the Lord's Prayer, the faith and canons of Nicea, an exposition on the mass, a sermon summarizing salvation history, a sermon on the eight vices, excerpts from the *Collectio Hibernensis*, the Acts of the Seven Sleepers of Ephesus, and sermon on the devil and hell. The large amount of moral instruction in this volume corresponds to the emphasis on this aspect of clerical education in the reform capitularies.[8] This small volume was created at Mondsee, in the archdiocese of Salzburg. Thus, it could indicate the help of that scriptorium in producing books for the secular clergy, perhaps under Archbishop Arno of Salzburg, whose pastoral instruction it contains.

Merseburg, Bibl. des Domstifts Hs. 136, ff. 2–21v. (Me) [262 x 165 mm. (approximately 10¼" x 6½"), 26 lines to a page], contains an exposition on the mass, a baptismal renunciation and profession of faith in Old High German, an *ordo* of baptism, and a baptismal instruction. Folios 2–21v. were written at the famous monastic scriptorium of Fulda, but the compiler of these folios was serving a bishop or abbot who had the needs of the secular clergy in mind. His inclusion of the baptismal formulas in Old High German corresponds to a capitulary, perhaps from a Mainz synod of circa 803, which stated that every priest must ask the renunciation and confession of faith in a language the people understand.[9] The presence of the Old High German and a liturgical *ordo* of baptism might suggest that ff. 2–21 were intended for a rural priest as he celebrated baptism. The fact, however, that these items are juxtaposed to a baptismal instruction consisting of nothing but a long list of Latin words taken from the baptismal prayers (not entirely the same prayers given in the adjacent *ordo*) with synonyms, to teach the cleric Latin vocabulary, shows that the book was intended for clerical study.

---

[8]See McKitterick, *The Frankish Church*, Chapter V, "The Florilegia," on the moral instruction of the clergy.

[9]"Nullus sit presbyter qui in ipsa lingua qua nati sunt baptizandos abrenunciationes vel confessiones aperte interrogare non studeat, ut intelligant quibus abrenunciant vel quae confitentur. Et qui taliter agere dedignantur (*lege* dedignatur) sed cedat in (*lege* secedat e [Dachéry]) parochia." Cap. XXVII of the so-called *Statuta Bonifacii*, cited by K. Müllenhoff & W. Scherer, *Denkmäler deutscher Poesie und Prosa aus dem VIII–XII Jhr.* (Berlin, 1864), p. 438.

Paris, BN lat. 1012 (P4) [194 x 129 mm. (approximately 7⅝" x 5"), 92 folios, 21 lines to a page with only four to six words to a line], contains two baptismal instructions, a homily from the collection of forty homilies of Pope Gregory I, a diocesan examination and capitulary, an exposition on the mass, expositions on the Apostles' and Athanasian Creeds, and a collection of sermons. Gregory's homily (on Lk. 10:1–9) is an exhortation to priests on their office as preachers and instructors. The diocesan examination asks the priest questions on his personal background (education, election) and his knowledge of the faith (Athanasian Creed). It is followed by fifteen *capitula* repeatedly copied in Carolingian reform legislation concerning the priests' moral conduct and the duties of their office. Carlo de Clercq says that this set of interrogations and *capitula* for priests does not seem to be a diocesan statute, but an exhortation to priests in preparation for an examination they must undergo before their bishop.[10]

Munich, Clm 14508, ff. 64–146 (Mu9) [226 x 154 mm. (approximately 8⅞" x 6"), 27 lines to a page], contains two expositions on the Lord's Prayer, three expositions on the faith, three baptismal instructions, a long excerpt from a canon law collection, the first diocesan capitulary of Theodulf of Orléans, a capitulary (probably of Garibald of Liège) beginning with what priests must know (the same capitulary as the capitulary of Sélestat cited in Chapter 1), an exposition on the seven clerical grades, *dicta* on seven and eight, and a canon law collection. McKitterick calls it an episcopal handbook because it contains two diocesan capitularies.[11] Whether the capitularies were intended for a bishop as a model for his own legislation, or whether they were intended to offer moral exhortation and admonition to a priest, they certainly are capable of the latter role, especially the capitulary of Theodulf.

(2) Bishops' Pastoral Manuals

Many of our codices that fit the qualifications of instruction-readers might as easily have belonged to bishops, whose concerns included collecting texts that would be useful for carrying out the educational reform of their clergy. They could have served as exemplars from which a compiler, working in an episcopal scriptorium (or monastic scriptorium whose abbot was a bishop or had close ties with a bishop), created instruction-readers for local priests. Or, a bishop might want a copy of the diocesan capitularies of his predecessor or a colleague as a model for composing his own diocesan capitulary. He might be interested in a colleague's letter responding to a circulatory questionnaire in order to compose his own response. He might desire an exposition on the

---

[10]C. de Clercq, *La législation religieuse franque de Louis le Pieux à la fin du IX siècle, 814–900*, (t. II), Anvers, 1958, p. 159. Because of the Tironian notes in this manuscript (f. 9, f. 59), perhaps it was a library exemplar from which instruction-readers were copied.

[11]*The Frankish Church*, p. 42.

dedication of a church, or sermons for feast days he would celebrate in his cathedral.

What sometimes distinguishes a bishop's pastoral manual from an instruction-reader for priests is the additional material inappropriate for, or superfluous to, the needs of a diocesan priest. El Escorial, Real Bibl. S. Lor. L. III. 8 (Es1) [approximately 216 x 152 mm. (approximately 8½" x 6"), 189 folios, 25 lines to a page (a thick, heavy volume)], for example, includes a letter of Bishop Herpuin to Archbishop Hincmar of Rheims and a brief form letter of Herpuin to Archbishop Wenilo of Rouen.[12]

Perhaps the catechetical material in Munich, Clm 14410 (Mu8) [258 x 173 mm. (approximately 10¼" x 6¾"), 102 folios, 25 lines to a page], indicates its user was a bishop. J. M. Heer says that the volume is entirely in one beautifully crafted Carolingian hand (except for the last folio) with initial letters in uncial and names of authors in the margins of its Ps.-Bede homiliary. Its fifteen canons of an unidentified Bavarian council are a collection of historical acts addressed to the lay folk and were intended, according to the preface, to be read out to them by their bishop on a certain feast day at the end of September.[13]

Vat. Pal. lat. 278 (V2) [approximately 203 x 178 mm. (approximately 8" x 7"), 88 folios, 25 lines to a page] contains Isidore's *De vocatione gentium libri II* and the treatise on baptism and first diocesan capitulary of Theodulf of Orléans. This work of Isidore was not mandatory knowledge for all clerics. The volume might have served as a bishop's pastoral manual, or its *two* works of Theodulf might show some bishop's interest in the author rather than the specific texts, a slightly different reason to produce this collection. It might as easily belong to the third type of book.

(3) Bishops' Reference Works

Some bishops had libraries and ran cathedral schools. Some bishops were also abbots and headed a monastery with a school, library, and scriptorium.[14] These men would be interested in collecting certain reference works. They may have wished to expand their libraries with works of famous authors as well as texts of personal interest for their own study and reflection. A bishop might have been a compiler of canon law or a participant in a theological debate. For this reason he may have wished to gather together many works or

---

[12]R. Kottje calls El Escorial L. III. 8 a "Sammelhandschrift für die seelsorgliche Praxis." He points especially to the letter of Bishop Herpuin of Senlis to Archbishop Hincmar of Rheims (his metropolitan) and the *littera dimissoria* of Herpuin for a deacon to Archbishop Wenilo of Rouen as evidence of the use of the codex as a bishop's manual for the pastoral needs of his flock. ("Zur Herkunft der Handschrift Escorial, Bibl. De S. Lorenzo L III 8, aus Senlis" in *Francia* 13 [1986 for 1985], pp. 623 f.)

[13]J. M. Heer, *Ein karolingischer Missions-Katechismus* (Freiburg i. Br., 1911), pp. 65 f.

[14]R. McKitterick has written on the development of Frankish libraries in *The Carolingians and the Written Word*, pp. 169–210.

expositions on the same theme. He may have sought works suitable to teach the students in his school. The volume was intended to be kept in the bishop's library. It is characterized by a lack of miscellaneous excerpted sentences and canons and by more complete works. The often substantial size of the volume, its good physical condition, lack of orthographical errors, inclusion of multiple expositions on the same topic, and sophistication of the texts also characterize this type of book. Whereas a bishop's pastoral manual would suit a bishop's essential and urgent needs as a pastor, the reference work would be for preserving, researching, teaching, and copying important texts.

Troyes, Bibl. mun. 804, ff. 1–79 (Tr1) [250 x 200 mm. (approximately 9⅞" x 7 ⅞")], for example, includes no less than nine expositions on the faith. It also includes the *De vivendo deo* of St. Augustine. J.-P. Bouhot says that in the theological debate over the beatific vision in the middle of the ninth century *De vivendo deo* was the principle defense used by theologians such as Hrabanus Maurus and Hincmar of Rheims.[15] The very condensed writing (35–39 lines to a page), all in one hand, suggests a library reference work. There are no *interrogationes sacerdotales* or episcopal capitularies as one might find in a bishop's pastoral manual.

Freiburg, Univ. Bibl. 8 (Fr) [305 x 265 mm. (approximately 12" x 10½"), 138 folios, 34 lines to a page], contains essentially the *Collectio Dionysio-Hadriana* with *addenda*. It is written in double columns with rubrics. Preceding the *Collectio* are the *Notitia Galliarum*, which are also found in canon law manuscripts from the famous archiepiscopal library and center of canon law studies at Salzburg.[16] This volume, written in eastern France, perhaps also was intended for study in the library of an archbishop.

Novara, Bibl. Arch. Stor. Dioc. e Capit. XXX (No) [457 x 305 mm. (approximately 18" x 12"), 282 folios, 36 lines to a page (some written in double columns)], also contains essentially a canon law collection with *addenda*. Probably written in northern Italy, the inclusion of the canons of the Synod of Milan of 864 points to the special interests of a bishop in northern Italy. From its size, one can assume it was intended to remain in a library or scriptorium.

(4) Schoolbooks

Schoolbook is a very general term, yet it is obvious that some of our volumes must have been used in schools. Sometimes brief items betray their schoolroom use, such as miscellaneous excerpts from pagan authors, alphabets, glosses, marginalia, catalogues of names, parts of chronicles, and *probationes*

---

[15]J.-P. Bouhot, "Les sources de l'Éxpositio missae' de Remi d'Auxerre in *Revue des Études Augustiniennes* 26 (1980), pp. 137 f.

[16]See R. E. Reynolds, "Canon Law Collections in Early Ninth-Century Salzburg" in *Proceedings of the Fifth International Congress of Medieval Canon Law, Salamanca, 21–25 September 1976*, ed. S. Kuttner and K. Pennington, *Monumenta Iuris Canonici*, ser. C, subsidia 6 (Vatican City, 1980), p. 30.

pennae.[17] In Monza, Bibl. Capit. E-14/127 (Mo), *dicta* on the five senses are a kind of frivolity not found in instruction-readers.

Some of our schoolbooks belonged to an episcopal schoolroom, while others were used in a monastic school. Wolfenbüttel, Herz.-Aug. Bibl. Helmst. 532 (W3) is an example of an episcopal schoolbook. It contains, among much else, the Bavarian law code and a fragment of the Lombard law code. The manuscript came from the archiepiscopal scriptorium at Salzburg, famous for its production of canon law manuscripts. Arno of Salzburg was probably the metropolitan under whom it was written. He wrote a pastoral instruction in which he ordered schools to be established in each bishop's city. Thus, he was concerned with clerical instruction as well as the collection and copying of canon law texts.[18] Presumably the clerics in his own school in Salzburg were exposed to a fair amount of canon law. This explains the Bavarian Law Code in a schoolbook from Salzburg, perhaps the copybook of a student who would one day serve in Arno's archdiocese. Other examples of episcopal schoolbooks are S5, B2, Z1, and Al1, already mentioned as *ordines Romani* exemplars padded with commentary, which Andrieu says were for study, not for liturgical use.[19]

To give some examples of monastic schoolbooks, in Montecassino, Archiv. della Badia 323 (Mc1) the *Physiologus*, a kind of vocabulary book of names of strange animals, takes up almost half the volume. The Greek origin or interpretation of names is an apparent theme of the whole volume, which includes Isidore's *Allegoriae*, a baptismal instruction consisting of explanations of Greek words in the rite of baptism, and *dicta* on the seven heavens, which explains Greek words like *tonitrua* (thunder). Munich, Bayer. Staatsbibl. Clm 6407 (Mu4) contains the famous "Munich Passages" discussed at length by John Marenbon.[20] The philosophical "dicta Albini" and "dicta Candidi" on the creation of man in God's image, as well as the numerous other theological texts on the Trinity, the nature of Christ, and the qualities of God, clearly indicate this volume was intended for study or teaching, the treasured possession of a highbrow monk and master.[21]

Intriguing are the schoolbooks used in monastic schools, but containing some items particularly suitable for the needs of the secular clergy. For example, Angers, Bibl. mun. 277 (An), a small volume, [170 x 115 mm. (approxi-

---

[17]For some examples, see the descriptions of W3, Z2, V3, Vi3, and Mo in volume II.

[18]See R. Reynolds, "Canon Law Collections, " pp. 17 f.

[19]See Chapter 1, p. 17.

[20]John Marenbon, *From the Circle of Alcuin to the School of Auxerre: Logic, Theology, and Philosophy in the Early Middle Ages* (Cambridge, 1981).

[21]Marenbon proposes the monk Candidus, the close friend and student of Alcuin, as the original author of the collection of passages copied at Verona in Mu4 (ibid., p. 43).

mately 6¾" x 4½"), 120 folios, 20–21 lines to a page], is perhaps the copybook of some student. It was mentioned that this contains a long "Himnum ante cibum" from the *Cathemerinon* of Prudentius, with profuse marginal glosses.[22] There is also a hymn to the Virgin Mary and a glossary of Hebrew words in Latin in question-response form. All of this might point more to monastic than clerical education, but the volume also contains two expositions on the faith, one on the mass, and three on baptism. The manuscript comes from the region of Lyons, and with its inclusion of the *De spe et timore* of Agobard of Lyons, it perhaps was the work of a student in a monastic school that undertook the training of secular clergy at the request of the archbishop of Lyons.

Another volume, St. Gall, SB Cod. sang. 124 (S2), contains largely scriptural exegesis. The inclusion of the annals of St. Gall suggests a monastic school. It contains the baptismal instruction of Jesse, Bishop of Amiens, to the priests of his diocese, and the manuscript was, in fact, produced in his diocese, so that a monastic school may have taken on the instruction of secular clergy at the bishop's request.

Another example is Vatican, Vat. Pal. lat. 485 (V3), written at the famous monastic school of Lorsch, though probably for the instruction of secular clergy. It contains liturgical *ordines* for baptism and confession, a confession formula in Old High German, a computus, two expositions on the mass, four baptismal instructions, four diocesan capitularies, a sermon of Ps.-Boniface on the renunciation in baptism, and four penitentials, as well as other material. This suggests a schoolbook designed for the education of the secular clergy who might serve in the Lorsch area. The manuscript continually received additions at Lorsch in the latter ninth century, when Lorsch was extending its holdings and jurisdiction over whole villages with parish churches.[23] Lorsch would be interested, then, in the preparation of secular clergy at its school or of its own monks, who would serve as parish priests (discussed below).

Paris, BN lat. 2328 (P61), contains Isidore's *Sententiae*, Alcuin on the virtues and vices, *Annotationes de lapidibus et gemmis*, an epitaph for Alcuin, and the Life of St. Marina, material that seems by its non-requisite nature most appropriate to monastic education. The volume, however, also contains a baptismal instruction, an exposition on the mass, and sermons suitable for the education of secular clergy. Perhaps the book was used at a monastic school that was also concerned with the education of future parish priests.

A pattern emerges among the following four codices. St. Paul im

---

[22]See Chapter 1, pp. 20 f.

[23]See F. Paxton, "Bonus liber: A Late Carolingian Clerical Manual From Lorsch (Bibliotheca Vaticana MS. Pal. Lat. 485)" in *The Two Laws: Studies in Medieval Legal History Dedicated to Stephan Kuttner*, ed. L. Mayali and S. A. J. Tibbetts (Studies in Medieval and Early Modern Canon Law), vol. I (Washington, D.C., 1990), p. 29.

Lavanttal, SB 5/1 (Sp1), contains Isidore's *De ecclesiasticis officiis* and *Differentiae*, followed by seven baptismal instructions. The volume was compiled at Reichenau by its librarian, Reginbert, with the help of a student.[24] Vienna, ÖNB 823 (Vi5) contains Isidore's *De ecclesiasticis officiis* and three baptismal instructions, followed by a brief instruction on Greek letter forms, a form letter for the transfer of a monk to another monastery, and a Greek-Latin alphabet. St. Gall, SB Cod. sang. 235 (S4) contains only Isidore's *Origines* and two baptismal instructions. Fourth, the tiny codex Verdun, Bibl. mun. 27 (Vd) [136 x 100 mm. approximately 5¼" x 6"] contains Isidore's *De natura rerum*, an exposition on the Lord's Prayer, seven expositions on the faith, two baptismal instructions, and an *interrogatio* on the interpretation of "letter." These codices all contain a major work of Isidore followed at the very end with baptismal instruction and sometimes lexigraphical material. The Verdun codex also includes instruction on the faith and the Lord's Prayer. Perhaps because knowledge about baptism was of basic importance in the education of a priest, it was the first kind of clerical instruction that was added to the curriculum in a school that took on the preparation of secular clergy.

From this brief survey of schoolbooks,[25] the question of schools for the secular clergy is raised. It seems from Carolingian legislation that bishops were told to set up parochial schools for educating future priests, or perhaps to make arrangements with monasteries in their dioceses. At the Council of Attigny in 822 it was decreed that every individual, youths and adults, with a view to occupying any position in the church, have a designated place (of study) and a suitable teacher. If the large size of the diocese prevented their meeting in one place, two or three places, or as many as necessary, should be provided.[26]

---

[24]See the description by A. Holder and K. Preisendanz, *Die Handschriften der Badischen Landesbibliothek in Karlsruhe: Bd. 3,2: Die Reichenauer Handschriften* (Wiesbaden, 1973), p. 112.

[25]The reader again must refer to Table 1 for further examples of schoolbooks. In some cases, the entire contents leave it ambiguous whether the volume was intended as a schoolbook or a bishop's personal volume. For example, F. Unterkircher believes Vi3 served the needs of Bishop Arno of Salzburg, containing texts of personal interest to him (*Alkuin-Briefe und andere Traktate: Codex Vindobonensis 795 der Österreichischen Nationalbibliothek, Faksimileausgabe* [Graz, 1969], p. 13). The comments, however, of B. Bischoff (*Die südostdeutschen Schreibschulen und Bibliotheken in der Karolingerzeit* II [Wiesbaden, 1980], pp. 117–19), point to its school use. He states that the exegetical excerpts, which fill over half the codex, were in part made for school level, and that Baldo corrected it and added explanatory titles, and perhaps himself acquired the Gothic alphabet (on f. 20v.) while in Ravenna.

[26]"Scolas autem, de quibus hactenus minus studiosi fuimus quam debueramus, omnino studiosissime emendare cupimus, qualiter omnis homo sive maioris sive minoris aetatis, qui ad hoc nutritur ut in aliquo gradu in ecclesia promoveatur, locum denominatum [denomit natum] et magistrum congruum habeat. . . . Si vero necessitas fuerit propter amplitudinem parroechiae, eo quod in uno loco colligi non possunt

In the following year Louis the Pious issued an "Admonitio Generalis" in which he confirmed the Attigny decision and ordered that schools be established in suitable places, wherever there was still need, to instruct and teach sons and ministers of the church.[27] The Council of Paris of 824 said that every bishop should henceforth apply himself more vigorously to preparing and educating knights of Christ for the service of the church in schools which they should have.[28] Louis's "Admonitio" is of special interest in that it might indicate schools for those who were already ordained and needed remedial education, not just future priests (although "sons and ministers of the church" could mean future ministers in training). It is not known, however, how many, if any, ordained parish priests actually went "back" to school.

It was noticed that some of the *monastic* schoolbooks include texts originally conceived for the instruction of secular clergy, and it was suggested that secular clergy might have been receiving education in monastic schools. Certainly, a number of bishops of the ninth century were educated in monastic schools, and perhaps also many *future* parish priests had started out with the intention of becoming monks. Did, however, most parish priests who had obtained some schooling receive it in a monastic school?

What our schoolbook codices suggest is that there was some concern to provide clerical education in certain monastic schools that had very close ties with bishops. Hrabanus Maurus composed his *De institutione clericorum* while he was Master of the monastery school at Fulda. He was a priest at the time (he had been ordained in 814) and had the education of the secular clergy in mind. Did he use the work as a guide for students at the school of Fulda? In 819 he gave a copy of it to his archbishop (of Mainz). Thus, he clearly saw himself serving the needs of the secular clergy, whether the archbishop would have sent students to Fulda or trained them in a separate school. Monastic schoolbooks suggest that monastic schools to some extent

propter administrationem quam eis procuratores eorum providere debent, fiat locis duobus aut tribus vel etiam ut necessitas et ratio dictaverit." *MGH Capit.* I, p. 357, Cap. III. Also the implication of Cap. XVIIII of Theodulf of Orléans's First Diocesan Capitulary (between 798 and 818), quoted below, note 36, is that these nephews of priests who are to be allowed to attend monastery schools in his diocese have a view of becoming priests. This is a different kind of schooling than Theodulf establishes in Cap. XX, parish schools run by his priests where all children can come and be taught to read. See P. Brommer, *Capitula Episcoporum*, p. 116.

[27] "Scholae sane ad filios et ministerios ecclesiae instruendos vel edocendos, sicut nobis praeterito tempore ad Attiniacum promisistis, et vobis iniunximus, in congruis locis, ubi necdum perfectum est, ad multorum utilitatem et profectum a vobis ordinari non negligantur." S. Baluzius, ed., *Capitularia regum Francorum*, t. I (Paris, 1870), col. 634, Cap. V.

[28] "V. Inter nos pari consensu decrevimus ut unusquisque episcoporum in scholis habendis, et ad utilitatem ecclesiae militibus Christi praeparandis et educandis, abhinc maius studium adhiberet." Ibid., col. 1137.

did have an agenda of study that included the needs of those preparing for parish ministry. There is no evidence that these were men already in parish ministry. All that can be said is that monasteries were participating in the general drive to spread learning to all of society during the period of the Carolingian Reform. They were instructing men for the active parish priesthood.

What role might the "external school" have had to play in the education of secular clergy? The recent study of M. Hildebrandt is a most welcome work for assembling all that has been documented about this elusive institution.[29] "External school" is a modern term. Of a school building which was outside the cloister but on the grounds of a monastery, served by monks of the monastery to educate outsiders (whether visiting monks, lay people, or those training for the secular clergy) there is only one documented example in the Carolingian period, St. Gall.[30]

Other ideas, however, emerge in Hildebrandt's study. One is monastery-run schools at rural parish churches. These were proprietary churches, owned by the monastery. The monastery appointed a monk-priest to the parish church and assistants, who became the nucleus of a small priory. A school was run there by the monk-priest for the training of parish priests.[31] Imbart de la Tour wrote long ago that, although it was not widespread in the ninth century, it could happen that the government of a parish was given to a monastery or chapter, whose church was then served by a community of monks or secular clergy under a rule. The abbot or provost or one of his delegates functioned as the parish priest.[32] If some of our monastic schoolbooks contain material suitable for secular clergy because some monasteries were training monks who would become priests in charge of churches owned by the monasteries, these monasteries nevertheless were contributing to the needs of the diocese in which they lay and must have had some arrangement with the bishop of the diocese. The monk-priest may have been ordained by him; in any case the monk-priest would be subject to the bishop and obtain the chrism for baptism and the sick from him. The monk-priest would instruct the people belonging to the parish church. Thus, our monastic schoolbooks would reflect what the people in the countryside may have absorbed through the teaching of their monk-pastor.

Both Hildebrandt and Imbart de la Tour show that the system of proprietary churches needs a great deal more investigation in relation to the solution of ignorant parish priests.[33]

---

[29]*The External School in Carolingian Society* (New York, 1992).

[30]Ibid., pp. 15, 18, 103–7, 140.

[31]Ibid., pp. 16, 119–29, 134–38.

[32]*Les paroisses rurales du IVe au XIe siècle* (Paris, 1900), p. 129.

[33]Thomas L. Amos, who has also written on monks who served as parish priests in churches owned by their monasteries, states, for example, that before 850 St. Germain-des-Prés owned thirty-six churches, St. Remi of Rheims thirteen, and St.

As to secular clergy studying with monks themselves in the monastery school, Hildebrandt believes that until circa 800 missionary activities in newly conquered areas necessitated monasteries, the only centers of culture in these areas, engaging in the training of parish priests.[34] This raises the question of the curriculum of studies in monastic schools.

One can only recall the very tantilizing evidence of, for example, An, clearly a monastic schoolbook with its glosses on a hymn of Prudentius and a glossary of Hebrew words, yet also containing two expositions on the faith, one on the mass, and three on baptism. Another example is S2, containing mostly scriptural exegesis and the annals of the monastery of St. Gall, but also containing Bishop Jesse of Amiens's baptismal instruction and originating in Jesse's diocese. Again, consider V3, written at the famous monastery of Lorsch, but containing liturgical *ordines* for baptism and confession, a confession formula in Old High German, and many more texts pertaining to the education of the secular clergy. Yet again, recall P61, combining texts suitable for monks and for priests, or Sp1, definitely composed at Reichenau, but containing seven baptismal instructions (which, it will be shown, reflect baptismal practice in the area). It should be noted that not all of these manuscripts originated in missionary areas. An comes from the area of Lyons and S2 from the diocese of Amiens. Thus, it was not only missionary activity that was forcing monasteries to engage in the education of parish priests.

There is no evidence that monasteries were acting as "night schools," however, for ignorant parish priests. Rather, the presence of our baptismal instructions in schoolbooks must reflect the character of the Carolingian Reform, which was not purely remedial, but looked to the future. The bishops were preparing a solid foundation for the future of the church through schools. The Reform looked forward to a day when every parish priest had gone to school.

The significance of our "schoolbooks" is not only that they are the very evi-

---

Germain of Auxerre ten. Mondsee, after losing its Bavarian parishes in legislation of 804, subsequently "acquired and staffed between ten and fifteen parishes in the Avar districts due to its participation in the Avar mission." ("Monks and Pastoral Care in the Early Middle Ages" in *Religion, Culture and Society in the Early Middle Ages: Studies in Honor of Richard E. Sullivan*, ed. Thomas F. X. Noble and John J. Contreni (Kalamazoo, Mich., 1987), p. 173.) Amos gives the impression that many parish priests of the ninth century were monk-priests. This, it seems, would have produced a rather high quality of parish priests, men educated both morally and intellectually. Furthermore, Giles Constable says churches owned by monasteries vastly outnumbered churches owned by lay-lords (see "Monasteries, Rural Churches and the Cura animarum in the Early Middle Ages" in *Settimane di studio devo* 28 [1982], pp. 367 f.), presumably meaning a fair number of good, abbot-appointed priests. The reform legislation, however, gives a very different picture of the state of the rural clergy.

[34]*The External School*, p. 140, and see also Amos, "Monks and Pastoral Care," pp. 171 f.

dence sought by modern scholars for the interrelationship of bishops and monasteries and the people, but that they show why the Carolingian Reform had an enduring effect. John Contreni, in the conclusion of his study of the cathedral school of Laon, said that "schools, such as that at Laon, were the most durable and influential product of the Carolingian renaissance." What he went on to say pertains equally to monastic schools. The flash of humanism, the study of Greek, the purity of the Carolingian script would wither after the ninth century, but "what did survive was the infrastructure of schools."[35] Baptismal instructions and other texts for the instruction of the secular clergy became part of the curriculum of monastic schools, which served more areas than a cathedral school could reach,[36] and thus greatly widened the possibility of every parish priest receiving a school education. That was what gave the Carolingian Reform its importance in history, for it was the local pastors who brought education to society at large.

Perhaps what is being seen in the four kinds of books is *two* dimensions of the Carolingian Reform. One is an immediate concern to reform the clergy who were already ordained and in charge of a parish. This concern is reflected in instruction-readers for priests, bishops' pastoral manuals, and some reference works so that baptismal instructions could be compiled and circulated. This immediate concern or remedial aspect of the Reform, educating installed pastors, probably was conducted in most places without schools, by means of clerical instruction readers, examinations by archdeacons and *missi*, episcopal visitations, diocesan synodal addresses, and circulatory letters. A few dioceses may have sent their pastors to school, as Louis's

---

[35]*The Cathedral School of Laon from 850 to 930: Its Manuscripts and Masters* (Munich, 1978), p. 167.

[36]Even though Bishop Theodulf of Orléans had a cathedral school at Orléans, he designated four monasteries or their dependencies in his diocese as places where priests could send their nephews or any relative to be educated. Cap. XVIIII of his First Diocesan Capitulary (between 798 and 818, but probably before the Council of Chalon-sur-Saône of 813) states: "Si quis ex presbyteris voluerit nepotem suum aut aliquem consanguineum ad scolam mittere, in ecclesia sanctae Crucis [in Orléans] aut in monasterio sancti Aniani [St. Aignan in Orléans] aut sancti Benedicti [Fleury (St. Benoit-sur-Loire)] aut sancti Lifardi [St. Liphard de Meung-sur-Loire] aut in ceteris de his coenobiis, quae nobis ad regendum concessa sunt, ei licentiam id faciendi concedimus." (P. Brommer, *Capitula Episcoporum*, pp. 115 f.) Hildebrandt notes that St. Gall educated secular clergy even though there was a school for training priests at the nearby bishopric of Constance, of which St. Gall was a dependency. She surmises St. Gall may have been one bishop's answer to educating the priests of his diocese, Constance taking care of local students while St. Gall took on those from a wider territory. (*The External School*, p. 107.) Also, see Hildebrandt's case study of six small dependencies of Fulda, "whose primary function appears to have been educational," and which were located where they were most likely "to serve the religious and charitable needs of the people in the vicinity." (Ibid., pp. 119–25.)

"Admonitio" of 823 might infer, but the problems with this idea seem immense. First of all, who would finance his leave of absence, and who would
replace him?[37] An argument, however, for the non-school form of education
that bishops had to devise are the clerical instruction-readers themselves.

The second dimension, seen through the fourth kind of book, "schoolbooks," is the concern to transform all of society through schools for the
clergy. Schools must be established throughout the dioceses, declares the legislation. Whether at monasteries or parish churches, those with training and
facilities were to lend their hand in the education of society. The Benedictine
reforms of Benedict of Aniane would try to restrict monastic involvement in
the world, but monastic schools continued to educate secular clergy after the
Aachen councils of 816 and 817.[38]

To summarize this attempt to explain the context of the baptismal instructions in four different kinds of books, at the grassroots level an effort can be
seen to provide parish priests with instruction through the use of readers. At
another level one sees the pastoral activity of individual bishops who instructed their clergy with the help of manuals containing reform decrees, sermons, synodal addresses, canonical norms, and diocesan capitularies. At still
another level one meets a highly learned circle of scholars, the leading bishops and abbots of the Carolingian Reform, who in their libraries collected
for study and re-copying erudite works on theological and liturgical questions. Finally, the manuscripts force one to take another leap in imagination
to the enclosure of the monastic or episcopal schoolroom, where bright, dili-
gent students took a serious interest in the works of the famous schoolmasters
and theologians such as Isidore, Alcuin, Amalarius, and Theodulf. Carolingian baptismal instructions are found in all of these contexts.

Until now, our vision of the Carolingian Reform or Renaissance has been
the tip of an iceberg. If it did consist in the effort to educate the whole of Christian society,[39] it has not been answered how those scholarly institutions of
monastery and cathedral schools, with their libraries, their specially gifted
masters and resident scholars from Ireland, their sophisticated curriculum of
studies, their "networking"[40] through a lively exchange of correspondence
and traveling students who asked one another questions on minute points of
grammar or biblical interpretation—how all *this* learning in any way related
to the preparation and education of the parish priest.[41] But the connection

---

[37]The external school of St. Gall envisioned boarders who would live at the school;
see M. Hildebrant, *The External School*, p. 9.

[38]Ibid., pp. 140 f. and Amos, "Monks and Pastoral Care," p. 171.

[39]See J. Contreni, "The Carolingian Renaissance," p. 59.

[40]Ibid., p. 72.

[41]Ibid., p. 72: "The burden of transmitting the Carolingian message to the world
outside the schoolroom fell on the students, only a few of whom became cathedral
or monastic masters in their own right. It was the job of the archdeacons and priests

between those elitist institutions and the education of "everyman" (starting with local pastors) *is* there, according to our manuscripts. In them we see monastic schools taking care of the needs of the dioceses in which they lay.

As more centers of learning continue to be studied and their manuscripts, masters, and contacts identified, there must be an attempt to address their role in their diocese in relation to the secular clergy. Manuscripts must be given attention that are not outstanding for one reason or another, but are books nonetheless, and required a commissioner, scriptorium, library, compiler, and scribe. These elements are found only in centers of learning with wealth and resources, such as Laon, Corbie, and Tours.[42]

When one reads the current scholarship on books, schools, scholars, and scriptoria in the Carolingian period, one senses a great hole. A virtual industry must have surrounded *all* of the kinds of codices represented in this study. Again, these are books, not just pamphlets or *libelli*. Each is a *liber*, even a *"bonus liber."*[43] They have covers, sometimes several hundred folios of parchment, occasionally even illustrations. Time and care went into their production, if perhaps not as much as went into some other volumes. Sometimes grammar mistakes abound. Often there is the sense that it is a student's edition of works his master has collected, or a bishop's manual he has personally put together for pure practicality, not with any pride of famous texts, or a cleric's instruction book whose compiler knew just what would be asked of the cleric by his bishop. Who was this ignorant parish priest, who somehow got ordained without adequate preparation? What role did the centers of

---

to bring Christian wisdom to their parishioners. We have no progress reports or reflections on this, the most important phase of the Carolingian program."

[42]Contreni must be given credit for his perception of the dichotomy between the kind of clerical educational reform program envisioned in the capitularies ("We read that men were to be trained to fulfill rather modest pastoral functions: e.g. to teach the Symbol, to be able to say mass, to be able to give instructions to candidates for baptism, to know and to teach the Lord's Prayer") and the course of studies pursued in the schools. The highbrows, however, like Theodulf and Hrabanus Maurus and Alcuin, it will be seen in this study also wrote baptismal instructions. Contreni puzzles that, while modern scholarship has focused on the sophisticated programs of the schools and paid less attention to the program of the capitularies, "However, the *ministerial* [my emphasis] requirements of the capitularies and the high scholarship of some masters were equally important in many schools. The library of Martin of Laon who taught during the third quarter of the ninth century contained books on Virgil, the liberal arts, and Greek. It also contained a collection of texts on basic Christian beliefs, a commentary on the Lord's Prayer, sermons denouncing idolatry, and a collection of canons relevant to marriage." ("Education and Learning in the Early Middle Ages: New Perspectives and Old Problems," Essay II, pp. 14 f., in *Carolingian Learning, Masters and Manuscripts*.)

[43]As some medieval hand wrote across the top of the first folio of V3. See F. Paxton, "Bonus liber," p. 1.

culture play in his, or his next generation's, education, which would directly effect the lives of the people?

How will such questions be answered? Whatever answers can be had lie in the manuscript evidence. There are approximately six thousand extant ninth-century volumes, according to B. Bischoff.[44] If his catalogue comes out, it will eventually be possible to categorize all of these manuscripts, and to identify even more of our four kinds of books, where and by whom they were copied, and where they circulated. There is a tremendous amount of work yet to be done on the aspect of the Carolingian Reform concerned with the instruction of the *people*, not the cultivation of the elite. If it happened through cooperation with that elite, through monastic schools willing to develop a curriculum for parish priests or monastic scriptoria willing to produce clerical-instruction readers, this is a phenomenon that has not yet received any systematic attention.

The most outstanding feature of the codices as a whole containing Carolingian baptismal instructions is their diversity. No two are entirely the same in their selection of material. Why this diversity? If the goal of educating society was officially supported with royal legislation, then why does not a more programmatic set of texts appear—one same canon law collection, penitential, creed commentary, grammar book, baptismal instruction? Quite the opposite is found:[45] The desire does not seem to have been to recopy carefully the same set of texts for dispersion throughout the realm. Instruction-readers for priests, for example, could be vastly different in their sophistication or interests. Why does one contain the *Collectio Dacheriana* and another the *Collectio Vetus Gallica*? Even at a quick glance, the survey of material in volume II is impressive for the diversity of texts on the same subject. Why twenty-four different expositions on the mass? Why forty-two different expositions on the faith? Why sixty-four different Carolingian baptismal instructions?

The individuality of each volume due to different selections of texts indicates what the Carolingian Reform actually meant to those who implemented it in individual archdioceses. In order to see why there is this diversity, in Part II the contents of the baptismal instructions themselves will be examined.

---

[44]"Über den Plan," p. 166. This number does not include fragments of Carolingian manuscripts, of which there are over a thousand.

[45]Contreni, "The Carolingian Renaissance," remarks on this diversity.

PART II: THE TEXTS

3

Introduction to the Baptismal Instructions
as Liturgical Expositions

One reason to read the Carolingian baptismal instructions is because there is information in them that has not been exploited. They describe what people believed about a large range of topics from the nature of the Trinity to the purpose of exorcism, salt, and oil. Regardless of whether the teaching was frequently that of Ambrose, Augustine, or Isidore, it is still necessary to know what was selected from the church fathers and how it was presented in a ninth-century context.

Another reason to investigate their contents relates to how baptism was celebrated in the Carolingian Empire. Most of them are quasi-liturgical expositions; that is, they explain a pre-determined series of ceremonies. They consist of a collection of mini-chapters on different topics corresponding to a stage or ceremony of the baptismal rite, such as "Concerning the catechumen" ("De catechumeno"), "Concerning the receiving of salt" ("De acceptione salis"), "Concerning exorcism" ("De exorcismo"). Depending on the topics (ceremonies) included and the order in which the topics are described, it is possible sometimes to discern the model used by the author of the baptismal instruction. His model might have been the *ordo* of baptism in a specific liturgical book or a description of baptism of an earlier writer or a florilegium on baptism. Even if his model was another baptismal instruction by an authority such as John the Deacon, Isidore, Alcuin, or Hrabanus Maurus, he was, of course, familiar with a specific *ordo* (rite) of baptism, the one he himself or the clerics for whom he wrote celebrated. Often his work is a rearrangement of his model so that it conforms more precisely to the baptismal *ordo* he knew. The sequence of the topics, then, he intended to be an important part of the baptismal instruction. The sequence itself taught a specific *ordo* of baptism.

There are thus two aspects of the contents of the baptismal texts which must be distinguished. One is the explanations they provide of various subjects relating to baptism, usually excerpted from patristic sources. The second is the liturgical *ordo* or rite which lies behind the baptismal instruction. Which *ordo* is not obvious, but must be brought to light by a comparison of its order of topics with various known rites of baptism in liturgical books. The rewards are very great when the specific liturgical *ordo* that guided the composer of the baptismal exposition is discovered. A small difference in the sequence of one or two topics, contrary to the norm, might not strike anyone as significant, until it is discovered that there is a liturgical *ordo* of baptism that has the very same sequence. In one of our baptismal instructions, for example, the topic of the touching of the nose and ears is discussed after the topic of the anointing of the breast and back, rather than before, contrary to all of our other baptismal instructions and most liturgical *ordines*. It would probably be best dismissed as a copyist's error, except that it is precisely the order of ceremonies described in *Ordo Romanus* XV of Andrieu's collection.

Sometimes the *ordo* behind the baptismal instruction is distinctly regional and shows where the composer wrote or for whom he wrote. It must be made very clear that there are these *two* aspects to the contents of the texts. This chapter and the next four will investigate not what the composer chose to say about baptism, but his selection and arrangement of topics, in order to attempt to discern the liturgical *ordo*, or rite, that guided him. To do this, it is necessary for a moment to speak about the celebration of baptism in the Carolingian period according to the liturgical books then in circulation.

The sources for the fifth through the tenth centuries show that its celebration differed in time and place due to such factors as the change by late antiquity to infant baptism as the norm; the Roman rite meeting with indigenous rites of northern Italy, Gaul, Spain, and Ireland; the missionizing efforts among adult heathens; and the spread of Christianity into the countryside far from a cathedral city and a bishop. Also, changes in the celebration of baptism in a specific area came about due to the presence of heresy or paganism or reformer bishops introducing unfamiliar practices.

The so-called "Roman" rite of baptism received numerous alterations when it was introduced into Frankish territory. There it was combined with so-called "Gallican" rites. The Carolingians themselves used the terms "Gallican" and "Roman" when referring to their liturgical books.[1] It may be that some employed the terms simply to mean that the book was being used in Rome or in Gaul. In any case, they were well aware of the differences among their ordinals, missals, and sacramentaries.

Even among sacramentary books considered "Roman," the rite of baptism is somewhat different in each. The significance of this fact should not be overlooked. It raises the question whether the Carolingians ever had in mind one fixed set of rubrics and prayers—a single text, when they referred, in reform legislation and elsewhere, to the Roman rite of baptism.

The Roman rite of baptism most well known to modern liturgists and historians is represented by *Ordo Romanus* XI (OR XI) of Andrieu's "Collection

---

[1]For some examples, see See Bernard Moreton, *The Eighth Century Gelasian Sacramentary: A Study in Tradition* (Oxford Univ. Press, 1976), p. 179, and Ann Freeman, "Theodulf of Orléans and the Psalm Citations of the 'Libri Carolini'" in *RB* XCVII (1987), p. 204 and note 59.

A" or "Roman" manuscripts, and by the *ordo* in the Reginensis Gelasian Sacramentary (Vat. Reg. lat. 316). In Rome at the end of the fifth century, infant baptism was the norm. At about this time, according to Andrieu, the Gelasian Sacramentary, the primitive archetype of Vat. Reg. Lat. 316 was written. Its main baptismal *ordo* was for infants, and there were three scrutiny masses held for them and their godparents on the last three Sundays before Easter. It included a supplementary *ordo* for adult pagan candidates. By the end of the sixth or beginning of the seventh century, OR XI was in circulation. This borrowed from the Gelasian Sacramentary some of the prayers and readings at the scrutiny masses but gave a far more detailed description of the scrutinies, which were increased in number to seven. Some time after this, before the mid-seventh century, a copy of the Gelasian Sacramentary was made that borrowed from the *ordo scrutiniorum* of OR XI. The Reginensis (Vat. Reg. lat. 316), written circa 750 perhaps at Chelles (near Paris) is a copy of this revised Gelasian Sacramentary, although still with three scrutiny masses, now also with a fuller description of the scrutiny procedure.

Andrieu edited OR XI using fourteen manuscripts dating from the beginning of the ninth century through the eleventh. Half the manuscripts belong to his "Collection A" or Roman manuscripts, half to his "Collection B" or Gallicanized manuscripts. Only the manuscripts of Collection A contain OR XI in its entirety; those of Collection B stop before the blessing of the font,[2] omitting this ceremony, baptism itself, and the post-baptismal ceremonies.

There are other differences between the Collection A and Collection B manuscripts, but Andrieu stresses that OR XI is truly a Roman *ordo*, as the Collection of manuscripts testify; Frankish copyists introduced alterations, and in these manuscripts OR XI is "Gallicanized."[3]

According to the Collection A manuscripts, baptism is observed as follows:[4] (The setting is Rome, the time Lent and Holy Week. A bishop [pontifex] presides over the final ceremonies on the Paschal Vigil, assisted by clerics of

---

[2]Nr. 89 in M. Andrieu, ed., *Les Ordines* II, p. 444. For the fourteen manuscripts see pp. 365 f. Andrieu found OR XI in one further manuscript of Collection B, which covers the first six scrutinies but not the final pre-baptismal ceremonies of Holy Saturday morning. It is tempting to conclude that to celebrate baptism according to the Roman *ordo* for those on Gallican soil meant to hold a series of scrutinies in the weeks before baptism. This will be dealt with in the next chapter.

[3]Ibid., p. 367 and note 2.

[4]The variations of the Collection B manuscripts and of the Reginensis will be noted. See Charts A1 and A2 for a summary of OR XI and the Reginensis Sacramentary. Technically, an *ordo* gives only the stage directions, or rubrics, for celebrating a liturgical rite and must be accompanied by a sacramentary, which gives the full texts of the prayers only indicated by incipit in the *ordo*. Some manuscripts of the B Collection of OR XI, however, also include the full texts of the prayers and other words spoken by the celebrant.

many grades. The candidates are infants accompanied by adult sponsors.) On Monday of the third week in Lent the time of the first scrutiny is announced. On Wednesday the names of the infants and their sponsors are taken down by an acolyte (enrollment/*descriptio nominum*),[5] and they are called into church in order, as their names are written, the males on the right side with male sponsors, the females on the left with female sponsors. A priest makes the sign of the cross on the infants' foreheads with his thumb (signing/*signum crucis*) and, extending his hand (one codex has "hands") over their heads, recites the "prayers for the making of a catechumen."[6] Salt is exorcized (blessed)[7] and placed on the infants' tongues (salt/*sal*) and they are then dismissed to await the hour of the first scrutiny (scrutiny/*scrutinium*).

In the first scrutiny (essentially a mass), after the entrance antiphon the infants' names are called out and they are brought forward by their sponsors who kneel (genuflection/*flectere genua*) and pray, then stand and make the sign of the cross on their infants' foreheads (signing/*signum crucis*). Then an acolyte signs the male infants and, extending a hand over their heads, recites an exorcism prayer (exorcism/*exorcismus*). Next he does the same to the female catechumens, signing them and reciting a different exorcism prayer. The whole process, from the sponsors' kneeling, is repeated two more times, each time with a different acolyte and different exorcism prayers (a total of six different exorcism prayers). The scrutiny is concluded by the sponsors kneeling, praying, then signing the infants a final (fourth) time. Mass continues, and after the first reading and response and before the Gospel, the catechumens are commanded to leave the church. (Presumably there were nurses outside to take the infants, because the sponsors stayed and participated in the offertory.)

The second scrutiny, on Saturday of the same week, is identical to the first. The third scrutiny is on an optional day (announced ahead) in the fourth week of Lent. This scrutiny is distinct. It is called both in the Reginensis and OR XI the *aurium apertio* ("opening of the ears"). At this scrutiny, following the usual exorcism prayers, the catechumens are introduced to the beginning of each of the four Gospels, to the Creed, and to the Lord's Prayer. First, following an introduction by the priest, the beginning verses of each of the four Gospels is read, each by a different deacon, and after each reading the priest explains the symbols of the man, lion, ox, and eagle (*traditio evangeliorum*).

---

[5]See Charts A1 and A2. In the following description the words in italics are topics in the baptismal instructions, which will be discussed later.

[6]"XXX. Orationes super electos ad caticumenum faciendum" is the title in the Reginensis, ed. by Leo Cunibert Mohlberg, *Liber Sacramentorum Romanae Aeclesiae Ordinis Anni Circuli (Cod. Vat. Reg. lat. 316/Paris Bibl. Nat. 7193, 41/56) (Sacramentarium Gelasianum)* Rome, 1960, (repr. 1981), p. 42, nr. 285.

[7]"Et postea benedicit sal hoc modo: 'Exorcizo te, creatura salis . . .'" Andrieu, *Les Ordines* II, p. 419, nr. 5.

The priest then gives an introduction to the Creed, and an acolyte takes in his arms a Greek-speaking male infant and recites the Nicene Creed in Greek, repeating it with a female infant. Then another acolyte takes a Latin-speaking male infant and recites the Creed in Latin, repeating it with a female infant (*traditio symboli*). Afterwards the priest gives a brief explanation of the words of the Creed.[8] Finally the priest recites the Lord's Prayer and gives an explanation of the words (*traditio orationis dominicae*).

The fourth, fifth, and sixth scrutiny meetings, on optional days during the fifth and sixth weeks of Lent, are identical to the first. The final scrutiny takes place on Holy Saturday morning.[9] Here the final pre-baptismal ceremonies are completed.[10] After the priest signs the infants (omitted in the Reginensis) (signing/*signum crucis*), he lays his hand on the head of each and says the exorcism prayer, "Do not lurk, Satan . . ." ("Nec te latet, Satanas . . ." (exorcism/*exorcismus*). Then he touches the nose and ears of each with his spittle and says into the ear of each, "Effeta . . ." ("Be opened . . .") (nose, ears/*nares, aures*). The anointing of the breast and back with exorcized oil follows, accompanied by a threefold renunciation of Satan, his works, and his pomps (omitted in OR XI) (breast, between the shoulder blades, renunciation/*pectus, inter scapulas, abrenuntiatio*).

Next (in both the Reginensis and OR XI) comes the return of the Creed by the priest, who imposes his hand while walking around the infants chanting the Creed (in Latin), first to the males and then to the females (return of the Creed/*redditio symboli*).[11] The catechumens are then dismissed to await the

---

[8]In the Reginensis both the Greek and Latin form of the Creed is the Nicene (the version sometimes known as the "Niceno-Constantinopolitan Creed"). Five manuscripts of Collection B of OR XI, however, give the Apostles' Creed in place of the Latin Nicene Creed. Two further manuscripts of Collection B give at least the incipit of the Apostles' rather than the Nicene Creed. Andrieu proposes that the primitive Gelasian Sacramentary contained the Apostles' Creed and that the Nicene Creed was substituted at the time of the Byzantine expansion into Italy after the Gothic War in the mid-sixth century (*Les Ordines* II, p. 394). The priest's introduction to the Creed does refer to the "symboli sacramentum . . . ab apostolis institutum," although this could apply to the Nicene Creed, which belongs to the apostolic tradition. Thus, the Apostles' Creed equally could be a later modification made on Gallican soil, where it was preferred to the Nicene.

[9]OR XI states: "Usque in sabbato sancto vigilia paschae, septem scrutinii esse debeant." Ibid., p. 442, nr. 81.

[10]Described under the rubric, "This is the order in which they are catechized." ("Ordo vero qualiter catecizantur ita est.") Ibid., p. 443, nr. 83.

[11]This recitation of the Creed by the priest replaced the ancient "redditio symboli," when adult catechumens proved that they had learned the words of the Creed. Four manuscripts of Collection B have the priest reciting the Apostles' Creed, not the Nicene, according to their incipits which state, "Credo in deum . . ." instead of "Credo in unum deum . . ." See Ibid., p. 443, nr. 86.

beginning of the Easter Vigil Mass. (At this point all the Collection B manuscripts cease).

To bless the font, the celebrant, (now in the manuscripts called the "pontifex" or bishop) proceeds from the church to the baptistery with all the clergy and two notaries bearing two man-sized candles. All the clergy and people assemble around the font. After two blessing prayers (the Reginensis has a rubric for signing the waters of the font during these prayers) the bishop pours chrism into the font in the form of a cross, mixes the water with his hand, and sprinkles some of it on the people, who are then allowed to collect some of the water in the font in small containers to sprinkle on their home and fields (blessing of the font/*benedictio fontis*).

OR XI very summarily states that the bishop baptizes a few of the infants and a deacon the remainder, although one manuscript gives the opening words of the threefold interrogation of faith. The Reginensis gives it in its entirety.[12] Following the third "Credo," the infant is immersed three times in the water.

Following baptism the infants are immediately given to a priest who anoints the tops of their heads with chrism (presbyteral anointing of head with chrism/*unctio capitis chrismate*). The bishop goes to his throne in the church (omitted in the Reginensis), where the infants are brought to him, and he gives each a stole (*stola*), chasuble (*casula*), chrism-cloth (*crismale*), and ten coins. Then the infants are vested (white vestments/*alba vestimenta*). Episcopal confirmation follows, with the bishop praying over the infants (the Reginensis says imposing his hand) a prayer invoking the seven-form gift of the Holy Spirit, and then signing each on the forehead with chrism (episcopal confirmation/*confirmatio episcopi*). After this the Vigil Mass continues, during which all the neophytes receive the Eucharist for the first time (eucharist/*corpus et sanguis domini*).

This skeleton description hardly conveys the richness of the rite when amplified by the words of its prayers. Nevertheless, one can now compare this Roman-rite baptism against some other rites of baptism. It was said that this rite was "Gallicanized" in some manuscripts. A careful distinction must be made between necessary changes in the Roman rite that took place on Gallican soil to accommodate the particular circumstances of individual locations, and baptismal *ordines* of longer-standing, indigenous tradition (for example, the ancient Milanese rite). Two unavoidable Gallicanizations of the Roman rite which did not lessen the Romanity of the rite in the eyes of some Caro-

---

[12]"Credis in deum patrem omnipotentem? Respondet: Credo. Credis et in Iesum Christum filium eius unicum dominum nostrum natum et passum? Respondet: Credo. Credis et in spiritum sanctum, sancta aecclesia (*sic*), remissionem peccatorum, carnis resurrectionem? Respondet: Credo." L. C. Mohlberg, *Sacramentarium Gelasianum*, p. 74, nr. 449.

lingians were the elimination of the scrutinies and the postponement of epis-copal confirmation.

To see these and certain other Gallicanizations that took place in the cele-bration of the Roman rite, one can turn to two *ordines* of baptism preserved in the tenth-century *Pontificale Romano-Germanicum (PRG)*.[13]

There are several baptismal *ordines* in the *PRG*.[14] One is the same as in Andrieu's *Ordo Romanus* L (OR L). OR L is a lengthy *ordo* describing the principal offices of the entire liturgical year, which was incorporated in its entirety into the *PRG* (number XCIX of Vogel and Elze's edition).

The part of OR L that covers the ceremonies of Lent and Holy Week is simi-lar to OR XI, but there are some differences (see Chart A3). Before the prayers for the making of the catechumen, OR L has a renunciation of Satan, his works and pomps, a threefold interrogation of faith (a shortened form of the Apostles' Creed), and an exsufflation with an exorcism ("Exi, immunde spiri-tus . . .").[15] In the *aurium apertio* all the manuscripts of OR L have the delivery of the Nicene Creed, not the Apostles', in Greek and in Latin.[16] In OR L the first event on Holy Saturday morning is the return of the Lord's Prayer and the Creed by the catechumens, if they are able, or by their sponsors.[17] OR L has a (third) renunciation of Satan, his works and pomps and threefold interroga-tion of faith immediately before the immersion in the font.[18] Finally, some manuscripts of OR L have the bishop giving the neophyte a stole, chrism-cloth, and ten coins (no chasuble, as in OR XI). Other manuscripts simply say that a cap (*cappam*) is placed on the neophyte's head.[19] One accommodation to a Gallican situation in manuscripts of OR L is the phrase, "If a bishop is pres-ent."[20]

The return of the Creed by the candidates or their sponsors on Holy Satur-day and the increased number of renunciations and professions of faith in OR L may reflect a special concern to make sure the candidates or their sponsors were not ignorant of the faith before they were baptized, and to give them more opportunities to denounce idolatry and assert their belief.

A further stage in the development of the Roman *ordo* on Frankish soil is seen in another *ordo* for baptizing an infant included in the *PRG* (PRG CVII;

---

[13]Cyrille Vogel and Reinhard Elze, ed., *Le Pontifical Romano-Germanique du dixième siècle*, 2 vols. (*Studi e Testi* 226, 227) Vatican, 1963.

[14]Although there are no extant ninth-century manuscripts of these baptismal *or-dines*, some of our Carolingian baptismal instructions examined below will show that, in fact, these *ordines* in the PRG are Carolingian.

[15]Andrieu, *Les Ordines* V, cap. XX, nn. 3–5, pp. 130 f.

[16]Ibid., cap. XX, nn. 74–79, pp. 152–54.

[17]Ibid., cap. XXIX, nr. 3, p. 262.

[18]Ibid., cap. XXIX, nr. 56, pp. 282 f.

[19]Ibid., cap. XXIX, nn. 66–69, pp. 286–88.

[20]"Si episcopus adest." See the *app. crit.*, ibid., pp. 287 f.

see Chart A4). It is found in only four manuscripts of the *PRG*.[21] The *ordo* it describes, or one very similar to it, must go back to the ninth century, because it is almost identical with the description of the *ordo* of baptism in the *De institutione clericorum* I, cap. XXV–XXX of Hrabanus Maurus.[22]

PRG CVII claims that it comes from the Roman Sacramentary of Pope Gregory.[23] In any case, it is not the Gregorian Sacramentary received by Charlemagne or its supplemented form by Benedict of Aniane.[24] The entire sequence of ceremonies, from the making of the catechumen to the reception of the Eucharist, takes place in the course of the Easter Vigil Mass. After a renunciation of Satan, his works and pomps, threefold interrogation of the faith, exsufflation three times upon the face with an exorcism, signing, imposition of hand (one manuscript has "hands") while reciting the prayers for the making of a catechumen (the same prayers as in the Reginensis, OR XI and OR L), and giving of exorcised salt, the priest again signs the infants, imposes a hand over the males and recites an exorcism prayer, then does likewise over the female infants. He repeats this three times, with six different exorcism prayers (the same as those in the Reginensis, OR XI and OR L). Then he immediately continues with the exorcism, "Do not lurk, Satan . . ." ("Nec te latet, Satanas . . .") said on Saturday morning in the Reginensis, OR XI, or OR L, and the "Effeta" ceremony of the touching of the nose and ears with spittle. A prayer of benediction to arm the catechumen against Satan (beginning, "Deus, inmortale presidium . . .") follows. After the anointing of the breast and the back with oil with the renunciation of Satan, his works and pomps, the priest blesses the font, during which he divides the water with his hand in the form

---

[21]Vogel and Elze, Le Pontifical II, pp. 155–64.

[22]M. Rissel at least suggests that there is a relation between the baptismal rubrics familiar to Hrabanus Maurus (who was archbishop of Mainz from 847 to 856) and the baptismal *ordo* of PRG CVII, which was incorporated into the PRG when it was compiled at Mainz a century later. Rissel states that Hrabanus used a model for his baptismal exposition in the *De institutione clericorum* that responds to the needs of priests in the eastern part of the Frankish empire who were engaged in missionary work. See M. Rissel, *Rezeption antiker und patristicher Wissenschaft bei Hrabanus Maurus: Studien zur karolingischen Geistgeschichte* (Lateinische Sprache und Literatur des Mittelalters, 7), Frankfort/M., 1976, pp. 220, 222.

[23]It begins, "Ex authentico libro sacramentorum sancti gregorii papae urbis Rome. Incipit ordo ad baptizandum infantes."

[24]Charlemagne tried to obtain a "pure" Roman sacramentary from Pope Hadrian. The so-called Gregorian Sacramentary that he received some time between 784 and 791 (Deschusses's "Hadrianum authenticum") was woefully inadequate, lacking many of the masses of the year and prayers of the rites, especially baptism. A supplement undertaken by Abbot Benedict of Aniane between 810 and 815 (Deshusses's "Supplementum Anianense") included a full set of prayers for the rite of baptism. These were drawn largely from an eighth-century-type Gelasian sacramentary, a type of Roman sacramentary characterized by Gallicanizations, some of which will be discussed later in this study.

of a cross at three different moments. The base of the paschal candle is immersed in the font with the invocation of the Holy Spirit. Chrism is also mixed in the water. The people are invited to take some of the water for sprinkling in their homes. The candidates are asked their names and if they desire to be baptized, then immersed three times in the name of the Trinity with the formula, "Et ego te baptizo in nomine Patris et Filii et Spiritus Sancti."[25]

Following baptism, the priest immediately anoints the infants with chrism on the top of their heads. He places a head cloth (*mitra*) on each, and they are vested. Finally, they receive the Eucharist in the Vigil Mass. After the words, "Let them enter into mass and communicate" the rubric states, "and if a bishop is present, let him confirm them."[26] Confirmation, however, would seem to come before Eucharist if a bishop was present because the *ordo* of confirmation begins, "The infants, *now having been vested*, are arranged in order.")[27] In the *ordo* of confirmation the infants are held by their sponsors, or, if older, stand on the feet of their sponsors. The bishop extends his hand over them all and recites the prayer invoking the seven-form gift of the Holy Spirit. Then, asking the name of each, he anoints each with chrism on the forehead.

In sum, the differences between OR L and PRG CVII are that, first, the latter condenses OR L into a single session. The seven scrutiny meetings over the weeks of Lent are eliminated, but the ceremonies of the first and last scrutinies are celebrated, so that while the word "scrutiny" does not appear, the six exorcism prayers of OR L are preserved. Second, there is no *aurium apertio* (delivery of the Gospels, Creed, and Lord's Prayer), nor is there a return of the Lord's Prayer and Creed by the candidates or their sponsors. Third, in PRG CVII a priestly benediction/exorcism prayer ("Deus inmortale presidium...") is included immediately after the "Effeta" ceremony. Fourth, PRG CVII has no repeated renunciation of Satan and interrogation of faith at the font immediately before immersion.[28] Finally, all the manuscripts of PRG CVII foresee the delay of episcopal confirmation.

A shortened catechumenate and the postponement of episcopal confirmation may not have developed solely out of the practical impossibility of frequent church gatherings or ready access to a bishop, although these are factors in the changes that took place when the Roman liturgy moved outside of Rome. Even, however, in the episcopal cities of the Carolingian period a reduced catechumenate and a deferred confirmation seem to have been normal. Indication of this will be seen in the baptismal instructions.

---

[25]Vogel and Elze, *Le Pontifical* II, p. 163, nr. 34.

[26]Ibid., p. 163, nr. 37: "Et si pontifex adest, confirmet eos."

[27]Ibid., p. 163, nr. 38: "*Induti* vero ordinentur per ordinem et infantes quidem."

[28]CVII is accompanied in the PRG by another *ordo* for a *paganus* (PRG CX). CX refers to CVII for the full text of the prayers when it says "ut supra," and is identical to CVII in almost all respects. One important difference, however, is that two of its manuscripts have a threefold interrogation of faith at the font. See ibid., pp. 170 f., nr. 29.

Having seen the ceremonies of baptism of the Roman rite, one can turn to the Bobbio Missal (circa 700) for an *ordo* of baptism that represents something closer to the Old Gallican Rite, although it has "Romanizations."[29]

In the Bobbio *ordo*, the candidates are infants and the first ceremonies mentioned begin on Palm Sunday, one week before Easter. On Palm Sunday the *aurium apertio* is held, which consists of the delivery of the Gospels and the Apostles' Creed, but not the Lord's Prayer. After giving various formularies which pertain to Holy Week ceremonies (no precise times are stated) the Bobbio text has a block of rubrics and prayers for baptism. First are given the prayers for the making of the catechumen (not the same as in the Reginensis), then a signing of the cross with a prayer that is the same as the one in the supplementary *ordo* of baptism for a pagan (*paganus*) in the Reginensis.[30] A sufflation three times into the infant's mouth with the words, "N., receive the Holy Spirit . . ." follows, then prayers for the blessing of the font, including some also found in the Reginensis, and a directive to pour chrism into the font in the form of a cross. (The prayer invoking the descent of the Holy Spirit is not in the Reginensis.) Next occurs the rubric: "Exorcism of a man before he is baptized," and an exorcism (not "Nec te latet, Satanas . . ."), followed by the touching of the nostrils and the words, "Effeta . . .". (There is no mention of the ears or the use of spittle). An anointing of the nose, ears and breast with oil follows. The candidate is asked if he/she renounces Satan, his pomps, his luxuries, and this present world, to which the sponsor replies: "May he/she renounce them." Next, in the threefold interrogation of the faith, the priest recites the Apostles' Creed in its entirety in the form of three questions, to which the sponsor replies: "May he/she believe." Baptism follows (the method is not specified) in the name of the Trinity with a non-Roman formula. After the font, chrism is poured over the infant's brow; then the infant is vested in a white garment and his/her feet are washed (the *pedilavium*). The collects in the Mass of the Paschal Vigil refer to the neophytes' receiving the Eucharist.[31]

In sum, the most distinctive features of the Bobbio in contrast to the Reginensis include no trace of any scrutiny masses, the delivery of the Gospels and Apostles' Creed on Palm Sunday, no salt, an exsufflation, its baptis-

---

[29]See J. D. C. Fisher, *Christian Initiation: Baptism in the Medieval West: A Study in the Disintegration of the Primitive Rite of Initiation* (London, 1965), p. 47.

[30]"Accipe signum crucis tam in fronte quam in corde." Mohlberg, *Sacramentarium Gelasianum*, p. 93, nr. 599.

[31]E. A. Lowe, ed., *The Bobbio Missal: A Gallican Mass-Book* (Ms. Paris. Lat. 13246): Text, London (HBS vol. LVIII), 1920, pp. 54–77. The non-Roman formula of baptism (nr. 248, p. 75) states: "Baptizo te in nomine patris et filii et spiritus sancti unam abentem (*lege*: habentium) substancia[m] ut [h]abias vitam aeternam parte cum sanctis."

mal formula, the *pedilavium*, and no episcopal confirmation (that is, second post-baptismal chrismation with an imposition of hand).

Having compared a Roman, two Gallicanized-Roman, and one Old Gallican rites of baptism, the Carolingian baptismal instructions as liturgical expositions may now be investigated. Because it is not possible in the length of this study to discuss all sixty-four baptismal instructions, a selection will be used to illustrate some of the reasons why there are so many different baptismal instructions. In Chapter 4, four are compared with OR XI. In Chapter 5, four are compared to a patristic florilegium; in Chapter 6, eight are compared to three Carolingian models; and in Chapter 7, three are compared with three non-Roman, indigenous rites of baptism.

4

The Carolingian Understanding of the Term "Roman Ordo*"*

Some, but not all, of the Carolingian reform legislation on baptism specifies that baptism should be celebrated according to the "Roman custom" or "*ordo.*"[1] Whether the Carolingian legislators had either the Reginensis or OR XI in mind is uncertain, but none of our baptismal instructions completely agrees with Vat. Reginensis lat. 316 or any of the manuscripts of OR XI. Below, the treatises by Jesse, Amalarius, Theodulf, and Leidrad show what these leading bishops of the Carolingian Reform taught on how baptism was to be celebrated in their dioceses.

Text 30 (Jesse)

Jesse, Bishop of Amiens (circa 799–836) addressed his explanation of the ceremonies of baptism (Text 30) to the clergy of his diocese.[2] The year is not

---

[1] *Admonitio Generalis,* 789, cap. LXX (and repeated in the *Capitulare Missorum,* ca. 802, cap. 28): "Ut episcopi diligenter discutiant per suas parrochias presbyteros, eorum fidem, baptisma et missarum celebrationes, ut et fidem rectam teneant et baptisma *catholicum* observent et missarum preces bene intellegant." Capitulary of 789, cap. XXIII: "Ut audiant episcopi baptisterium presbyterorum, ut secundum *morem* Romanum baptizent." (*MGH Capit.* I, pp. 59, 103, 64.) Constitution of Arno of Salzburg, ca. 798, cap. IV: "Et hoc consideret episcopus, ut ipsi presbyteri non sint idiothae, sed sacras scripturas legant et intellegant, ut secundum traditionem Romane aecclesiae possint instruere et fidem catholicam debeant ipsi agere et populos sibi commissos docere, missas secundum consuetudinem caelebrare, sicut Romana traditio nobis tradidit. Baptismum publicum constitutis temporibus per II vices in anno faciat, in Pascha, in Pentecosten; et hoc secundum ordinem *traditionis* Romanae debet facere." (*MGH Conc.* 2, p. 198.) *Interrogationes Examinationis,* ca. 803: "IV. Missam vestram secundum ordinem Romanam quomodo nostis vel intellegitis. . . . VII. Officium divinum secundum ritum Romanorum in statutis sollemnitatibus ad tecantandum [*lege:* decantandum] quomodo scitis. VIII. Baptisterium quomodo nostis vel intellegitis." (*MGH Capit.* I, p. 234.) The Council of Mainz of 813, cap. IV: "Sacramenta itaque baptismatis volumus, ut, sicut sancta vestra (Charlemagne's) fuit ammonitio, ita concorditer atque uniformiter in singulis parrochiis *secundum Romanum ordinem* inter nos celebretur iugiter atque conservetur, *id est scrutinium ad ordinem baptismatis,*" (Conc. II, p. 261). None of the episcopal capitularies from the ninth century newly edited by P. Brommer in *Capitula Episcoporum* (including Theodulf of Orléans's First Diocesan Capitulary) specifies that baptism should be celebrated according to the Roman *ordo* or custom.

[2] "Sacris sacerdotibus et in Christo omnibus dioecesi nostrae digne militantibus . . ." (vol. II, p. 405).

52

known. Some scholars have assumed that Jesse's address was stimulated by Charlemagne's baptismal questionnaire to his metropolitans of circa 812,[3] but he probably wrote it at least ten years earlier.[4]

Jesse may have been motivated to address his clergy by a circulatory letter from Charlemagne urging the bishops to admonish their clergy about baptism, or by a royal capitulary containing clerical reform legislation regarding baptism. There were circulatory letters on baptismal instruction before Charlemagne's inquiry of 812. A letter of Charlemagne in a form addressed to Bishop Garibald of Liège, written some time before Garibald's death in 809, warned him about the duty of teaching and was especially concerned that baptismal sponsors could recite the Lord's Prayer and the Apostles' Creed before they received anyone from the font. Finally, he warned Garibald that diocesan synods should be held with his priests on all these matters.[5] Garibald

---

[3]Carlo de Clercq says of Jesse's treatise: "Le document doit être mis en rapport avec l'interrogatoire de Charlemagne sur les rites baptismaux et les préoccupations des conciles de 813 à leur sujet. Il n'est pas une résponse d'un archevêque à l'interrogatoire impérial, mais une instruction d'un évêque à ses prêtres, sur le sens et les cérémonies du baptême, conformément au désir exprimé par Charlemagne." (*La législation religieuse franque de Clovis à Charlemagne, 507–814*, vol. I, Louvain/Paris, 1936, p. 282.) Friedrich Wiegand says that Jesse wrote his treatise probably at the same time as the other bishops wrote their responses to Charlemagne's questionnaire. (*Erzbischof Odilbert von Mailand über die Taufe: Ein Beitrag zur Geschichte der Taufliturgie im Zeitalter Karls des Grossen,*Leipzig, 1899, p. 5, n. 2.) Wiegand was perhaps following the words in Migne: "Abfuisse videtur anno 812 cum . . . scripsit epistolam . . . hanc enim scripsit eodem fere tempore quo suas Amalarius et Theodulfus lucubrationes exarunt." (*PL* 105: 781 f.) Also Friedrich Stegmüller counts Jesse's treatise among the extant responses to Charlemagne's inquiry. ("Bischof Angilmodus über die Taufe: Ein Beitrag zur spätkarolingischen Tauftheologie" in *Römische Quartalschrift für die christliche Altertumskunde und für Kirchengeschichte* 52 1957, p. 14, n. 6.)

[4]Andrieu dates Jesse's treatise to circa 800, but does not give his reasons (see *Les Ordines* II, p. 409, note 2). Professor Bischoff more recently discovered a *membrum disiectum* of Paris, BN lat. 13373 (P18) containing Jesse's treatise: Florence, Bibl. Med. Laurenz. Ashb. App. 1923 (F2), which he says was written at Corbie at the beginning of the ninth century. David Ganz has studied P18 closely and dates this manuscript to the very first years of the ninth century. Another manuscript of Jesse's treatise, St. Gall, Stiftsbibl. Cod. sang. 124 (S2), could have been written as early as 804.

[5]"Monuimus de praedicatione in sancta Dei ecclesia, ut unusquisque vestrum secundum sanctorum canonum auctoritatem et praedicare et docere deberet: primo omnium de fide catholica, ut et qui amplius capere non valuisset tantummodo orationem dominicam et simbolum fidei catholicae, sicut Apostoli docuerunt, tenere et memoriter recitare potuisset, et ut nullus de sacro fonte baptismatis aliquem suscipere praesumeret, antequam in vestra aut ministrorum vestrorum sacri ordinis praesentia orationem dominicam et simbolum recitaret . . . et conventum habeatis cum vestris sacerdotibus et diligenter omnem rei veritatem requirite et examinate . . ." *MGH Capit.* I, pp. 241 f.

did convene a diocesan synod as a result of this letter[6] and probably other bishops received the letter and addressed their clergy on their duty to instruct the people commissioned to them.

Jesse was absent from his diocese when he wrote his address to his clergy, as he explains in his preface.[7] He worked closely with Charlemagne between 799 and Charlemagne's death in 814, and was absent from his diocese on a number of occasions before 812.[8] His absence in Constantinople during 802 and 803 might explain, "by reason of impossibility I am prevented from speaking to you." Also, a profusion of reform capitularies were issued circa 802,[9] which might have inspired his baptismal address to his clergy. On the other hand, it is possible that Jesse took his own initiative in the reform of his diocesan clergy. His action may even have inspired Charlemagne to issue circulatory letters.

One reason why it is important to establish when Jesse wrote his baptismal instruction is that the *ordo* of baptism he describes, which presumably was the *ordo* used in the diocese of Amiens, differs somewhat from OR XI.

For his first topic on how one is made a catechumen, Jesse turned to a liturgical book and essentially copied the rubrics for the *ordo* of the catechumen.[10] Parallels between Jesse's *ordo* and OR XI led a number of scholars to say it was OR XI that Jesse inserted into his instruction, "sometimes word for word."[11] In fact, there are some important differences between Jesse's *ordo* and OR XI. Most striking are Jesse's different times for the scrutinies, especially the *aurium apertio*. Jesse says the first scrutiny is held on Monday (not Wednesday) of the third week in Lent. One could perhaps explain this as a simple confusion, since the title of OR XI refers to "secunda feria" (Monday) as the day on which the first scrutiny is *announced* (not held). There is no possibility, however, of simple confusion in Jesse's times for his other scrutinies:

Scrutiny I: OR XI: Wednesday, third week in Lent
             Jesse: Monday, third week in Lent

---

[6]*MGH Capit.* I, pp. 242–44.

[7]See vol. II, p. 405.

[8]In 799 he was a *missus dominicus* and met with Pope Leo III; at Christmas, 800, he was present at Charlemagne's coronation in Rome; in 802 he was sent by Charlemagne to Empress Irene in Constantinople, returning in 803; in 805 he distributed a capitulary of Charlemagne as a *missus dominicus*; circa 808 Charlemagne sent him to Pope Leo III in Ravenna; in 809 he was present at the Council of Aquileia; and in 811 he subscribed to Charlemagne's "ordinationi testamenti" at Aachen. (See Migne, *PL* 105: 779–81 and B. Scholz, *Carolingian Chronicles*, pp. 82 f.)

[9]See C. de Clercq, *La législation*, I, p. 380.

[10]"Tertia ebdomada in quadragesima, II feria, hora tertia, veniant ad ecclesiam et antequam in aecclesiam introeant scribantur nomina infantum et eorum qui eos suscepturi sunt ab acolito."

[11]M. Andrieu, *Les Ordines* II, p. 409, n. 2.

Scrutiny II: OR XI: optional day, third week in Lent
    Jesse: optional day, third week in Lent

Scrutiny III: OR XI: optional day, fourth week in Lent: *AURIUM APERTIO*
    Jesse: before Wednesday of the fifth week in Lent: the same
        scrutiny as the first

Scrutiny IV: OR XI: optional day, fifth week in Lent
    Jesse: before Wednesday of the fifth week in Lent

Scrutiny V: OR XI: optional day, fifth week in Lent
    Jesse: Wednesday, fifth week in Lent

Scrutiny VI: OR XI: optional day, sixth week in Lent: the same scrutiny as the
    first
    Jesse: Friday, fifth week in Lent: *AURIUM APERTIO*

Scrutiny VII: OR XI: Holy Saturday morning
    Jesse: no seventh scrutiny

One can actually find in another Roman *ordo*, Andrieu's OR XV, a parallel with Jesse's *ordo*. In OR XV the first scrutiny does take place on *Monday* of the third week in Lent.[12] This part of OR XV is extant in only one manuscript written at the end of the eighth century.[13]

One can also find a parallel in the Gellone Sacramentary. Gellone contains five different *ordines* relating to baptism. The first three include the Roman *ordo* of the scrutinies; the fourth is for one who is sick (*infirmus*); and the last is an *ordo* for making a pagan (*paganus*) a catechumen.[14] The rubric at the beginning of the second of these five separate *ordines* states that the first scrutiny takes place on Monday of the third week in Lent.

Jesse's *ordo*, however, does not agree entirely with OR XV or the Gellone Sacramentary. Gellone clearly prescribes seven scrutinies. The seventh is on Wednesday of the sixth week in Lent, according to the rubric for the mass of that day.[15] Jesse mentions only six scrutinies, and the last, on the Friday before Palm Sunday, is the *aurium apertio*. Jesse's *ordo* indicates that he attempted to implement the Roman *ordo* of scrutinies in his diocese in northern France. It is not known what liturgical book Jesse worked from, but it contained a different Roman *ordo* than any currently known.

Had whoever compiled Jesse's *ordo* (probably in the eighth century) adapted OR XI, or had he worked from another *Ordo Romanus*?[16] Besides the

---

[12]See Andrieu, *Les Ordines* III, p. 116, nn. 85–86.

[13]St. Gall, Stiftsbibl. Cod. sang. 349.

[14]A. Dumas, ed., *Liber Sacramentorum Gellonensis: Textus* (*CCSL* CLIX), Turnhout, 1981, pp. 48 f., 64 f., 312 f., 339 f., and 347 f.

[15]"Hic conples septimo scrutinio." Ibid., p. 75.

[16]The earliest manuscripts of OR XI are from the beginning of the ninth century. See

time and number of the scrutinies, Jesse's *ordo* differs from OR XI in lacking any mention of the delivery of the Creed in Greek. Also, three times in place of "patrini et matrinae" he calls the sponsors "susceptores."

For his second topic, "De competente" (see Chart B1), Jesse paraphrases Isidore on the etymology of the word "competens,"[17] but then disagrees with Isidore on when the catechumen becomes a competent. Isidore says it is before the Creed is delivered,[18] but Jesse says that one does not become a competent until after he has received the Creed and the Our Father. One wonders if this was not due to the place where the word "competens" appears in the liturgical book used by Jesse.

After the topic of salt, Jesse proceeds to describe the final pre-baptismal ceremonies. For the topic of exorcism ("*Exorcizatur sive catecizatur infans*") Jesse refers to the exorcism prayer "Nec te latet, Satanas." (Thus, one has reached the Holy Saturday morning ceremonies of OR XI.) Jesse includes the topic of exsufflation after exorcism, even though there is no mention of an exsufflation of the catechumens anywhere in OR XI or the Reginensis.

The next topic, touching of the nose and ears with saliva (the "Effeta" ceremony), follows the order of the Reginensis and OR XI, although Jesse seems to suggest that the Holy Spirit is invoked at the touching of the nose.[19] There is no prayer invoking the Holy Spirit at this point in the Reginensis or OR XI. Another difference is that in the Reginensis the renunciation of Satan, his

---

Andrieu, *Les Ordines* II, pp. 365 f., for his dates, and see vol. I for further information on the manuscripts. Some of the "Collection A" manuscripts were written in northern France. OR XI in its entirety in the "Collection A" type is in a beginning ninth-century codex probably from Tours (Montpellier, Bibl. Interuniver. Section Médecine 412). Another "Collection A" manuscript, although it ceases in the middle of the blessing of the font (nr. 91 in Andrieu) is our Lg (s. IX$^{ex.}$, north-eastern France, perhaps in or near Jesse's own diocese).

[17]In the fourth century, people often remained catechumens for years. Thus, to distinguish them from others who wished to receive baptism at the upcoming Easter, the latter were called *competentes*. By the sixth century, John the Deacon in Rome distinguished competents from catechumens as those who are ready to receive the Creed ("iam meretur verba [symboli] suscipere, ut qui paulo ante solum catechumenus dicebatur, nunc etiam vocetur competens vel electus;" ed. A. Wilmart, "Un florilège sur le symbolisme du baptême avec un appendice sur la lettre de Jean Diacre" in *Analecta Reginensia*, [*Studi e Testi* 59], Vatican, 1933, p. 173). When infant baptism became the norm the term lost any real meaning, although by the Carolingian period it had acquired didactic importance. This was due to the circulation of baptismal florilegia containing John's definition of the word and to the use of Isidore as one of the chief sources of baptismal instruction, who in his *De ecclesiasticis officiis* II.xxi–xvii divides all the ceremonies of Christian initiation into three stages: the catechumen, the competent, and the baptized.

[18]*De ecclesisticis officiis* II. xxii. 2 (*CCSL* CXIII, p. 97).

[19]"Nares etiam tanguntur ut per invocationem sancti spiritus odorem bonorum operum . . . percipiant." Vol. II, p. 418.

works, and pomps is said simultaneously while the breast and back are anointed. Although Jesse's next topic after anointing of the breast and back is renunciation, this renunciation takes place later, at the moment of baptism itself.[20]

Jesse's first words for the topic of triple immersion ("*de trina mersione*") are: "Having renounced the works of the devil and having received the mystery of the faith, the infant is immersed in the water." A renunciation followed by a profession of faith at the moment of baptism is also described by Isidore,[21] but not described in the Reginensis and OR XI nor in most of the liturgical sources. It is a feature, however, of some, but not all, of the manuscripts of OR L.[22] Jesse's words, "et interrogatur de credulitate christi..." may directly refer to the rubric in OR L: "Item de *credulitate*. Interr. : 'Credis in deum.'" Jesse may have possessed one of the still unidentified sources used by the compiler of OR L.[23]

Jesse has two topics between renunciation and Creed ("*De symbolo*").[24] The first is white garments ([*De albis vestibus*]). The position of this topic *before*,

---

[20]"Prolibato hoc ordine officio, perducitur infans ad baptismi sacramentum et interrogatur de credulitate christi, et abrenuntiatione diaboli; pompas autem . . . abrenuntiat." Vol. II, p. 420.

[21]After describing the font into which the catechumens will descend, and the presence of the Trinity there, Isidore says: "Duae sunt namque pactiones credentium. Prima enim pactio est in qua renuntiatur diabulo et pompis et universae conversationis illius; secunda pactio est in qua se credere in patrem et filium et spiritum sanctum profitetur." *De ecclesiasticis officiis* II.xxv.5 (*CCSL* CXIII, p. 104).

[22]Andrieu's crochets < > indicate an addition found "in only one recension or a special category of manuscripts." Following the blessing of the font OR L reads: "et tenente eo infantem a quo [the sponsor] suscipiendus est . . . Interrogat pontifex < item si Satanae abrenuntient et si firmiter symbolum in Deum habeant sic: 'Abrenuntias Satanae?' Et compatrini vel commatrinae sic respondeant: 'Abrenuntio.' Interr. : 'Et omnibus operibus eius?' Resp. : 'Abrenuntio.' Interrog. : 'Et omnibus pompis eius?' Resp. : 'Abrenuntio.' Item de credulitate. Interr. :> 'Credis in Deum patrem omnipotentem, creatorem caeli et terrae?' Resp. : 'Credo.' Interr. : 'Credis et in Iesum Christum filium eius unicum dominum nostrum, natum et passum?' Resp. : 'Credo.' 'Credis et in spiritum sanctum, sanctam ecclesiam catholicam, sanctorum communionem, remissionem peccatorum, carnis resurrectionem et vitam aeternam <post mortem>?' Resp. : 'Credo.' 'Vis baptizari?' Resp. : 'Volo.' <Tunc accipit eum et dicit:> 'Et ego te baptizo in nomine patris...'" (*Les Ordines* V, pp. 282–84, nn. 55–60).

[23]Andrieu identifies OR XI, OR XXVIII, the Reginensis, and the Hadrianum among the sources of OR L, but says there are others still not identified. See *Les Ordines* V, pp. 49–71.

[24]For most of the Texts the topic "De symbolo" refers to the delivery of the Creed rather than the profession of faith at the font. Although for this topic Jesse wrote about the Creed in a general way and did not refer to its profession at the edge of the font, he chose to put the topic immediately before triple immersion, so that his order of topics would reflect a profession of faith (perhaps the entire Creed in response to three questions) at the font.

rather than after, immersion in the font is unique among our collection of baptismal instructions, but it is intentional. Jesse's words leave little doubt that he sees the infant dressed in white as it approaches the font.[25] Despite the fact that the donning of the white garment is described *after* baptism in every known liturgical *ordo* of baptism and all didactic tradition, Jesse chose to place the topic before the font. Perhaps he was simply describing the real situation. It is highly unlikely that the infants were brought to the church naked. For the Easter Vigil celebration their parents would have dressed them in white in anticipation of the font. Reinforcing the idea that the infant is already clad in white as it is being baptized is Jesse's comparison of the infant in the font to the Lord wrapped in a new white linen shroud when he is laid in the tomb.[26]

The second topic inserted between renunciation and Creed is the new name "Christian" ([*De novo nomine 'Christianus'*]) that he makes it clear all receive upon emerging from the font. Jesse probably put the topic here because it goes with his theme of "putting on the new man" in baptism, but he is unique in connecting the reception of the name "Christian" with the font rather than with the post-baptismal chrismation. Jesse's liturgical model may have had an interrogation of the name of the infant at the font, as, for example, in PRG CVII,[27] that he wished to indicate by putting the topic of the new name in this place.

Following the topic of baptism itself (*"De trina mersione"*), the order of the post-baptismal ceremonies is characteristic of the Roman *ordo*, in that there are two chrismations and the second one (episcopal confirmation) comes before Eucharist. Jesse shows deliberate care in placing confirmation before Eucharist. His explanation of Eucharist is taken from Alcuin's baptismal *ordo* (Text 9), but whereas Alcuin has Eucharist before episcopal confirmation, which begins, "Novissime per inpositionem manus . . ." Jesse says, "Novissime" ("lastly") and then gives Alcuin's explanation of the Eucharist, reversing Alcuin's order.

In conclusion, Jesse never says that he is following "the Roman *ordo*" in so

---

[25]"[A]brenuntiat, ut, reiectis diaboli operibus et vitiis veternosis, renovandus expoliatusque pannis sordidis et conscissis, mundatur (mundatus), induatur albis et novis vestibus, currat cum desiderio ad fontes." Vol. II, p. 420. Jesse may have used *fontes*, plural, because he was intentionally echoing the baptismal Psalm 42, which begins "Quemadmodum desiderat cervus ad fontes aquarum, ita desiderat anima mea ad te, Deus." Or perhaps *fontes* is due to the liturgical book he used. *Fontes* for *fontis* (*lege*: [*aquas*] *fontis*) is found in some liturgical manuscripts.

[26]"Dominus autem in sepulchro novo sepultus, et in sindone munda obvolutus est; et quicumque consepeliri vult christo per baptismum, abiecta vetustate et inmunditia, mundatus et novus induatur sindone nova." Vol. II, p. 421.

[27]"'Quis vocaris?' Resp. 'Ille.' Interrog. 'Vis baptizari?' Resp. 'Volo.'" (Vogel and Elze, *Le Pontifical* II, p. 163, nr. 33.)

many words.[28] His *ordo* for the catechumen is *not* word for word an excerpt from OR XI. There is a new *ordo* here, a distinct variation of OR XI. Jesse took obvious pains to encourage Roman features of baptism in his diocese, but J. D. C. Fisher's statement must be corrected that, "In fact, the order of initiation which Jesse expounds is exactly that found in OR XI." Fisher goes on to say: "Hence the effects of Charlemagne's decree in the diocese of Amiens was to cause the introduction of the Roman rite with as little modification as possible."[29] There is, however, no indication in the Capitulary of 789 that Charlemagne had OR XI in mind.

Text 23 (Amalarius)

Text 23 (see Chart B2) was composed by Amalarius of Metz (Archbishop of Trier, 809– circa 814) in response to Charlemagne's questionnaire (circa 812). Three times Amalarius uses the expression, "just as we find written in the Roman *ordo*." All three times, he is referring to action in the scrutinies.[30]

According to his sequence of topics, Amalarius outlines an *ordo* of baptism somewhat different from OR XI. This is partly due to the influence of Charlemagne's order of questions, but not entirely. For his first topic, "*De catecumino*," Amalarius refers to the prayer for the making of the catechumen and quotes two phrases from it, indicating he probably had the actual sacramentary book or ordinal under his eyes to which he was referring when he said, "just as we find written in the Roman *ordo*."

His next topic, "*De scrutinio*," corresponds with OR XI, since all the ceremonies for the catechumen take place within the context of a scrutiny meeting and his next ten topics describe ceremonies that are done in a scrutiny. The sign of the cross is placed on the infants' foreheads by priests, acolytes, godfathers and godmothers, as in OR XI. As to why the scrutiny is done seven times, however, the explanation Amalarius gives is entirely different from that in OR XI. He makes no mention of the seven gifts of the Holy Spirit. It seems likely that Amalarius would have used the explanation in OR XI had he known it. Since he did not use it, it may be that his *ordo* was a variation of

---

[28]Jesse did not write all of what is printed under his name in *PL* 105: 781–96. Andrieu says that Jesse did claim to follow the "Roman" *ordo*, but Andrieu was under the impression that Jesse was the author of what is, in fact, an anonymous baptismal tract mentioning "Roman" which Migne (following Cordesius) included under Jesse's name.

[29]Fisher, *Christian Initiation*, p. 68. Fisher was referring to the Capitulary of 789, cap. XXIII (quoted above in note 1); see his p. 57, note 2.

[30]"In scrutinio quippe facimus signum crucis super pueros, sicut invenimus scriptum in romano ordine. . . . Ipso die facimus scrutinium septimum, sicut in romano ordine invenimus scriptum. . . . Deinde perscrutamur patrinos vel matrinas, si possint cantare orationem dominicam et symbolum, sicut praemonuimus, ac postea per ordinem, sicut in romano ordine scriptum est, sacrum officium peragimus usque ad sacratissimum opus baptismatis." Vol. II, pp. 339, 344, 346.

OR XI without the explanation. OR XV, for example, has the first part of OR XI's phrase that says seven scrutinies must be done, but does not have the second part explaining that this is because there are seven gifts of the Holy Spirit.[31]

Amalarius puts the topic of delivery of the Lord's Prayer before delivery of the Creed, the reversal of OR XI. Also, he does not mention any delivery of the Gospels.[32] In OR XV the delivery of the Lord's Prayer also comes before the delivery of the Creed: however, OR XV does have the delivery of the Gospels.[33] For the topic of Creed ("*De symbolo*") Amalarius gives an exposition on the Apostles' Creed. It was said that some Gallicanized manuscripts of OR XI have the Apostles' rather than the Nicene Creed. (OR XV has the incipit of the Nicene Creed.) Amalarius in any case did not perceive the Apostles' Creed as contrary to the "Roman *ordo*."

The Reginensis and OR XI have no mention of an exsufflation. Amalarius may know of one in the scrutinies, or he simply may be responding to Charlemagne's question on exsufflation.

His next topic on salt is clearly out of liturgical order. Amalarius knows this because he begins his explanation of salt by saying that this ceremony is done after the first prayer for the making of a catechumen. Amalarius is simply following Charlemagne's order of questions here, which asks about salt after exorcism and exsufflation.

Amalarius moves to the seventh and last scrutiny on Holy Saturday morning with the topic, "*Quando fiat novissimum scrutinium.*" The word "novissimum" is not in OR XI, but it is in OR XV.[34] Also, both Amalarius and OR XV have no mention of the signing of the cross on Holy Saturday morning, contrary to OR XI.

Amalarius agrees with the Reginensis in describing the touching of the nose and ears with spittle, anointing of the breast and back, and renunciation of Satan, his works, and pomps.[35] In his explanation of touching of the ears,

---

[31]See M. Andrieu, *Les Ordines* III, p. 119, nr. 112.

[32]In his *Liber officialis*, L. I, c. 8, 2, when summarizing the events of the *aurium apertio*, he mentions the delivery of the Gospels before he mentions the delivery of the Lord's Prayer and the symbol together as items which must be recited back on Holy Saturday. See J. M. Hanssens, ed., *Amalarii episcopi opera liturgica omnia*, vol. II (*Studi e Testi* 139), 1948, Vatican City, p. 52.

[33]See M. Andrieu, *Les Ordines* III, p. 118, nr. 105.

[34]"In ipsa autem novissima [vice], quod est in sabbato sancto." Ibid., p. 119, nr. 113).

[35]OR XI omits anointing of the breast and back and renunciation, but other *ordines Romani* for baptism have them (OR XV, XXVIII, XXXI). Not all of the other *ordines Romani* of Andrieu covering Holy Week mention any meeting of the catechumens on Holy Saturday morning. These include OR XXIII–XXV, XXVII (except one manuscript which states: "Sabbato sancto mane reddant infantes symbolum et post haec catecizantur ipsi infantes;" see Andrieu, *Les Ordines* III, p. 359, note 51), XXIX, XXXA, and XXXB. OR XXXII refers the reader to another *ordo* for the ceremonies regarding the

however, he appears to quote a prayer taken directly from the baptismal *ordo*, which does not seem to be found in any extant liturgical book.[36]

For renunciation (*"De abrenunciatione"*), Amalarius says that after the infants have renounced Satan, his works, and pomps, the godparents must show that they know the Lord's Prayer and the Creed.[37] In the Reginensis and OR XI there is a chanting of the Creed by the priest over the infants ("redditio symboli").[38] In Amalarius it seems that this ceremony has become an opportune time for the sponsors to demonstrate their knowledge of the Lord's Prayer and the Creed.[39] Amalarius's topic describing the return of the Creed and the Lord's Prayer by the godparents is very close to what is in OR L, although there it is the first, rather than the last, ceremony on Holy Saturday morning.[40] Amalarius uses the same terms as OR L for the sponsors ("patrini" and "matrinae"), which are not terms used in the Reginensis, OR XI, or OR XXVIII (OR XV uses "matres" and once "parentes vel patrini").

Also for renunciation Amalarius again seems to quote a phrase directly from the liturgy when he says: "Dicimus illi: 'Contradic satanae?'" This is a different formula from "Abrenuncias satanae?" in the Reginensis, and again it does not seem to exist in any extant liturgical book.[41]

Amalarius has no topic on the baptismal immersion itself, perhaps because Charlemagne did not pose a question on it. Amalarius gives a *"recapitulatio"* at the point between the pre-baptismal and post-baptismal ceremonies to clarify the liturgical order of events, which he altered somewhat because of Charlemagne's order of questions. In his recapitulation he puts salt in liturgical order (according to OR XI); he eliminates exsufflation, which is not described in the Reginensis or OR XI; and now he mentions a final profession of

---

"parvulos" on Holy Saturday morning. In Jesse's *ordo* there is no seventh scrutiny on Holy Saturday. It may be that some of these *ordines Romani* do not mention any Holy Saturday morning ceremonies for the catechumens because none were celebrated in the geographical region where they were compiled.

[36]"Et iterum dicat [presbiter] auribus: 'Aures iste [*sic*], deo miserante, semper aperte [*sic*] sint ad intellegenda verba disciplinae dei.'" Vol. II, p. 345.

[37]"Deinde perscrutamur patrinos vel matrinas, si possint cantare orationem dominicam et symbolum." Vol. II, p. 346.

[38]See Charts A1 and A2, and Chapter 3, note 11.

[39]Carolingian capitularies demanded that the godparents be able to recite these two prayers before they lifted anyone from the font, but they do not say precisely if or when they are examined. See P. Brommer, *Capitula episcoporum*, p. 26, Cap. III and note 5 in this chapter.

[40]"Post tertiam denique horam sabbati procedunt ad ecclesiam qui baptizandi sunt simul cum patrinis et matrinis . . . et tunc qui possunt reddunt orationem dominicam et symbolum sive patrini pro ipsis atque matrinae eorum, qui eos suscepturi sunt." (M. Andrieu, *Les Ordines* V, pp. 261 f., Cap. XXIX, nn. 2–3.)

[41]Amalarius does quote "Abrenuntias satanas?" from a sacramentary book ("sequitur in eodem sacramentario") in his *Liber officialis* L. I, c. 23, 7 (Hanssens, ibid., p. 127).

faith before the baptismal immersion, as in the Reginensis (and one manuscript of OR XI).[42] Amalarius's recapitulation shows his concern that his baptismal exposition reflect a specific liturgical *ordo* he has before his eyes.

His post-baptismal topics agree with the Reginensis, except that he does not include episcopal confirmation. This may be due to the fact that Charlemagne did not ask about it.[43] Amalarius's use of the word "linteo" for headcloth is not common.[44] It may reveal a feature of the specific book he had under his eyes, another now lost version of the *ordo Romanus*.

To summarize, Amalarius was following a book that, unlike OR XI or the Reginensis, had the delivery of the Lord's Prayer before the delivery of the (Apostles') Creed; no delivery of the Gospels; a totally different explanation as to why there are seven scrutinies; the return of the Lord's Prayer and Creed by the godparents after the renunciation on Holy Saturday; a different version of the threefold profession of faith at the font; and the use of "linteo." Only some of Amalarius's features have been found in OR XV or OR L. Nevertheless, whatever *ordo* Amalarius followed, at least for the scrutinies, was clearly "the Roman *ordo*" in his eyes. What has now been seen from both Jesse and Amalarius is plenty of room for variation within the *ordo Romanus*.[45]

Text 16 (Theodulf)

Some 400 kilometers southwest of Trier, Theodulf, Bishop of Orléans, also responded to Charlemagne's questionnaire at the request of his metropolitan, Archbishop Magnus of Sens. He reiterated Charlemagne's questions in the titles of his chapters (see Chart B3), but he rearranged their order and added topics about which Charlemagne had not asked. His sequence of topics is not

---

[42]In the Reginensis the catechumen is asked: "'Credis in deum patrem omnipotentem?'. . . 'Credis et in Iesum Christum filium eius unicum dominum nostrum natum et passum?'. . . 'Credis et in spiritum sanctum, sancta aecclesia (*sic*), remissionem peccatorum, carnis resurrectionem?'" (Mohlberg, *Sacramentarium Gelasianum*, p. 74, nr. 449). Amalarius says: "confiteatur se credere in deum patrem omnipotentem, et in iesum christum filium eius, natum ex patre ante omnia saecula, factum ex muliere in tempore, et in spiritum sanctum, et reliqua." Vol. II, p. 347.

[43]Had episcopal confirmation, for both of these men, become disassociated from all the other ceremonies of baptism because of its delay? Alcuin speaks of the episcopal confirmation which is done eight days after baptism. (See *Ep*. 143 in *MGH Epp*. IV, p. 226, lines 18–20. Also this is stated in the Prague Sacramentary (ed. A. Dold, *Das Prager Sakramentar: II: Prolegomena und Textausgabe*, Beuron in Hohenzollern, 1949, p. 62).

[44]Many of the liturgical books do not mention a head covering at all (the Reginensis, the Gellone Sacramentary, OR XV, XXIII, XXIV, XXVII, XXIX, or XXXA). Others have "chrismale" (OR XI, XXXI, and XXVIII). Some manuscripts of OR L have "cappam." The *PRG* has "mitram." In OR XXXI "linteo" appears but refers to the white garments with which the infant is vested.

[45]This is only confirmed by differences between Amalarius's description of baptism in Text 23 and in his *Liber officialis*, where he also quotes from a sacramentary book. (See *Liber officialis*, L. I., c. 23, 1–10, ed. Hanssens, *Amalarii* II, pp. 125–28.)

entirely in agreement with the Reginensis or OR XI.[46] Theodulf says: "The priest exsufflates on his face . . . then the evil spirit is exorcized . . . when it has been exorcized salt is given to him [the catechumen] . . . then the Creed is delivered to him."

An exsufflation with an exorcism among the initial ceremonies for the catechumen, although not in OR XI, is found in a number of baptismal *ordines*.[47] A specific liturgical book Theodulf had in mind may be revealed by his words, "Then the evil spirit is exorcized so that he goes out and departs from that creature."[48] He was undoubtedly echoing the words of the exsufflation prayer itself. "Ut exeat et recedat" is a phrase commonly found in the exorcism prayers of the scrutinies. The word "plasmate" appears more than once in baptismal prayers, although in only one case, in a Spanish *ordo* of baptism, does it seem to appear with "Recede" in an exorcism-with-exsufflation prayer. This Spanish *ordo* is edited by M. S. Gros from a manuscript from Lagrassa (s. XI). It represents, according to Gros, the baptismal rite celebrated in Narbonne at the beginning of the ninth century. It is the Roman *ordo*, but with Spanish variations, combining elements found in OR XI, the Gellone Sacramentary, the León Antiphonary, and the *Liber Ordinum*.[49] Theodulf, it may be recalled, was a Visigoth from Spain. Ann Freeman has recently shown that Theodulf's knowledge of Spanish sources is echoed in the *Libri Carolini*.[50] Theodulf's familiarity with the words of a Spanish baptismal *ordo* may have been consciously or unconsciously written into his description of the exsufflation.[51]

---

[46]Unlike Amalarius, he nowhere says he is following the "Roman *ordo*."

[47]OR L, for example, states: "Tunc exsufflat in faciem eius tribus vicibus, dicens: 'Exi, inmunde spiritus, et da locum spiritui sancto paraclito.'" (M. Andrieu, *Les Ordines* V, p. 131, nr. 5). Also, PRG CVII, the Fulda Sacramentary, the Bobbio and Stowe Missals, the Ambrosian Manual, and the León Antiphonary all have an exsufflation of the catechumen. In the Reginensis, the Gellone and Rheinau Sacramentaries, OR XXXI and the sacramentary fragment of Brussels, Bibl. Roy. 10127–10144 (see *CCCM* XLVII, p. 100), there is an exsufflation of the catechumen, but only in their supplementary rites for a sick or a pagan catechumen.

[48]"Unde et exorcizatur idem malignus spiritus ut exeat et recedat ab illo plasmate." Vol. II, p. 285.

[49]The Spanish *ordo* states: "Tunc sufflet sacerdos tribus vicibus in vultum eius dicendo: 'Recede inmunde spiritus in sanctae trinitatis nomine ab hoc dei plasmate,'" ed. M. S. Gros, "El Antiguo Ordo Bautismal Catalano-Narbonense" in *Hispania Sacra* 28 (1975), p. 80, nr. 2.

[50]Ann Freeman, "Theodulf of Orléans," pp. 195–224.

[51]As to other Spanish or Spanish-related *ordines*, the description in the *Liber Ordinum* of the exsufflation on the catechumen with an exorcism prayer includes the word "plasmate," but not "ut exeat et recedat" (see M. Férotin, *Le Liber Ordinum*, coll. 25 f.) The Fulda Sacramentary has an exsufflation on the catechumen with the words, "Recede, diabole, ab hac imagine dei et da locum spiritui sancto." (no "plasmate") (ed. G. Richter und A. Schönfelder, *Sacramentarium Fuldense*, Fulda, 1912, p. 343, nr. 2680). The Mozarabic liturgies share many features in common with the Ambrosian (Mila-

For his seventh topic, on belief ("*VII. De credulitate*"), Theodulf gives an exposition on the Apostles' Creed. There is no mention of an *aurium apertio*. Here he adds an explanation regarding the baptism of infants who cannot yet speak or understand.

For scrutiny ("*VIII. De scrutinio*") Theodulf offers two explanations. First, a scrutiny is a literal examination in which people old enough to understand give reason for their belief.[52] Second, Theodulf explains scrutiny in the sense of the scrutiny meetings of OR XI, as occasions of instruction.[53]

His explanations for touching of the nose and ears, anointing of the breast and back, and renunciation of Satan do not include any direct reference to liturgical formulas. The next topic is baptism (there is no mention of a return of the Creed or blessing of the font). He begins with Isidore's words on the renunciation and profession of faith. Theodulf may have known a second renunciation at the edge of the font (as in OR L), after the one that accompanies the anointing of the breast and back, because he mentions the renunciation under the topic of baptism ("*XIII. De sacramento baptismi*") as if it is directly associated with immersion in the font.[54]

Theodulf's order of topics corresponds to OR XI for the post-baptismal ceremonies, except that he has anointing of the top of the head after, rather than before, donning of white garments. This may be due to Charlemagne's order of questions.

In sum, Theodulf was describing a Roman *ordo* of baptism, but it was not exactly OR XI. In three places his description agrees with OR L contrary to OR XI (exsufflation-with-exorcism; return of the Creed by the sponsors; and probably a second renunciation at the edge of the font). There is one striking parallel between his description of the exsufflation-with-exorcism and the Romano-Spanish *ordo* of Narbonne. This may only point to Theodulf's Spanish origins, not the *ordo* he used in Orléans, but in any case Theodulf, like Jesse

---

nese) rites. In a north-Italian baptismal *ordo* in Milan, Bibl. Ambros. T. 27. sup., an exsufflation of the catechumen is followed by, "Recede ergo maledicte sathana a famulis dei et da locum spiritui sancto, quia in ipsius nomine tibi interdicimus" (no "plasmate"), ed. Dom C. Lambot, *North Italian Services of the Eleventh Century* (Milan, Bibl. Ambros. T. 27. Sup.) London (HBS vol. LXVII), 1931, p. 16.

[52]"Qui vero illius sunt iam aetatis ut rationem credulitatis suae reddere possint, diligenti examine scrutandi sunt." Vol. II, p. 293.

[53]"Hunc enim morem [scrutiniorum] ecclesia servare consuevit, ut per aliquot dierum spatium hi qui in sollemnitate paschali baptizandi sunt scrutentur, ut instructis et doctis… ." Vol. II, p. 293. His words give the impression that the scrutiny meetings are a bit archaic, but something one attempts to observe before Easter out of tradition.

[54]"Morimur ergo peccato quando abrenuntiamus diabolo et omnibus quae eius sunt; consepelimur christo cum sub invocatione sanctae trinitatis sub trina mersione in fontem lavacri quasi in quoddam sepulchrum descendimus." Vol. II, p. 303.

in Amiens and Amalarius in Trier, had in Orléans his own version of the Roman *ordo* of baptism.[55]

Text 25 (Leidrad)

Archbishop Leidrad of Lyons (798–814?) also replied to Charlemagne's baptismal questionnaire. As can be seen from Chart B4, he gave little attention to the initial ceremonies. He was far more interested in explaining the symbolic interpretation of baptism than in describing a liturgical order of events. Leidrad's order of catechumen; exorcism-with-exsufflation; salt; and competent is taken directly from Isidore. For scrutiny he says, "All this action which is celebrated over the catechumens and the competents some people call a scrutiny, for no other reason, I suppose, except that the word comes from 'to scrutinize.'"[56] It is a suggestive remark, as if "scrutiny" was a word not generally used. It recalls Theodulf's same difficulty with explaining the term and his double explanation of it as a literal examination and as a traditional meeting of catechumens for instruction. Leidrad knew this latter meaning, but even though he wrote from the ancient see of Lyons, it seems only "some people" were familiar with the latter meaning. Also, both Leidrad and Theodulf placed the topic of scrutiny at the end of all the topics pertaining to the initial ceremonies of the catechumen, whereas Jesse and Amalarius, who described an *ordo* of scrutinies, placed it first.

Leidrad positioned the topics of Creed ("*Cap. IIII. De symbolo*") and belief ("*Cap. V. De credulitate*") directly before baptism ("*Cap. VI. De baptismo*"). This suggests he had in mind an *ordo* without a formal delivery of the Creed in a scrutiny meeting. Its only recitation would be its profession by question and response at the font.[57]

For holy unction ("*Cap. VII. De sacra unctione*") he covered the ceremonies of the presbyteral anointing of the head with chrism as well as episcopal confirmation with imposition of hand and chrismation on the forehead, following Isidore's treatment of these topics one after the other in chapters XXVI and XXVII of *De ecclesiasticis officiis* II.[58] (Leidrad's omission of any mention of

---

[55]In support of the influence of the Spanish liturgy on liturgical books in France, R. Reynolds has informed me that many more texts of Benedict of Aniane's Supplement to the Gregorian Sacramentary came from Spain than Deshusses knew; for example, the texts on holding councils.

[56]"Haec tota actio quae super caticuminis et conpetentibus celebratur a quibusdam scrutinium nominatur, non ob aliud, ut putamus, nisi a scrutando." Vol. II, p. 359.

[57]"De his igitur quibus caticuminos interrogamus quando baptizantur, sic credimus." Vol. II, p. 366.

[58]Regarding the imposition of hand (singular) or hands (plural), the manuscripts of Leidrad are not consistent the three times he mentions this action (See vol. II, pp. 373 f). Also, the manuscripts of Isidore are not consistent. See *De ecclesiasticis officiis* II.xxvii; *CCSL* CXIII, p. 107 and the *apparatus criticus*.

the head covering may be due to the fact that Isidore does not mention it, although this topic is omitted in Texts 17 and 5 perhaps for liturgical reasons).

Like Amalarius, Leidrad's final topics address the problem of infants who cannot speak for themselves. The inclusion of a topic on the infants' belief at some point in Leidrad, Amalarius, and Theodulf is noteworthy, since Charlemagne asked nothing about infants whose faith is professed by godparents.[59]

In sum, Leidrad's interest was much more in the symbolic meaning of certain ceremonies than in a step-by-step exposition of the liturgical *ordo* of baptism. His decision, however, to group all of the initial ceremonies of the catechumen at the end of his first chapter while giving greater treatment to the ceremonies he located immediately prior to and after the moment of baptism, especially his placing the topics of Creed and belief where they correspond to a final profession of faith at the font, may reflect an *ordo* without scrutiny meetings, in which all the essential ceremonies take place on the day of baptism.

Leidrad may have avoided too exact a description of a specific liturgical *ordo* because the priests of his diocese were using different ones. (Charlemagne's questionnaire asked him, "how you and your suffragans teach the priests and the people . . . about baptism.") Probably in many parishes baptism was celebrated without a series of Lenten scrutiny meetings.

In fact, there is another baptismal instruction, this one anonymous, that may have originated in Leidrad's archdiocese. Except for the first sentence, the anonymous composer of Text 26 simply extracted passages from Leidrad's lengthy treatise; however, he rearranged Leidrad's topics in three cases and omitted three topics in order to describe an *ordo* suitable for a rural parish priest. (See Chart B5.) He put competents before salt and equated its meaning with the term catechumens, omitting Isidore's definition, quoted by Leidrad, of a competent as one who receives the Creed; he omitted Leidrad's topic of scrutiny altogether; and he omitted both of Leidrad's topics on Creed and belief, perhaps to avoid Leidrad's explanation of a Nicene-type Creed. Finally, he repositioned the topic of the imposition of hands[60] for the bestowal of the Holy Spirit *after* Eucharist, indicating a situation where the minister of baptism was a presbyter and episcopal confirmation was necessarily delayed until a bishop could come. Thus, with a few significant changes he made Leidrad's sequence of ceremonies make sense for clerics in a rural parish setting where baptism was celebrated in a single session and without the presence of a bishop.

---

[59]Charlemagne's interest in the quality and preparedness of sponsors expressed in his legislation, however, may have been on the minds of these bishops.

[60]Text 26 quotes the passage from Leidrad where Leidrad has hands (plural). See note 58 of this chapter.

In sum, the term "Roman *ordo*" or any reference to "Roman" is used by only one of these four leading bishops of the Carolingian Reform. The rites of baptism they describe are not uniform, and none of them is the same as OR XI. It is tempting to conclude that one reason some baptismal instructions differed from others is because there was no single *ordo* of baptism commonly recognized as being "the Roman *ordo*." Is this remarkable? Should it be expected that these four bishops would describe the same rite? The reform legislation is what has led some liturgical historians to state that the goal of the reformers was the conformity of the liturgy according to the Roman rite.[61] The legislation regarding baptism, however, ranges from saying nothing at all about "Roman," to vague terms, such as "the Roman custom" or "the Roman tradition," to certain imprecisely defined rites, such as the rite of the scrutinies, or the Paschal and Pentecost rite. In the legislation quoted above in note 1, Charlemagne's *Admonitio Generalis* of 789 said only that priests should observe "catholic baptism." A royal capitulary of the same year said that priests should baptize according to "the Roman custom." The Constitution of Arno of Salzburg ca. 798 stated that priests should celebrate public baptism twice a year, at Easter and at Pentecost, and this [*public* baptism] should be done according to "the order of the Roman tradition." A priest's examination of ca. 803 asked how they knew and understood the Roman *ordo* of the mass and the Roman divine office, but only "baptism," with no reference to "Roman." The Council of Mainz of 813 stated: "We wish, just as in your admonition (a reference to Charlemagne's capitulary of 789, *cap.* XXIII, perhaps), that the sacrament of baptism be celebrated and kept in each of our parishes concordantly and uniformly according to the Roman *ordo*, that is, the scrutiny in the *ordo* of baptism."

It is this last *capitulum* that deserves attention in light of the four baptismal instructions. They suggest that "the Roman *ordo*" may have referred to *any* rite that included a distinctly Roman element, the *ordo* of scrutinies. It is this element that appears to be the essential ingredient for any rite being called Roman. Amalarius (Text 23) uses the expression, "just as we find written in the Roman *ordo*" three times, and all three times it is in reference to action done in the seven scrutinies. Also, Amalarius indicated "Roman *ordo*" meant what was done "up to" the time of baptism. When referring to the seventh scrutiny on Holy Saturday morning, he described a first event, the return of the Creed by the godparents, and then said, "After that, we observe the sacred office in order, just as it is contained in the Roman order, *up to* the most sacred work of baptism."[62] Thus, in Amalarius's eyes, celebrating baptism ac-

---

[61]See, for example, A. Angenendt, "Die Liturgie und die Organisation des kirchlichen Lebens auf dem Lande" in *Settimane di studio del centro Italiano di studi sull'alto medioevo* 28 (Spoleto, 1982), pp. 173 f. and C. Vogel, "La réforme liturgique sous Charlemagne" in *Karl der Grosse*, ed. W. Braunfels, Bd. II, p. 217.

[62]See note 30 in this chapter.

cording to the Roman *ordo* meant including the scrutinies. It did not mean the observance of some one standard rite of baptism from its first to last ceremony.

Theodulf of Orléans (Text 16) had two explanations of a scrutiny: a literal examination of the faith of the candidate and the Roman series of meetings in the weeks prior to Easter. He called the latter a custom (*morem*) the church "was accustomed" (*consuevit*) to observe but did not say he observed it. He seemed quite removed from it. Since he never said he was following the "Roman *ordo*," nor described the *aurium apertio*, it is possible that he, too, thought the Roman *ordo* of baptism referred to the Roman scrutinies.

The same may apply to Leidrad of Lyons (Text 25), who distanced himself completely from the Roman scrutinies with the curt remark that all the action involving catechumens and competents "some people" call a scrutiny, "for no other reason, I suppose, except that the word comes from [the verb] 'to scrutinize.'" He did not use the term "Roman *ordo*" in his treatise.

If some Carolingians understood the "Roman *ordo* of baptism" to refer to a pre-baptismal *ordo* of scrutinies, there were still a variety of these. Maybe it was OR XI for some. It was not for Jesse (Text 30), who did not observe the *OR* XI-type of seven scrutiny meetings with an *aurium apertio* on the third and a *redditio symboli* on the seventh.

In conclusion, the Roman *ordo* of baptism referred to in the fourth *capitulum* of the Council of Mainz quoted above, that which was to be observed "uniformiter" by all, was a Lenten program of scrutinies. There is no evidence that the "Roman *ordo* of baptism" referred to a specific rite of baptism, from start to finish, while there is evidence that it meant an *ordo* of scrutinies.[63] If this is correct, then it is not necessary to debate whether Charlemagne intended to impose a single, complete rite of Roman baptism on the Carolingian empire when in the Mainz *capitulum* it states: "We wish, just as you [Charlemagne] admonished, that the sacrament of baptism be celebrated concordantly and uniformly by all according to the Roman *ordo*, that is, the *ordo* of scrutinies." The expression "uniformiter" in the Mainz *capitulum* refers to the Roman *ordo* of scrutinies. Anyone observing this *ordo* would be keeping similar Lenten observances of meetings, readings, and prayers.

This conclusion helps to explain the continued diversity of liturgical rites of baptism throughout the period of the Carolingian Reform. Historians have been fascinated by this diversity because the opposite was supposed to be true. The Carolingian Reform was supposed to have achieved standardization and conformity in its liturgical practice. No legislation, in fact, ever attempted such a feat regarding baptism in its entirety. Rather, it sought to include one Roman element in the process of Christian initiation. By exten-

---

[63]Observing public baptism only twice a year, at Easter and Pentecost (see the legislation cited in note 1 of this chapter) in itself might imply observing the scrutinies, since Paschal or Pentecost baptism in the sacramentary books includes the *ordo* of scrutinies.

sion, anyone observing the scrutinies could be said to be observing Roman baptism, but in fact the legislation did not seek to put an end to current rites of baptism. The explanation as to why there was such a diversity of rites of baptism is not because the Reform "failed" when it tried to suppress individualism. It never sought to impose a model for the entire rite on all the dioceses. Its suggestion and even urging to include a distinctive Roman Lenten program is a more accurate way to envision liturgical reform regarding baptism than to imagine an entire rite of baptism which should replace those in use.[64]

This chapter has shown four bishops' descriptions of baptism in their dioceses, and these rites differed. There was no one model Roman rite commonly recognized by them. A broad interpretation of "the Roman *ordo*," however, was not the only reason for diversity among some Texts. The next chapter will look at why Carolingian baptismal instructions still differ even when they are derived from one same model.

---

[64]It may have been far more problematical for the Carolingians to think of conformity in regard to baptism than conformity in regard to the mass or monastic liturgies.

5

The Creative Use of a Patristic Florilegium

One important source for the composers of Carolingian baptismal instructions was John the Deacon of Rome. At the beginning of the sixth century he wrote a letter to one Senarius, describing the rite of baptism.[1] The text gained importance because of its use by Alcuin in his own widespread description of the *ordo* of baptism, which is largely a series of extracts, almost *verbatim*, from John the Deacon (see Chapter 6). John's text received explicit approval from Alcuin, yet other Carolingian composers who used John were not content simply to regurgitate him in baptismal instructions for the clergy.

This chapter will show the creative rearrangement of a patristic florilegium by four Carolingian redactors, arising from their desire to use a Roman model, yet to describe different liturgical *ordines*.

Texts 1, 2, 3, and 4 are derivations of a florilegium based on John the Deacon's letter to Senarius. The composer of this florilegium interspersed sentences from Isidore, Augustine, Cyprian, Pope Celestine, Pope Leo, and Scripture with sentences from John the Deacon. The florilegium is not extant, only its derivatives, but from the passages that Texts 1, 2, 3, and 4 share in common, it seems safe to say that they derived independently from this florilegium.

Texts 1, 2, 3, and 4 each differs somewhat from the other three in its sequence of topics. One would, of course, like to know what the sequence of topics was in the now-lost florilegium archetype in order to see where our composers varied from their model. J.-P. Bouhot's reconstruction of the order of topics in this archetype is only hypothetical, since no two of its derivations have exactly the same order of topics. Bouhot's order agrees, however, with the order of ceremonies described by John the Deacon.[2] Probably the

---

[1]John the Deacon was perhaps the future Pope John I (523–26), according to F. Stegmüller, "Bischof Angilmodus," p. 14. The letter of John to Senarius is edited by A. Wilmart in "Un florilège carolingien," pp. 170–79. It is preserved on ff. 24–31v. of Vat. Reg. lat. 1709A in a mid–ninth-century hand. See Wilmart, ibid., p. 156.

[2]J.-P. Bouhot, "Un florilège sur le symbolisme du baptême de la seconde moitié du VIIIe siècle" in *Recherches Augustiniennes* XVIII (1983), pp. 151–82. He attempted to reconstruct the florilegium archetype according to the tracts he believed derived from it, our Texts 1, 2, 3, and 42. He did not know of the existence of Text 4. Text 42 is a variation of Text 9 (Alcuin's *ordo*) and could have derived from Text 9 rather than the florilegium archetype.

composer of the florilegium archetype was guided in the arrangement of his topics by John's order of ceremonies. He certainly used much, if not all, of John's text. (John is quoted under sixteen out of twenty-one topics in Text 1, for example.) Furthermore, the sequence of topics in Text 2 agrees perfectly with that of John the Deacon. (The author added topics not in John and omitted some in John, but the order of John's topics has not been rearranged.)

Puzzlingly, Bouhot states that the order of ceremonies in his reconstruction of the florilegium archetype is identical to OR XI,[3] and Antoine Chavasse has argued that John the Deacon's description "coincides perfectly" with the Reginensis.[4] Even if it is allowed that John passed over some of the ceremonies because he was not attempting a step-by-step liturgical exposition in his letter to Senarius, there are some fundamental differences between the *ordo* he describes and OR XI or the Reginensis.

As can be seen on Chart C1, after some opening words on why one is made a catechumen ([*De catecumenis*]),[5] the first ceremony John refers to is the renunciation of Satan ([*De abrenuntiatione*]). It appears to take place at the very beginning of the catechumenate;[6] in any case, it certainly takes place before the delivery of the Creed,[7] unlike the Reginensis and OR XI.

Next, John defines the word catechesis ([*De catechesis*]) to mean instruction that is given "through a blessing of the one imposing his hand" ("*per benedictionem inponentis manum*"). After summarizing this catechesis, in which the catechumen is told how he will become holy from damned, just from unjust, and a son from a slave,[8] John states that the catechumen is

---

[3]J.-P. Bouhot, "Un florilège," p. 162, note 27.

[4]Antoine Chavasse, "Les deux rituels romain et gaulois de l'admission au catéchuménat que renferme le sacramentaire Gélasien (Vat. Reg. 316)" in *Études de critique et d'histoire religieuses* (Lyons, 1948), p. 86.

[5]The words in italics in the following paragraphs refer to the words on Chart C1.

[6]"Priusquam aliquis renascatur in Christo, diabolicae (sic) potestate teneatur adstrictus, cuius laqueis nisi inter ipsa primitus fidei rudimenta veraci professione renuntians exuatur ad salutaris lavacri gratiam non accedit." (A. Wilmart, "Un florilège," pp. 171 f.).

[7]"Dehinc quodam profectu atque provectu ille qui dudum exsufflatus diabolicis laqueis pompisque renuntiaverat symboli ab apostolis traditi iam meretur verba suscipere." And later: "Perscrutamur enim eorum corda per fidem utrum menti suae post renuntiationem diaboli sacra verba definxerint." (ibid., p. 173).

[8]There are some striking parallels between John's description of "catechesis" and the words of a catechetical sermon delivered to the catechumens at the very beginning of the rite of admission immediately after the registering of their names in the Fulda Sacramentary. T. C. Akeley, *Christian Initiation in Spain c. 300–1100* (London, 1967), p. 149, says the sermon in the Fulda Sacramentary is of some antiquity and is in a homiliary in London, BM Add. ms. 30853 (s. XI). The homily collection is from Silos and Dom Morin suggests that with its dependence on Caesarius of Arles, and lacking any post-Isidore material, it may have originally come from Arles. (See *Liber commicus sive lectionarius* (Maredsous, 1893), p. 115.)

exsufflated and exorcized ([*De exsufflatione*]), ([*De exorcismo*]). The two actions of breathing on the face of the catechumen and demanding that the devil depart go together. They occur before the giving of salt. In OR XI and the Reginensis, however, there is no mention of an exsufflation with an exorcism before the giving of salt.

Next, the catechumen receives salt ([*De salis acceptione*]), "in which he is signed" ("in quo signatur"). John finishes the first stage of the catechumenate by referring to the frequent imposition of hand and thrice repeated blessing of the Creator ([*"frequens impositio manus et tertio benedictio conditoris"*]).[9]

For John, a new stage begins after the catechumens receive the Creed ([*"De symboli traditione"*]). Then they are called "competents" or "elect." The Creed may be the Apostles' Creed ("symboli ab apostolis traditi"), not the Nicene, of the Reginensis.

The scrutinies (*"De scrutiniis"*) for John are something that occur only after the catechumens have received the Creed.[10] John knows only three scrutinies. He may have been familiar with the early Gelasian Sacramentary; it is not possible to know from the Reginensis form of the Gelasian Sacramentary whether the delivery of the Creed primitively took place before, during, or after its three scrutinies.

Among the final pre-baptismal ceremonies John includes, first, the touching of the ears and nose with oil ([*De tactu aurium cum oleo*]), ([*De tactu narium cum oleo*]). In the Reginensis and OR XI this is done with spittle, not oil. Second, John describes the anointing of the breast ([*De pectoris unctione*]), but says nothing about the anointing of the back, nor does he put the renunciation of Satan, his works and pomps with this ceremony. Also, he does not mention a return of the Creed. Third, John brings in a final ceremony that he says is not found in the liturgical books but nevertheless has a long tradition: the removal of the shoes of the catechumens so that they approach the font bare-footed ([*De nudis pedibus*]).[11] This may be a remnant of the ancient

---

[9]"Hoc ergo agit frequens impositio manus et in reverentia trinitatis invocata super caput eius tertio benedictio conditoris." (Ibid., p. 172). (A. Chavasse believes that the "frequent imposition of hand" refers to the series of six exorcism prayers of the scrutiny, all accompanied by hand-laying, which follow the giving of salt in the Reginensis, and that the "blessing of the Creator" refers to the final prayer of the minister, "Aeternam ac iustissimam pietatem," which concludes the exorcisms. It is said "three times" according to Chavasse because the Reginensis has provision for three scrutiny meetings. ("Les deux rituels," p. 85.)

[10]"Tunc fiunt illa quae ab aecclesiastica consuetudine scrutinia dictitantur. Perscrutamur enim eorum corda per fidem utrum menti suae post renuntiationem diaboli sacra verba definxerint, utrum agnoverint futuram gratiam redemptoris, utrum se credere fateantur in deum patrem omnipotentem." (A. Wilmart, "Un florilège," p. 173.)

[11]"Haec igitur aecclesiastica sollicitudo per successiones temporum cauta dispositione constituit, quamvis horum vestigia vetus pagina non ostendat." (Ibid., p. 174.)

catechumenate with a stripping of the garments and shoes of the candidates before their renunciation of Satan and profession of faith prior to the font.[12]

John does not mention the blessing of the font or the threefold interrogation of faith immediately before baptism. Following baptism ([*De trina mersione*]) he first says that the baptized receive white vestments,[13] but after describing the anointing of the head with chrism ([*De unctione chrismatis*]) and the head covering ([*De linteola vel mystico velamine*]) he says, "Then they are dressed in white vestments."[14] ([*De albis vestibus*]).

A brief allusion to the reception of the Eucharist ([*De communicatione corporis et sanguinis*]) completes John's description of the ceremonies. Although he does not include episcopal confirmation, he does know it because later in the letter he answers a further question of Senarius as to whether it will prevent one's salvation if one dies baptized but "without the episcopal chrismation and benediction."[15] John's answer (he does not think the lack of confirmation can subtract from the totally regenerated state of the neophyte) suggests that Senarius and John were both familiar with a situation where the episcopal confirmation was not always done integrally with baptism, before the reception of the Eucharist, as in the Reginensis. Already at the beginning of the sixth century, confirmation might be delayed, even in episcopal cities. Baptisms presumably were being done at many parish churches in Rome, so that a bishop was not always the celebrant.

In sum, there are obvious differences between John and the Gelasian Sacramentary in its Reginensis form. The major *ordo* of baptism in the Reginensis is for infants, whereas John seems to have had adult converts in mind. At the close of his description he adds a sort of postscript regarding infants ([*De confessione parvulorum*]) in which he says that, "all these [ceremonies] they *also* do with infants who still do not have the use of reason."[16] Perhaps the way to explain John's sequence of ceremonies is to assume he had an adult pagan convert in mind. His order for the initial ceremonies of the catechumenate has parallels with the additional rite in the Reginensis for a pagan. This rite has "catechize" in the beginning, an exsufflation and reference to an exorcism, and salt given with a sign of the cross,[17] which agrees

---

[12]See E. C. Whitaker, *Documents*, pp. 39, 69, 72, 74.

[13]"Sumptis dehinc albis vestibus" (Wilmart, "Un florilège," p. 174).

[14]"Utuntur igitur albis vestibus." (Ibid., p. 174).

[15]"Sine chrismatis unctione ac benedictione pontificis." (Ibid., p. 179).

[16]"Illud autem ne praetermissum videatur, ante praedicamus, quod ista omnia etiam parvulis fiant, qui adhuc pro ipsius aetatis primordia nihil intelligunt" (Ibid., p. 175).

[17]"Gentilem hominem cum susceperis, in primis *catacizas* eum divinis sermonibus et das ei monita, quemadmodum post cognitam veritatem vevere [*sic*] debeat. Post haec facis eum caticuminum: *exsufflas* in faciem eius et facis ei crucem in fronte; *inponis manum* super caput eius his verbis: 'Accipe signum crucis ... evasisse te *laquaeos* mortis ... agnosce ...' Postquam gustaverit medicinam *salis et ipse se signaverit*, benedicis eum." (L. C. Mohlberg, *Sacramentarium Gelasianum*, Cap. LXXI, p. 93.)

with John's words, "salt, in which he is signed" ("sal in quo signatur"). The parallelism is not exact, but it seems John may have had these rubrics in mind.[18] The order of topics in Texts 1, 2, 3, and 4 can now be compared to John's order of ceremonies.

Text 1

The composer of Text 1 quoted John heavily, but changed his order of sentences. Almost all of his rearrangement makes Text 1 conform more closely to OR XI. (See Chart C2.) To Isidore's standard explanation of the competents the composer added: "On these competents they do the scrutinies according to the seven gifts of the Holy Spirit," the same explanation as in OR XI.[19] He seems to have known, then, OR XI or a similar Roman *ordo* that prescribed seven scrutinies. He put the delivery of the Creed *after* the topics of competents and scrutiny, corresponding to OR XI where (unlike John) it is not the purpose of the scrutinies to be tested on the Creed.

He combined the topics of catechesis and delivery of the Creed ("*VIIII. De cathacesis vel symboli traditione*"). He may have had in mind the instruction (catechesis) given at the *aurium apertio* in OR XI when the Creed is delivered. He probably did not know any earlier occasion of instruction of the catechumens such as John knew for his adult candidates.

He stated that the nose and ears are touched with spittle, not oil. This follows the prescription in OR XI. Moreover, he included a separate chapter citing Pope Gregory I on the use of spittle, as if he objected to John's use of oil.

He included the anointing of the back in addition to the breast. John may have omitted the anointing of the back for brevity, but in any case by adding it the composer brought Text 1 into closer conformity with the Roman rite.

He placed the topic of the renunciation of Satan after the anointing of the breast and back, where it is found in the Reginensis, and not where John placed it, at some point before the delivery of the Creed. Because of this switch, John's words do not at all fit where the composer positioned the topic.[20] It indicates that he was above all concerned with having the order of topics right—that he had a certain *ordo* in mind.

He transferred John's last statement on the confession of infants, which concerns the profession of faith by their sponsors, to the place immediately

---

[18]A. Chavasse, "Les deux rituels," pp. 79, 93–98, believes that the rite for a pagan in the Reginensis is a Romano-Gallican composition of the fifth century and was included in the primitive Gelasian Sacramentary written, he believes, ca. 500.

[19]See M. Andrieu, *Les Ordines* II, p. 442, nr. 81.

[20]"Nisi aliquis inter ipsa primitus fidei rudimenta . . . renuntians . . . ad salutaris lavacri gratiam non accedet, et ideo hunc oportet primum cathecuminorum adiutorium introire." Vol. II, p. 164.

before triple immersion, thus indicating that he knew a profession of faith at the edge of the font, as in the Reginensis.

He included a topic on episcopal confirmation with the imposition of hand. In OR XI it comes before the reception of the Eucharist, whereas he placed it after. This variation of the Roman *ordo*, due to the delay of episcopal confirmation, is spelled out in some liturgical books, as was seen, for example, in the manuscripts of PRG CVII.[21]

Finally, the composer of Text 1 shifted John's topic on bare feet ([*De nudis pedibus*]) to last place ("*XXII. De pedum nuditate*"). Perhaps, not familiar with the ceremony of the candidates taking off their shoes before they approached the font, he did not know what to do with it, yet felt compelled to include it because the Roman John did. (He did not omit any one of John's topics). F. Weigand believes he was trying to suggest the *pedilavium*; however, the *pedilavium* in the north-Italian and Gallican books takes place before the donning of the white garments.[22]

In conclusion, almost all the changes from John's order make Text 1 conform better to OR XI and the Reginensis. As to where and when Text 1 was redacted, its oldest manuscript was written at St. Gall circa 800, but the orthography suggests that it was copied from an earlier manuscript written in an insular or insular-influenced hand.[23] Insular-influenced manuscripts are well attested in the Swiss and north-Italian area in the eighth century. In one manuscript Text 1 is in the form of a letter of Archbishop Odilbert of Milan to Charlemagne in response to Charlemagne's baptismal questionnaire. It is not known whether Odilbert himself used Text 1 to write his response, or a later editor attached Odilbert's preface to Text 1.[24] Also, Text 1 includes a number of citations of Ambrose of Milan not in Texts 2, 3, and 4, and in all of its manuscripts Text 1 is juxtaposed to Text 6, consisting largely of Ambrose and Ps.-Maximus of Turin and probably of north-Italian origin. Thus, Text 1 probably reflects a Romanized north-Italian celebration of baptism. Another example of such a rite will be seen in Text 38.

Text 2

Text 2 seems also to have been redacted in the north-Italian area. Three of its ninth-century manuscripts are from northern Italy or Switzerland/northern Italy. As in Text 1, John the Deacon is quoted heavily, but in Text 2 John's order of topics is not rearranged. Some of John's topics are omitted, however, and further topics are added.

---

[21]See Chapter 3, pp. 47–49.

[22]See S. Keefe, "The Claim of Authorship in Carolingian Baptismal Expositions: The Case of Odilbert of Milan" in *Fälschungen im Mittelalter*, MGH Schriften Bd. 33, V, Hannover, 1988, p. 394.

[23]See ibid., pp. 386 f.

[24]See ibid., pp. 391–99.

Topics of John rearranged in Text 1 were competents, scrutiny, catechesis, confession of infants, and bare feet. All of these topics are absent in Text 2. (See Chart C3.) Is this a coincidence? It was seen that their order was unsatisfactory to the composer of Text 1 and that by rearranging them he was able to describe an order of ceremonies closer to OR XI and the Reginensis. The composer of Text 2 may have omitted them because he was puzzled by their order, or because he wished to describe a briefer, "quolibet tempore" rite of baptism for the clerics for whom he wrote. If, for example, the pre-baptismal ceremonies were all condensed into a single meeting on the day of baptism, references to catechesis, competents, and scrutinies might well be omitted. Although he omitted a separate chapter on confession of infants (John's [De confessione parvulorum]), he included John's explanation of the sponsors speaking for the infants under the topic of renunciation, some evidence that his omission of topics was not simply due to a desire for brevity, but to unhappiness with his model's order of topics.

Like Text 1, Text 2 has episcopal confirmation after the Eucharist. In sum, the sequence of topics in Text 2 suggests its composer had in mind a rite in which the celebrant would not be a bishop and confirmation would be delayed. If Text 2 was used in northern Italy, then a second post-baptismal chrismation by the bishop apparently had not dropped out everywhere in this region,[25] or had been restored under the influence of Romanization. The care to include instruction on the devil's works and pomps and to provide more explanation on the Eucharist than John provided might indicate its intended use for some rural parish priest who would be baptizing people with little or no catechetical preparation.

Text 3

Text 3 has far more topics than Texts 1, 2, or 4. It is divided into five sections, each beginning with a Roman numeral "I." (See Chart C4.) The first three sections pertain to the stages of the catechumen, competent, and baptism respectively; the fourth contains instruction on the Eucharist; and the fifth consists of one brief chapter on penance.

There are only two alterations in John's sequence of topics. As in Text 1, the topic on the confession of infants follows renunciation. Second, the delivery of the Creed ([De symbolo tradendo]) is mentioned after, rather than before, competents. (The composer quotes Isidore, not John the Deacon, at this juncture, who describes competents and then says they are given the Creed.)

Text 3 has a topic on the return of the Creed ([De reddendo symboli]) immediately before baptism ("De baptismo"). Four of its seven manuscripts state only: "Concerning the return of the Creed, the forty-sixth chapter of the Council of Laodicea should be read."[26] Three, however, have the decree itself: "that those

---

[25]See Chapter 7, p. 109.
[26]"VIII. De reddendo symbulo in concilio apud laoditium congregato cap. XLVI

who come for baptism ought to learn the faith and return it to the bishop or to the priest(s) on Thursday of Holy Week."[27]

Holy Thursday is the day Ildefonsus of Toledo prescribes for the return of the Creed,[28] as does the Second Council of Braga of 572.[29] Outside of Spain, however, there seems to have been no area in the west that had a return of the Creed on Holy Thursday. J.-P. Bouhot says it is plausible that Text 3 was redacted at Tours in the entourage of Fridegisus, circa 820/25.[30] Perhaps, then, at the scholarly center of Tours, the redactor had an interest in retaining the canon for curiosity or edification. Some copyists of Text 3, however, knew that this canon about returning the Creed on Holy Thursday contradicted the practice in their area, and perhaps omitted it for this reason. They had the pastor-reader of Text 3 in mind.[31]

Text 4

The earliest manuscripts of Text 4 are eleventh century. One is from Polirone in northern Italy, the same area of circulation as Texts 1 and 2. Text 4 contains material not in Texts 1, 2, or 3, and it also has a slightly different sequence of topics from any of them (see Chart C5). It has renunciation and confession of infants ("*Quod parvuli per se abrenuntiare non possunt*"), immediately before baptism, suggesting an *ordo* with a renunciation and profession of faith at the edge of the font. Omitted, as in Text 2, are topics on catechesis and bare feet. Like Texts 1, 2, and 3, a topic is added on the episcopal imposition of hand after Eucharist, but unlike them a topic on the head covering is omitted.[32]

In sum, four redactions of a florilegium show the different preferences of their composers. Some of these must be due to the way they knew baptism to

---

legitur" in Es1, V4, P9, or "legite baptizandis" in Mi2. Vol. II, p. 189.

[27] "Quod oporteat eos qui ad baptisma veniunt fidem discere et quinta feria septimane maioris episcopo aut presbiteris reddere" in Mu9, Z2, Vm. Vol. II, p. 189 (in *app. crit.*).

[28] The text in his *De cognitione baptismi* states: "Caput XXXIV. Quod quinta feria ante Pascha reddendum est symbolum. Hoc symbolum, quod competentes in die unctionis [Palm Sunday] accipiunt, aut per se, si maiores aetate sunt, aut per ora gestantium, si parvuli sunt, quinta feria ante Pascha sacerdoti recitant atque reddunt." *PL* 96: 127.

[29] In the Acts of the Second Council of Braga of 572 Martin of Braga listed separately some canons from ancient eastern councils. Canon XLVIIII of this group says, "Non liceat ante duas septimanas Paschae sed ante tres babtismum suscipere; oportet autem in his diebus ut hii qui babtizandi sunt symbolum discant et quinta feria novissimae septimanae episcopo vel presbytero reddant." (J. Vives, *Concilios*, p. 99.)

[30] J.-P. Bouhot, "Un florilège," p. 160.

[31] As to the presence of the canon from the Council of Laodicea in the florilegium archetype, perhaps the compiler of the archetype used a Spanish collection of canons containing the canons of the Council of Laodicea.

[32] One manuscript (V1) omits the topic of exorcism (perhaps unintentionally, because it has the preceding topic of exsufflation).

be celebrated in the liturgical books familiar to them. Otherwise, it is hard to explain why two Texts have some of the very same variations from their archetype as well as differences. Since there was no necessary reason for any of the redactors to alter the sequence of the archetype, the fact that they did demands an explanation.

The composer of Text 1 desired to make John the Deacon conform to an *OR* XI-type rite of baptism. It is astonishing how clearly the influence of *OR* XI is seen behind every alteration. The fact that Odilbert of Milan became associated with Text 1 perhaps attests that it was considered a good model of the Roman *ordo* of baptism. Odilbert, from northern Italy, specifically wanted to prove his Romanity to Charlemagne.[33] Whether Odilbert himself used Text 1 as his response, or a later copyist associated it with Odilbert's preface, Text 1 was recognized as being more than an arbitrary collection of sentences. Its sequence of topics was very important to its users. More attention needs to be paid to liturgical commentaries that are florilegia. Text 1 supports a view that this type of literature, so heavily disseminated for the instruction of the clergy, was compiled with deliberation and selectivity, with the desires and needs of its intended readers in mind.[34]

In Text 2, its composer transformed the same archetype florilegium as the composer of Text 1, but so that it describes a "quolibet tempore," short *ordo* of baptism. He omitted topics such as the scrutinies and the competents but added information particularly suitable for a rural parish priest facing baptismal parties which had little or no preparation for the sacrament.

In Text 3, some of its manuscripts omit the words of the Council of Laodicea demanding a return of the Creed on Holy Thursday, perhaps because this would have confused the priests for whom the copies were intended. Its earliest manuscripts show its use perhaps at Tours, but it is also these manuscripts in which the inapplicable decree of Laodicea is omitted. One way to explain this is that this scholarly monastic center also had the practical needs of secular clergy in mind, whether secular clergy were being trained at Tours or books for their instruction were being compiled there.

Text 4, with different variations than Texts 1, 2, and 3, but redacted from the same archetype, forces one to ask why its composer also bothered to change his model, unless he had the needs of specific recipients in mind.

In conclusion, these four composers were aware that the education of the clergy involved more than the mere copying of a patristic florilegium. They understood that to educate the clergy effectively they would need to create

---

[33]His preface praises Charlemagne for his defense of orthodoxy and love of the apostolic tradition, but Odilbert never uses the expression "the Roman *ordo*" or the word "Roman." See Wiegand, *Erzbischof Odilbert*, pp. 25–27.

[34]R. McKitterick, *The Frankish Church*, pp. 164 f., asserts this regarding ethical florilegia.

texts that spoke to their needs. Educational reform would only carry the element of urgency if the texts of instruction were pertinent. This could only happen at the local level, because a single standard model could not take into consideration a variety of individual needs. The implementation of the Carolingian Reform lay here, in the hands of those who locally shaped the texts of instruction.

The significance of these four Texts is that they show the nature of the Carolingian Reform in its actual implementation by individuals. It was not simply the cranking out of more, same florilegia for clerical instruction, but it involved the careful consideration of the text and its appropriateness, the adding and exchanging of other sources, and the rewriting of the order of topics. Such time-consuming editing has been noted among famous highbrows of the Carolingian Renaissance, such as Radbertus and Ratramnus of Corbie,[35] but it has never been credited to the composers of the myriad obscure texts produced for the education of the secular clergy. Yet these anonymous composers would eventually far outweigh the Gottschalks and John Scottuses of the Carolingian era in their contribution to the cultural transformation of society as a whole.

In the following chapter some further examples of the care taken by composers of baptismal instructions for the education of the secular clergy will be shown.

---

[35]See D. Ganz, *Corbie*, pp. 85, 91.

6

The Reworking of Three Carolingian Models

The Carolingians are well known for their love of authoritative texts. Works falsely attributed to giants such as Jerome, Augustine, Gregory, and Isidore abound in Carolingian manuscripts.[1] The baptismal instructions betray this penchant for collecting authoritative sources. In fact, almost all of them are florilegia in a sense, although not all of them so clearly boast the format as Texts 1, 2, 3, and 4, examined in Chapter 5.

By far the most frequently copied of all the baptismal instructions was Text 9. It received the highest authority by its association with Alcuin, who probably composed it and certainly used it and endorsed it (see below). This study lists thirty-one manuscripts of Text 9, and there are undoubtedly more. Despite its authority and approval in official eyes, it was apparently not satisfactory for many who had to compose baptismal instructions for their clergy. Thirteen of our Texts are evidence of this. Most of them contain every word of the brief Text 9, while further explanation from other sources has been added. Also, sometimes the order of topics has been changed. The reworking of the order of Text 9 demands an explanation, if only because Text 9 was such a widely copied, almost formulaic tract, which one would not expect to have been given extra consideration. Below, a particularly striking adaptation of Text 9, Text 38, will be used to show one composer's initiative to present baptismal instruction that responded to the needs of clergy in a specific area.

Text 9 is associated with the name of Alcuin because in its earliest manuscripts it is contained in two letters of Alcuin, one to monks in Septimania and one to a priest named Oduin, both written circa 798. Whether Alcuin himself composed "Primo paganus" at the time of the letters, or only incorporated it into them, he certainly endorsed its description of baptism.[2] Despite his refer-

---

[1] One only has to glance through Lambert's *BHM* or Machielsen's *CPPM*, or the articles in *Fälschungen im Mittelalter* edited by H. Fuhrmann, for example.

[2] Following it in the letter to the monks in Septimania he states, "You see how faithfully, reasonably, and prudently all these things [the ceremonies of baptism] were handed down to us to observe. Let no Catholic dare to struggle against the authority of the church, no sane man against reasonable custom, no faithful person against wise piety. Lest a schismatic and not a Catholic he be found, let him follow the most approved authority of the Roman church. ("Videtis, quam fideliter rationabiliter et prudenter haec omnia tradita sunt nobis observanda. Nemo catholicus contra ecclesiae

ence to the Roman church, the *ordo* of baptism he outlines is a far cry from *OR XI* or the Gelasian Reginensis Sacramentary. Alcuin's *ordo* is very brief and may be paraphrased in its entirety so that the sequence of topics can be seen.[3]

1. (*caticuminus et renuntiatio*) First a pagan coming to baptism becomes a catechumen so that he renounces the evil spirit and all his damning pomps.

2. (*exsufflatio*) He is also breathed upon (exsufflated) so that, with the devil having fled, an entrance is prepared for Christ our God.

3. (*exorcismus*) The evil spirit is exorcized, that is, conjured, so that he goes out and departs, giving place to the true God.[4]

4. (*sal*) The catechumen receives salt so that his filthy and dissolute sins are cleansed with salt, the divine gift of wisdom.

5. (*traditio symboli*) Then the faith of the Apostles' Creed is delivered to him so that the home, empty and abandoned by its former inhabitant, is decorated with the faith, and a dwelling place is prepared for God.

6. (*scrutinia*) Next, scrutinies are done so that he is examined often whether, after the renunciation of Satan, he has fixed the sacred words of the given faith deeply in his heart.[5]

7. (*nares*) His nostrils also are touched so that as long as he draws breath he may endure in the received faith.

8. (*pectus*) His breast is also anointed with the same oil so that with the sign of the holy cross an entrance for the devil is closed.

---

auctoritatem, nemo sobrius contra rationabilem consuetudinem, nemo fidelis contra pietatis intellegentiam certare audeat. Et ne scismaticus inveniatur et non catholicus, sequatur probatissimam sanctae Romanae ecclesiae auctoritatem." *MGH Epp.* IV, p. 215.) The triple immersion is the focal point of Text 9. Its emphasis can be explained if the original context of Text 9 was indeed to the monks in Septimania circa 798, at the height of the controversy between Spain and the Franks over the Adoptianist heresy. See W. Heil, "Der Adoptianismus, Alkuin und Spanien" in *Karl der Grosse*, ed. W. Braunfels [Düsseldorf, 1965], Bd. II, pp. 95–155). Alcuin took the leading role against Elipandus of Toledo and Felix of Urgel. His views of these heretics extended to his views of any Spanish liturgical customs that went against the orthodox, Roman tradition. His letter to the monks in Septimania is a warning to avoid Spanish errors, including immersing only once. Also, if Alcuin did compose Text 9 himself, this might explain its almost total dependence on John the Deacon, an early *Roman* authority.

[3]For theLatin, see Text 9 in vol. II, pp. 240–245. The numbers and italicized words (not in the Text) refer to the sequence of topics on Chart D1.

[4]Another reading (see V5) is: "He [the catechumen] is exorcized, that is, conjured, so that the evil spirit goes out and departs."

[5]See, however, the alternate readings in the *app. crit.*

9. (*scapulae*) His shoulder blades are also signed so that he is armed on all sides. Also [or "again"] in the anointing of the breast and shoulder blades firmness of faith and perseverance in good works is signified.

10. (*trina mersio*) And thus in the name of the Holy Trinity with a triple immersion he is baptized. And rightly man, who was made in the image of the Holy Trinity, is renewed to the same image through the invocation of the Holy Trinity; and who died through the third grade of sin, that is, by deed, raised three times from the font through grace rises to life.

11. (*alba vestimenta*) Then he is dressed in white vestments because of the joy of his rebirth, his chastity of life, and his angelic beauty.

12. (*caput, mysticum velamen*) Then his head is anointed with sacred chrism and covered with a mystic veil so that he realizes by this diadem that he bears the dignity of the kingdom and the priesthood, as the Apostle said: "You are a royal and priestly people, offering yourselves to the living God, a holy sacrifice pleasing to Him."

13. (*corpus et sanguis domini*) Thus he is confirmed with the Lord's Body and Blood so that he is a member of that One who suffered for him and rose.

14. (*impositio manus a summo sacerdote*) Finally, he receives the septiform gift of the Holy Spirit through the imposition of the bishop's hand, so that he is strengthened through the Holy Spirit to preach to others, who through grace in baptism was bestowed with eternal life.

The differences between the order of ceremonies in Text 9 and OR XI and the Reginensis (compare Charts D1, A1, A2) are that the renunciation of Satan seems to come at the beginning (this corresponds to the first ceremony in OR L and PRG CVII); there is an exsufflation with an exorcism before salt (this also corresponds to OR L and PRG CVII); the Apostles' Creed, not the Nicene, is delivered to the catechumens; the scrutinies occur after the delivery of the Creed to test its retention; there is no touching of the ears, only the nose; there may be a double anointing of the breast and back (shoulder blades);[6]

---

[6]This is not unique. In Text 58 one finds: "We are ordered to make the sign of the cross on the breast *two times*." ("Nam *bis* in pectore oleo exorzizato crucem facere iubemur."). In *OR XV* one finds precisely this directive: "Inde tangit ipse presbiter de oleo benedicto pectus infantum, ficiens (*sic*) bis crucem in eorum pectus, dicendo: 'Abrenuncias.'" (M. Andrieu, *Les Ordines* III, p. 119, nr. 114.) The directive to anoint the breast is given twice in the *ordo* for a sick (*infirmus*) catechumen in the Gellone Sacramentary (ed. A. Dumas, *Liber Sacramentorum Gellonensis: Textus*, nr. 2306, pp. 331 f.) and in the excarpsus of Brussels, Bibl. Royal 10127–144 (ed. C. Coebergh and P. de Puniet, "Liber Sacramentorum Excar[p]sus (Cod. Bruxellensis 10127–144, s. VIII–IX)" in *CCCM* XLVII, Turnhout, 1977, pp. 102 f.). Thus, the double signing of the breast in Text 9 may reflect a specific liturgical book.

white garments are donned before the head is anointed; and episcopal confirmation by hand-laying alone (not chrismation) comes *after* reception of the
Eucharist.

Text 9 is based on John the Deacon (see Chapter 5), but omitted are John's
topics on catechesis, frequent hand-laying and three-times blessing of the
Creator, competents or elect, touching of the ears, and bare feet. Added to
John's topics are the touching of the shoulder blades (back) and episcopal
hand-laying (confirmation). Do these changes represent the composer's
(Alcuin's or someone else's) effort to describe a specific liturgical *ordo* known
to him? If the composer had in mind a non-paschal, "quolibet tempore" rite of
baptism in which all the ceremonies for the catechumen took place at a single
session on the day of baptism itself, this could explain his omission of the topics of catechesis, frequent hand-laying and triple blessing of the Creator, and
competents or elect. The bare feet one can probably assume was dismissed as
an archaism.

In a shortened rite the topic of scrutinies might still have value if they referred to the examination of the sponsors on their knowledge of the Creed
and the Lord's Prayer. Amalarius (Text 23), it may be recalled, stated, "In the
scrutiny . . . we teach the godfathers and godmothers the Lord's Prayer, so
that they also can teach those whom they receive from the font. Similarly we
teach the Creed." Also for Leidrad (Text 25) the term "scrutiny" meant a literal examination.

The omission of the touching of the ears, almost always found with the
touching of the nose, is more difficult to explain liturgically. John the Deacon
has the touching of the ears before the touching of the nose, and that is why
Text 9, quoting John, reads, "His nose is *also* touched." The ears do not seem
to have been omitted simply for brevity (allowing nose to represent ears and
nose). The composer does not abbreviate the anointing of the breast and the
shoulder blades. In fact, John the Deacon did not mention the shoulder blades
at all, but the composer of Text 9 thought it important to add them. The omission of the touching of the ears, then, may mean that Text 9 describes the *ordo*
of a specific liturgical book which does not have a touching of the ears but
only a touching of the nose.

Although the liturgical book that precisely corresponds to the entire sequence of ceremonies in Text 9 may never be found, one that comes close,
and, most strikingly, has a rubric directing the priest to touch the nose without any mention of the ears, is the Sacramentary of St. Martin of Tours (Tours,
Bibl. mun. 184, s. $IX^{4/4}$, with Paris, BN lat. 9430, s. X^{in}). This is intriguing from
the point of view of Alcuin as the composer of Text 9, or at least of its being
composed at Tours. Deshusses says that these two manuscripts together
transmit, up to a certain point, the missal that Alcuin compiled for his abbey
of St. Martin's circa 800. Not only does its "ordo baptisterii" have the touching of the nose and no mention of the ears, but it also specifically describes a

sufflation and exorcism before the giving of salt; a delivery of the Creed after salt and before Holy Saturday without a formal *aurium apertio*; and the covering of the head with a chrism cloth ("chrismale;" John the Deacon and Text 9 have "mysticum velamen"). In all of these points the Sacramentary of St. Martin of Tours is different from the *Hadrianum Supplementum* (representative of many eighth-century-type Gelasian sacramentaries). The agreement between the rubrics of the Sacramentary of St. Martin of Tours and the sequence of topics of Text 9 is not perfect, but their similarities contrary to the *Hadrianum Supplementum* strongly suggest a link between them.[7] Especially, it is possible to explain the omission in Text 9 of the touching of the ears as an intentional omission. It could have been due to the use of a specific liturgical book in a particular area.

An important reason to be able to explain the sequence of topics in Text 9 liturgically, in respect to some specific *ordo* of baptism in use in the Carolingian period, is because of its numerous adaptations. Text 9 was seen as a summary of a specific liturgical book, and so it had to be adapted where a different liturgical book was in use. The most vivid example is Text 38.

Text 38

Text 38 contains all the words of Text 9 (with variations), but its order of topics for the pre-baptismal ceremonies is very different. The order, however, has remarkable parallels with a most distinctive *ordo* for the scrutinies from northern Italy preserved in an eleventh-century manuscript (Milan, Bibl. Ambros. T 27 sup.). Its editor, Dom Lambot, believes it was in use in a cathedral city in northern Italy in the eighth century.[8]

First, in Text 38 the topic of the delivery of the Creed (*traditio symboli*)[9] is placed *after* the topic of the scrutinies, whereas in Text 9 the delivery of the Creed comes *before* the scrutinies. In Lambot's *ordo* the delivery of the Creed does not take place until all the scrutinies are over.[10] This would

---

[7]J. Deshusses gives the rubrics of the Sacramentary of St. Martin of Tours (cod. Tu1) in *Le Sacramentaire Grégorien, ses prinicipales formes d'après les plus ancièns manuscrits*, vol. III (Spicilegium Friburgense 28) Fribourg/Sw., 1982, pp. 108 f. The touching of the nose without mention of the ears is in three other baptismal *ordines* (and maybe more), but they do not come close to Text 9 in other respects. They are: the fragment of Brussels, BR 10127–144 in C. Coebergh and P. de Puniet, "Liber Sacramentorum Excarpsus," p. 102; the variation of codex "P" (Paris, BN lat. 820) of PRG CVII, ed. C. Vogel and R. Elze, *PRG* II, p. 159, nr. 24; and the Bobbio Missal, ed. by E. A. Lowe, *The Bobbio Missal*, p. 74, nr. 241.

[8]See C. Lambot, *North Italian Services*, p. xxxiv. The *ordo scrutiniorum* is on pp. 7–31.

[9]See Chart D2.

[10]This is a feature common to northern Italy. See M. Magistretti, ed., *Manuale Ambrosianum ex codice saec. XI*, 2 vols. (Monumenta veteris litiurgiae Ambrosianae 2–3) Milan, 1904, repr. 1971, pars altera, pp. 168 f. and M. Magistretti, ed., *Beroldus sive*

explain the reversal of the delivery of the Creed to after the scrutinies in Text 38.

Second, exsufflation has been repositioned immediately before the delivery of the Creed. In Lambot's *ordo* the third and last scrutiny session is especially solemn and the number of exorcisms is increased. After the usual signings of the catechumens, the celebrant places himself in their midst and proclaims the three-part exorcism prayer, "Do not lurk, Satan." ("Ne te lateat, inmundissime Sathana."), before each part making an exsufflation on the catechumens in the form of a cross.[11] These solemn exsufflations, marking in a special way the last exorcistic preparations before receiving the Creed, would explain the decision to put the topic of exsufflation immediately before the topic of the delivery of the Creed. Third, the anointing of the breast (*pectus*) is put *before* nose, immediately after the delivery of the Creed. This is striking because the anointing of the breast and shoulder blades (*scapulae*) are topics invariably found together in our other Texts. In Lambot's *ordo*, however, on the very day of the delivery of the Creed[12] there is provision for catechumens who were not able to attend any of the previous scrutinies. They receive the same enrollment ceremony (see note 16 below), then a special scrutiny is conducted for them on the spot, consisting of prayers, exorcisms, signings, and exsufflations. Three separate times the priest anoints their breasts with oil.[13] This could explain the position of the anointing of the breast beside the delivery of the Creed and removed from its usual companion, the anointing of the shoulder blades, in Text 38.[14] It would also suggest that the composer of Text 38 had in mind rural priests who would follow this provisional scrutiny, having parishioners who did not attend the regular scrutiny meetings held in a cathedral city. (The reality even in a cathedral city may have been that most people did not attend the full series of scrutinies.)

The composer of Text 38 once more disrupts the order of topics in Text 9 by placing renuntiation (*abrenuntiatio*) and an additional topic on the interrogation of the faith (*interrogatio fidei*), before baptism itself (*trina mersio*). He states that when the candidates come to the font, they should renounce "in the usual

---

ecclesiae Ambrosianae Mediolanensis kalendarium et ordines saec. XII (Milan, 1894), pp. 94–96. In Lambot's *ordo* the *traditio symboli* begins on p. 25.

[11]C. Lambot, *North Italian Services*, pp. 16, xxii. The "Ne te lateat" exorcism is essentially the same as the "Nec te latet" in the Reginensis and OR XI, but there it is done long after the day of the *traditio symboli* and it is accompanied by a hand-laying, not exsufflations.

[12]Ibid., p. 18.

[13]Ibid., pp. 19 f.

[14]See L. Mitchell, *Baptismal Anointing* (London, 1966), p. 146, on the pre-baptismal anointing in the Gallican rites being the "climax," along with the delivery of the Creed, of all the catechumenate ceremonies.

custom," and should be interrogated on the faith of the Creed "again." This recalls OR L, in which there are two renunciations before the one at the font, and two previous interrogations of the faith (on the day of the first scrutiny and at the return of the Creed on Holy Saturday morning; see Chart A3).

Dom Lambot's *ordo* was originally only an *ordo* for the scrutinies and was combined at some point in history with a Roman *ordo* of baptism to make it a complete rite.[15] Text 38 does not agree with the addition to Lambot's *ordo scrutiniorum* (the addition does not describe a renunciation at the font). Our composer knew Lambot's *ordo scrutiniorum* before it was completed by a Roman *ordo* that does not have a renunciation at the font, or he preferred another *ordo*.

There are some other striking parallels between Text 38 and Lambot's *ordo scrutiniorum*. The composer of Text 38 added a topic on competents (*competentes*), not in Text 9. He explains that catechumens become competents when they have given their names and the names of their sponsors to an acolyte at the doors of the church. In Lambot's *ordo* there is a detailed description of the enrollment ceremony. The "catechumens" give their names and those of their sponsors at the front of the church, assisted by an acolyte, and then proceed up to the choir where they are addressed as "competents" for the first time.[16]

Another connection between Text 38 and Lambot's *ordo scrutiniorum* are certain distinctive phrases found in both. One that occurs repeatedly in the *ordo* and which Lambot calls "la plus notable curiosité de notre rituel"[17] is the formula, "Omnia recta." The celebrant proclaims these words after exsufflations.[18] "Omnia recta" is pronounced twice during the special scrutiny for

---

[15]Lambot identified it as "one very close to Hittorp's *Ordo Romanus Antiquus*," that is, Andrieu's OR L. See *North Italian Services*, pp. xxxiv f. It begins with the blessing of the font (pp. 31–35 in Lambot).

[16]Lambot, *North Italian Services*, pp. 7 f.: "Cum vero statuto die advenerint, iussi a ministro veniant in aecclesiam, et interroget presbyter illos qui ipsos catecuminos in brachiis tenent, qui vocentur. . . . At illi ut annuntiaverint nomina catecumini presbytero interrogato, tunc invocet presbyter nomina praefatorum catecuminum [*sic*], 'Illi et illi et illae . . .quid desiderant?' R. accolitus: 'Gratiam dei.' Sequatur presbyter: 'Gratia dei quid illis confert?' R. accolitus: 'Remissionem peccatorum, vitam aeternam'. . . . Eant omnes ad summos choros . . . et dicat [diaconus] excelsa voce: 'Orate competentes, cervicem flectite'. " This definition of a competent as one who gives his name will be encountered in Text 7, which comes from Spain. It is only in the Spanish and north-Italian liturgical sources that one finds this same connection between the enrollment of names and the cry, "Orate, competentes." Compare the León Antiphonary, L. Brou & J. Vives, ed., *Antifonario Visigotico Mozarabe de la Catedral de León* (Monumenta Hispaniae Sacra V, 1) (Barcelona/Madrid, 1959), pp. 203 f., with Lambot, *North Italian Services*, p. 8. On the closeness of the Mozarabic and Ambrosian liturgies, see W. C. Bishop, *The Mozarabic and Ambrosian Rites* (London, 1924).

[17]Lambot, *North Italian Services*, p. xxi, note 2.

[18]Ibid., pp. 11, 16, 19, 20, 21. Lambot thinks "Omnia recta" refers to the exorcisms which have been accomplished in good and proper form. (See p. xxi, note 2.)

those who missed the normal three. Another phrase is "more solito" ("in the usual custom").[19] The composer of Text 38 uses both of these phrases when he interjects his own explanation of the events at the font, almost as if he had adopted them subconsciously while thinking of the *ordo scrutiniorum* he had described.[20] It is not necessary, of course, that these phrases come from the liturgy, but it adds to the probability that he had Lambot's *ordo scrutiniorum* under his eyes, given the other parallels between it and Text 38. Text 38, preserved in a manuscript from the first third of the ninth century, is the first actual evidence that Lambot's *ordo scrutiniorum* was used in the Carolingian period.[21]

In conclusion, although Text 38 is essentially Text 9 as far as its words of explanation are concerned, its composer intentionally reworked it to describe a specific Romanized north-Italian *ordo*, presumably the *ordo* in use where he was writing. There is a correlation between Text 38 and its one known manuscript. The manuscript comes from northern Italy or Bavaria and it also contains another baptismal instruction (Text 33) definitely composed in northern Italy because its author is known, Archbishop Maxentius of Aquileia.

Another authoritative model for Carolingian composers of baptismal instructions was the questionnaire Charlemagne sent to his archbishops on baptism circa 812 (Text 14). In it he said, "We wish to know, through your writings or through you yourself, how you and your suffragans [that is, bishops] teach and instruct the priests of God and the people commissioned to you on the sacrament of baptism." Then he listed a long series of questions on the individual ceremonies: "That is, why is an infant first made a catechumen, and what is a catechumen? Then, in order, everything that is done: concerning the scrutiny, what is a scrutiny? Concerning the Creed," and so forth.[22]

Political and liturgical historians cite this famous letter wherever one turns in works on Charlemagne, mostly as evidence of the extent of his concern for liturgical reform. Its chief importance is the baptismal literature it caused to be written across the Carolingian empire at relatively the same time. This one

---

[19]Ibid., p. 20.

[20]"Cumque *more solito* abrenunctiaberint [*sic*] iterum de fide symboli sciscitantur. Et cum per ordinem *omnia recte* responderint . . ." Vol. II, p. 536.

[21]Lambot thought that it was not combined with a Roman *ordo* until the tenth century or later because the *ordo* was "very close" to Hittorp's *ordo* (Andrieu's OR L), which is known only in tenth-century manuscripts of the *PRG* (see Lambot, *North Italian Services*, pp. xxxiv f.). Text 38 is evidence that the north-Italian *ordo* of scrutinies had already been combined with a variation of OR L's rite for baptism by the first third of the ninth century.

[22]See Text 14 in vol. II, pp. 261 f. Throughout this study the questionnaire is called "Charlemagne's," although it was probably composed by someone at his court and only approved by him.

document gave rise to a great many of the Carolingian baptismal instructions collected here, either in the form of direct replies of archbishops to Charlemagne, indirect responses of suffragans to their archbishops, diocesan synodal addresses and statutes describing how baptism ought to be taught and celebrated, or anonymous clerical instructions. They have special value as a corpus for the study of the Carolingian Reform because they allow a picture of the Reform across Carolingian Europe at relatively the same moment. How did Charlemagne's questionnaire inspire so much baptismal literature?

It is almost certain that the questionnaire was connected with the five regional reform councils of 813, and that through these councils' decrees on baptism the questionnaire quickly became a model for diocesan legislation and for baptismal instructions aimed at parish priests. Charlemagne sent his questionnaire to his archbishops shortly before he convened the five regional synods at Arles, Rheims, Mainz, Tours, and Chalon-sur-Saône in the Spring of 813. The date of the questionnaire, circa 812, is determined by the bishops who responded. It must lie between 811, when Maxentius became Archbishop of Aquileia, and the very beginning of 813, when Amalarius departed for Constantinople.[23]

The five councils, presided over by archbishops and bishops but convoked and guided by Charlemagne, have often been cited because of the important influence they had on subsequent legislation. The acts of the councils are all addressed to Charlemagne, and the canons of each are very similar in theme. There are indications from Carolingian chronicles that a convocation of bishops was held at Aachen before the five councils. A. Werminghoff suggests it was here that Charlemagne gave the bishops an agenda of topics he wished to be discussed.[24] Whether Charlemagne referred to his baptismal questionnaire in this agenda is not certain, but the bishops were unquestionably told that baptism was to be discussed, as the canons of the councils attest.[25] The very

---

[23]Amalarius had written his response before he left, because he mentioned it to Abbot Peter of Nonantula on his sea voyage, who later requested it. See Hanssens, *Amalarii* I, p. 65 and the letter of Peter, p. 229.

[24]*MGH Conc.* II, pp. 245–47.

[25]Council of Mainz of 813, "IIII. cap. Sacramenta itaque baptismatis volumus, ut, sicut sancta vestra fuit *ammonitio*, ita concorditer atque uniformiter in singulis parrochiis *secundum Romanum ordinem* inter nos celebretur iugiter atque conservetur, *id est scrutinium ad ordinem baptismatis*." Council of Arles of 813, "III. De baptismo et mysterio sanctae fidei: ut unusquisque archiepiscopus suos suffraganeos diligenter studioseque admonere curet, quatenus, per studium sacrae lectionis imbuti, et de mysterio sanctae fidei et de sacramento baptismatis, unusquisque illorum in propria parroechia perfecte studioseque presbyteros et universum populum docere et instruere non neglegat." Council of Rheims of 813, "VII. Baptisterii et caticuminorum ventilata est ratio, ut sacerdotes plenius intellegerent, qualiter *condignis ordinibus* efficerent Christianum." Council of Tours of 813, "XVIII. Episcoporum sit magna sollicitudo presbyteris suis tradere baptismi sacramentum et quid in eodem renuntiandum quidve credendum sit." (*MGH Conc.* II, pp. 261, 250, 254, 288).

first concern of the capitulary that Charlemagne issued after the five councils, summarizing their acts, was baptism: "Canon I. Concerning baptism, that every archbishop diligently and studiously warns his suffragans that each one does not neglect to examine his priests plainly as to how they baptize, and that [the bishops] teach them this earnestly, so that [baptism] is done in order."[26]

If, as a result of the council activity of 813, archbishops urged their suffragan bishops to call local diocesan synods and relate the decrees to their parish priests, then the bishops had to provide baptismal instructions for them, either through diocesan circulatory letters, oral addresses, or manuals for archdeacons or for individual priests. What was to serve the bishops as a model for these instructions? Conveniently, many could turn to their archbishops' recent responses to Charlemagne's questionnaire, or possibly their own reports to their archbishops answering Charlemagne's questionnaire, or at least to a copy of the questionnaire.

But how satisfactory was the questionnaire as a model? The composers who did choose to use it as their model made changes. Partly this was due to the fact that Charlemagne's series of questions does not reflect any liturgical order. (See Chart E1.) His order of Creed (*symbolum* and *credulitas*) followed by renunciation, insufflation (exsufflation), exorcism, and salt, for example, is found in no liturgical *ordo* of baptism.

There is no indication that he sought to promote liturgical conformity to any particular *ordo* of baptism by means of his questionnaire. Even though his series of questions on the ceremonies of baptism is largely identical in wording to Alcuin's *ordo* (Text 9), the questionnaire was not created from Text 9 directly, but from a florilegium that made use of Text 9. A close comparison of Texts 14 and 9 confirms this (compare Charts D1 and E1). For example, first Charlemagne asks a double question regarding the catechumen: "Why is an infant first made a catechumen and what is a catechumen?" Text 9, however, does not say *what* a catechumen is; it says only why. A hypothetical florilegium that also included Isidore's oft-quoted definition of the catechumen ("id est, audiens") would explain Charlemagne's double question. Second, Charlemagne asks a simple question, "What is a scrutiny?" Text 9, however, does not define the term "scrutinium." It says only *why* scrutinies (plural) are done. Also, Text 9 has the topic of "scrutinia" in a different place. Third, Charlemagne asks, "Concerning the Creed, what is the translation of the Greek term 'symbol' in Latin?" Text 9 does not say what "symbol" means in Latin, only why it is delivered to the catechumens. Again, a hypothetical florilegium including Isidore's oft-quoted explanation of what the *symbol*

---

[26]"I. Cap. De baptismo, ut unusquisque archiepiscopus suos suffraganeos diligenter ac studiosae admonere studeat, ut unusquisque suos presbiteros puriter investigare non neglegat, baptismatis sacramentum qualiter agant, et hoc eos studiose doceant, ut ordinabiliter fiat." (*MGH Conc.* II, p. 294).

means in Latin[27] would explain Charlemagne's question. Also, Text 9 has this topic in a different place.

In other words, Charlemagne composed the questionnaire from an anonymous didactic instruction, one typical of the kind that had multiplied since Alcuin's promotion of Text 9 fourteen years earlier. What was foremost in Charlemagne's mind was baptismal instruction, not a specific liturgical order of topics. This is important to stress in its own right, before examining Texts modeled on the questionnaire. The main reason Charlemagne sent out his questionnaire was not to promote the Roman rite of baptism, but baptismal instruction. The education of the clergy, not liturgical conformity to a specific *ordo*, was uppermost in his mind. The canon quoted above, which he issued after the five regional councils, does not mention the word "Roman." His questionnaire does not outline any liturgical *ordo*, and, in fact, it omits questions on two topics that were controversial in regard to the Roman rite: the triple immersion (in Spain some practiced single immersion) and episcopal confirmation (in northern Italy some omitted). His concern to list a long series of specific questions reflects only the kind of response for which he was looking. His request that they respond "in order" ("per ordinem") simply indicates he wished them to respond to each topic one by one. He sent out his questionnaire to stir interest in the teaching of baptism. He may have even thought of disseminating the archbishops' responses. He read them carefully. In one case, he wrote back to Leidrad, not reproving his order of ceremonies (see Chapter 4), but demanding a fuller explanation of the topic of renunciation.[28] Why would he have done this, unless to foster more literature for the education of the clergy?

Our Texts show how Carolingians interpreted the intent of the questionnaire. Perhaps some of the now anonymous baptismal instructions were originally composed by archbishops, but most of the anonymous tracts whose order of topics and wording are partially identical with Charlemagne were never direct responses to him. The following texts, whether direct responses or not, show how Charlemagne's model was accommodated.

Text 15

Text 15 was written by Archbishop Magnus of Sens in response to the questionnaire. Magnus did not rearrange Charlemagne's order of topics. (See Chart E2.) He was aware, however, that they did not follow a liturgical order because under the topic of the scrutiny he explains that the scrutiny is done to

---

[27]"Symbolum enim grece et indicium dici potest et conlatio." (*De ecclesiasticis officiis* II. xxiii. 3; *CCSL* CXIII, p. 98) and in *Origines* VI. xix. 57: "Symbolum per linguam Graecam signum vel cognitio interpretatur." (W. M. Lindsay, ed., *Isidori Hispalensis Episcopi Etymologiarum sive Originum*, 2 vols. [Oxford, 1911].)

[28]Leidrad's second letter to Charlemagne on renunciation is extant. See *PL* 99: 873–84.

see if the catechumens have retained the Creed, which they have recently received, even though he put the topic of the Creed *after* the topic of the scrutiny, following Charlemagne's order. Again, under the topic of the renunciation he says that after the renunciation "rightly follows the confession of the Holy Trinity," even though his next topic is insufflation, following Charlemagne's order.

Magnus could not altogether resist making Charlemagne's list more liturgically complete. He treated the triple immersion under an introductory topic on baptism and added explanations of the touching of the ears and episcopal confirmation, placing the latter before Eucharist (thus following OR XI and the Reginensis, not Text 9).

In sum, Magnus revealed three features of the rite of baptism known to him. One was no scrutiny of the Roman type, but a simple examination of the catechumen to see if he had learned the Creed. Another was the profession of faith after the renunciation. (This corresponds to the renunciation followed by the profession of faith at the beginning of OR L and PRG CVII.) Finally, since Magnus added "iterum" ("again") to Charlemagne's second question on the anointing of the breast and back, he may have known a second anointing of the breast and back.[29]

There seems to be no liturgical book possessing all three of these features. Would it be odd for Magnus, as an archbishop with a cathedral, to have an *ordo* in mind that lacked a formal series of scrutiny meetings? It is not certain that all the cathedral cities celebrated the scrutinies, but in any case Magnus composed his response to Charlemagne from the replies of the suffragan bishops around his archdiocese, and his remarks may reflect the normal practice in the dioceses. In fact, Text 17 is an actual witness that the scrutiny in Magnus's dioceses was a single-day event before baptism to test the sponsors on their knowledge of the Creed and the Lord's Prayer.

Text 17

Text 17 is a response to Charlemagne's questionnaire not addressed to the emperor, but written by a suffragan bishop of Sens at the request of Magnus, in the same manner as his suffragan Theodulf of Orléans (Text 16).[30]

The only differences between Text 17 and the questionnaire are the omission of mystic veil and two additional topics (placed at the end) on triple immersion and the invisible effect of baptism. (See Chart E3.) The composer has several interesting comments about the celebration of the ceremonies in his

---

[29]See Text 58 and note 6 of this chapter. The double signing of the breast may have been common, but the use of "bis" and "abrenuntiat" in Text 58 reveals a specific liturgical book, possibly a version of OR XV.

[30]See S. Keefe, "An Unknown Response from the Archiepiscopal Province of Sens to Charlemagne's Circulatory Inquiry on Baptism" in *RB* XCVI (1986), pp. 54 f. (Text 17 is there called "the Troyes Anonymous.")

diocese, but since his task is to answer the questionnaire (he begins, "We are asked why that one who comes to baptism first is made a catechumen."), he simply takes Charlemagne's topics as they come and then describes the action each involves, not trying to create a liturgical sequence of topics. His omission of mystic veil may indicate that he simply did not know the ceremony of the covering of the head with a veil.[31]

One of several distinctive features of Text 17 is the explicit description of the touching of the nose with oil, rather than spittle. The use of oil for the nose and ears is in John the Deacon, and the use of oil for the ears is implied in Alcuin's *ordo* (Text 9). The Roman sacramentaries and *ordines*, however, prescribe spittle. Apparently many areas even in the heartland of the Reform continued to use oil. This ancient custom in Spain (Ildefonsus and the León Antiphonary) will be seen in Text 7, and it is in the Bobbio Missal. Leidrad of Lyons (Text 25) was not only referring to Spain, apparently, when he said regarding the touching of the nose that in different places different customs were held: Some use oil, some use spittle, and some use no liquid at all.[32]

Another noteworthy remark in Text 17 regards the scrutiny. This, it says, is an inquiry performed by an archdeacon, whether baptism is done in the city or in the diocese. Baptism should be celebrated at Easter and Pentecost, and the archdeacon should make his inquiry of the sponsors twice a year: on the second Saturday in Lent, in preparation for Easter baptisms, and the second Monday after Easter, in preparation for Pentecost baptisms. This "scrutiny" is not the Roman *ordo* of scrutinies but a single examination of sponsors on their knowledge of the Creed and the Lord's Prayer before they are allowed to receive anyone from the font.

The ending of Text 17 seems curious if the bishop who wrote it was responding to Charlemagne's questionnaire, for it states: "It is asked why one is immersed three times in the sacred font," which Charlemagne did *not* ask. Also, there is a question on the invisible effect of baptism, posed as if by a priest to his bishop.[33] Probably Text 17 was a suffragan's response to the questionnaire later adapted to serve as a clerical instruction. The composer has

---

[31]OR XI, some manuscripts of OR L, and OR XXVIII mention a *chrismale*, but neither the Reginensis nor OR XV, XXIII, XXIV, XXV, XXVI, XXVII, XXIX, nor XXXB have an explicit reference to any head covering. They either simply say that the infant is vested or do not mention vesting at all. Nor do the Prague Sacramentary, Rheinau Sacramentary, excarpsus of Paris 2296, excarpsus of Brussels 10127–144, *Hadrianum ex authentico*, or *Hadrianum Supplementum* have any mention of a head covering. Texts 4, 25, and 5 also omit this topic.

[32]Vol. II, p. 360.

[33]"Est questiuncula parva quam me satis delectat audire: si cum baptizatur homo qui visibilis est et visibili mergitur lavacro, quomodo potest invisibilem animam mundare qui visibilis [*lege*: invisibilis] est et inpalpabilis? Volo et ego in quantum michi vires suppetunt et dominus ministrare iusserit vobis sub brevitate perstringere." Vol. II, p. 326.

added a question on the threefold immersion, which Charlemagne omitted, but without which a clerical instruction on baptism would hardly be complete. He has also added a question on the invisible effect of baptism. This concern echoes a similar concern about the invisible effect of the Eucharist in an episcopal capitulary of Bishop Haito of Basel (806–23)[34] showing the kind of questions about the sacraments priests were expected to be able to answer.

Text 14A

Text 14A is the opening section of a diocesan statute, perhaps of Waltcaud of Liège (810–31), which repeats Charlemagne's questions. Some changes have been made, however, both in the selection and order of Charlemagne's list of topics.[35] "Waltcaud" omitted the topics of scrutiny and Creed and put renunciation, works, pomps, and belief (*credulitas*) at the place where baptism would occur. (See Chart E4.)

In short, he transformed Charlemagne's sequence into a liturgical *ordo* of baptism in which there is a renunciation followed by a credal interrogation at the edge of the font, as in OR L. "Waltcaud" sought to make liturgical sense out of Charlemagne's series of questions. (He began: "Concerning the *ordo* of the baptismal rite, how every priest should know . . .") He may have omitted the topics of scrutiny and Creed because he was familiar with a shortened rite in which there were no formal scrutinies or a delivery of the Creed. It was seen above that Text 26, a variation of Leidrad's treatise (Text 25) rearranged to suit parish priests, also omitted these topics.[36]

Whether Liège was the place of origin of Text 14A or not, one bishop's effort to turn Charlemagne's questionnaire into a useful instruction for his priests shows the actual implementation of the Reform.

Texts 34 and 35

It has been argued by A. E. Burn that Texts 34 and 35 (an abbreviated form of Text 34) represent the response of Archbishop Arno of Salzburg (d. 816) to Charlemagne. Seven of the titles (in question form) in Texts 34 and 35 are identical with seven of the questions in the questionnaire (see Charts E5 and E6). Even if the author of the original form of Texts 34 and 35 did not write in

---

[34]"V. Quinto, ut sciant quid sit sacramentum baptismatis et confirmationis, et quale sit mysterium corporis et sanguinis domini, quomodo in eisdem mysteriis visibilis creatura videtur   tamen invisibilis salus ad aeternitatem animae subministratur, quod in sola fide continetur." (Brommer, *Capitula Episcoporum*, pp. 210 f. Brommer thinks (p. 204) this capitulary was probably written between 806 and 813.)

[35]The attribution to Waltcaud is explained by P. Brommer, *Capitula Episcoporum*, p. 43. It is based on the association of this diocesan statute with works of Garibald of Liège in a single manuscript tradition. Caution is necessary, however, because there were a number of reasons for combining anonymous statutes with authorized ones, and similarities in capitularies from far-separated dioceses are common.

[36]See Chapter 4, p. 66.

direct reply to Charlemagne, at least he knew the questionnaire and used it as a model for a baptismal instruction. Klaus Gamber believes Text 35 represents a small handbook compiled by Arno for his missionary priests.[37]

Text 34 is known in only one manuscript, written at Mondsee, and Text 35 is known earliest in a codex from Freising (both in the archdiocese of Salzburg). A long introductory topic on catechizing those new to the faith might suggest that they were written for priests in a missionary situation. The title and content of the topic is borrowed from Augustine's *De caticizandis rudibus* and outlines how one should instruct an adult not yet founded in the faith. Arno's archdiocese, bordering pagan territory, would fit well as the place of origin of the Texts. Another topic added to Charlemagne's topics is episcopal confirmation. It is placed *after* the topic of the Eucharist, corresponding to the necessary delay of confirmation in missionary territory (although also in non-missionary areas confirmation was being delayed).

In conclusion, none of these baptismal instructions follows Charlemagne's sequence of topics without some additions, omissions, or rearrangement. Magnus of Sens (Text 15) reveals a rite without a series of formal scrutiny meetings, the type of rite probably used throughout his archdiocese. Text 17, from his archdiocese, confirms that a formal series of scrutinies was not done in one place. It has the touching of the nose with oil, not spittle, and no veiling after baptism. In Text 14A "Waltcaud," addressing his priests, tried to make liturgical sense of Charlemagne's series of questions. This also occurred in Texts 34 and 35, where renunciation is placed before, rather than after, belief and Creed (corresponding to the order in OR L and PRG CVII of an initial renunciation followed by the profession of faith).

It is clear that these composers were conscious of a liturgical model. If they chose Charlemagne's questionnaire as their model, they also adjusted it to correspond to the real pastoral needs of their readers. Some recipients, such as "Waltcaud's" priests, would only be familiar with a rite of baptism without scrutiny meetings. The evidence of these texts suggests that differences from their models were often due to particular liturgical books, even when the specific book is not known.

A final authoritative model that will be looked at now is Hrabanus Maurus's baptismal instruction in his *De institutione clericorum*.[38] In Book I, chapters XXV–XXX, he describes an *ordo* of baptism in which all of the cere-

---

[37]Klaus Gamber, *Niceta von Remesiana, Instructio ad Competentes, Frühchristlichen Katechesen aus Dacien* (Textus Patristici et Liturgici I (Regensburg, 1964), pp. 17 f. R. McKitterick, *The Frankish Church*, p. 212, thinks it more probable that it was composed at Freising, perhaps by Bishop Hitto (811/2–836).

[38]Ed. A. Knöpfler, *Rabani Mauri de institutione clericorum libri tres* (Veröffentlichungen aus dem kirchenhistorischen Seminar München Nr. 5) (München, 1900). Hrabanus wrote it in 819 while master of the monastery school of Fulda (he had been consecrated priest in 814), before becoming Archbishop of Mainz (847–56). On abbreviated versions of the work, see Knöpfler, pp. xx–xxiv.

monies are condensed into a single session. Hrabanus says his *ordo* is for a *paganus*. It is almost identical with the rite for infants of PRG CVII and for a pagan of PRG CX.[39] Hrabanus is so close to their descriptions that there can be no doubt he was describing the rite or the prototype of the rite which was included in the Mainz PRG approximately one hundred and thirty years later.[40]

Hrabanus may have written with a missionary situation in mind, offering the clergy for whom he wrote a short *ordo* for their work among the heathen, where it was not possible to go through weeks of scrutiny meetings, nor to wait for the once a year Easter Vigil, nor for the candidates to memorize the Creed and "return" it. Hrabanus's description was equally suitable, however, for non-missionary clergy within the Carolingian empire, where a short rite of baptism was the more common throughout the parishes.[41]

Five of our baptismal instructions are mere variations of him. Texts 44, 45, and 46 consist exclusively of extracts from chapters XXV–XXX, while Texts 47 and 48 also contain some explanation from elsewhere. (Only Text 44 is represented in a ninth-century manuscript, but because of the similarity of Texts 45 and 46 to it, and because of the ninth-century material surrounding Texts 47 and 48 in their manuscripts, all of these Texts are probably Carolingian compilations.)

The Texts do not have entirely the same set of extracts, and no one of them can be entirely dependent on any other. All five differ from one another in their sequence of topics. It is this phenomenon which deserves attention, for the very reason that all five are essentially simply extracts of Hrabanus, and two are semi-dependent on two others. By examining two of them, it will be seen that their composers did not extract thoughtlessly.

---

[39]See Chapter 3, note 22.

[40]Compare Charts A4 and F1. Especially striking is that after the touching of the nose and ears, as in PRG CVII and PRG CX, and before he describes the anointing of the breast and back, Hrabanus states: "Then he is fortified with a priestly benediction" ("Deinde benedictione sacerdotali munitur;" Knöpfler, *Rabani Mauri de institutione clericorum libri tres*, p. 49). Precisely at this point in PRG CVII and PRG CX is a benediction beginning, "Deus inmortale presidium omnium postulantium." (Vogel and Elze, *Le Pontifical* II, p. 160, nr. 25 and p. 169, nr. 21.) This prayer is not in the Reginensis, the Gregorian Sacramentary (*Hadrianum ex authentico*), or in OR L. It is in the *Hadrianum Supplementum*, the Gellone Sacramentary, and the excarpsus of Brussels, Bibl. Roy. 10127–144, but in these it does not come after the touching of the nose and ears. Rather, it is the second prayer recited over the males ("super masculos") in the scrutiny meetings (see J. Deshusses, *Le Sacramentaire Grégorien* I, p. 374, nr. 1074). "Deus inmortale presidium" after the touching of the nose and ears seems to appear only in PRG CVII and PRG CX; yet Hrabanus's description, especially his choice of the word "munitur" ("fortified") recalling its word "presidium" ("defense," "protection"), reflects his knowledge of this benediction prayer after the touching of the nose and ears.

[41]See "A Note on Rites for an *Infirmus* or a *Paganus* as the Normal Rite of Infants" on pp. 156–58.

Text 45

In Text 45 seven topics in Hrabanus are eliminated and the position of one, "Concerning infants who cannot renounce or believe" is repositioned immediately before "triple immersion." (In Text 45 it is called *Parvulorum salus adimpletur per fidem patrinorum"*; see Chart F2.) It was seen earlier that in Texts 1 and 4 John the Deacon's topic "on infants who could not confess" (his last topic; see Chart C1) was repositioned immediately before "triple immersion." It is surprising that this occurs in all three Texts because Texts 1 and 4 have a different model than Text 45. There is no indication that the composer of Text 45 knew Text 1 or Text 4. The same repositioning of this topic in all three Texts attests that the changes Carolingian composers made from their models were due to their own reflection on the proper liturgical order. Placing a topic on the faith of infants just before baptism corresponds to the sponsors having to say "credo" for the infants in *ordines* that have an interrogation of faith at the edge of the font.

Even if the omission of seven topics in Text 45 was due to a desire to abbreviate, one must still explain why the composer chose to eliminate the topics that he did and not others. While it has not been possible to identify one liturgical book that in all respects is identical with Text 45, some of its omissions are found in specific manuscripts. For example, in Text 45 the prayer "Deus inmortale presidium" is omitted and there are no references to any exorcisms. These features are also found in an *ordo* for a pagan ("gentilem hominem") in OR XXXI.[42]

In sum, the composer of Text 45 knew a different version of the *ordo* known to Hrabanus, and adjusted his excerpts accordingly. Our tracts, especially the brief, anonymous, and unoriginal ones merely condensing other authors, have never been appreciated as evidence for the existence of specific liturgical books. Even if the composer's primary purpose was to offer his reader a briefer baptismal instruction than that of Hrabanus, he still revealed his use of a specific *ordo* that guided him in his omissions or rearrangement of topics. Even a mere extracted form of Hrabanus's chapters is an important witness of the use and circulation of a specific liturgical book.[43]

---

[42]M. Andrieu, *Les Ordines* III, pp. 506–8, nn. 114–20. Andrieu dates the *ordo* to the second half of the ninth century (see ibid., p. 487). The omission of any mention of exorcisms should be stressed, given that a number of liturgical historians insist that baptism had almost become a "rite of exorcism" by the ninth century. See A. Angenendt, *Kaiserherrschaft und Königstaufe: Kaiser, Könige, und Päpste als geistliche Patrone in der abendländischen Missionsgeschichte* (Arbeiten sur Frühmittelalterforschung, Bd. 15) (Berlin/New York, 1984), p. 52: "Es kann also gar keinem Zweifel unterliegen, welche Richtung die Entwicklung von der Antike zum Mittelalter hin genommen hat; es ist eine massive Exorzisierung."

[43]Manuscripts B and G of PRG CX also have the same omissions as Text 45. Although they have differences from Text 45 in other respects (they describe the conse-

Text 47

Among other changes from Hrabanus's sequence, Text 47 has two topics dealing with the blessing of the font—the immersion of candles and the insufflation of the water. (see Chart F3.) In many of the liturgical books the blessing of the font is by far the longest and most detailed of all the baptismal ceremonies. The liturgical books differ considerably on how much detail they include; many include both of the actions just mentioned, but not all have candles (plural). The Gellone Sacramentary spells out very clearly exactly what is found in Text 47.[44] Also, a number of manuscripts of the Gregorian Sacramentary[45] have candles (plural) and a sufflation. Thus, the description in Text 47 of candles (plural) and an insufflation of the water are features of *some* liturgical manuscripts. It allows the probability that other alterations in Text 47 reflect a specific liturgical book, even if it is not possible to identify it.

To summarize, in this chapter it has been seen how merely didactic, semi-florilegia tracts, little more than variations of one of their three models, nevertheless are intentional reworkings, revealing different liturgical practices. First, Alcuin of Tour's *ordo* (Text 9), the most frequently copied of all the Carolingian baptismal instructions, was itself shown to bear distinctive characteristics of a local sacramentary of the abbey of St. Martin of Tours. The composer of Text 38 used all the words of Text 9, but altered its sequence of topics. His order, as well as certain expressions he added, agree closely with a north-Italian *ordo* of scrutinies (edited by Lambot), of which there is only an eleventh-century witness, even though Lambot would like to believe it goes back to the eighth century. Text 38 is the first witness that Lambot's *ordo scrutiniorum* or one very close to it, was in use in the ninth century. The composer of Text 38 was from northern Italy. He adapted Text 9 to describe an *ordo* in use in his area. The clergy for whom he wrote knew a Romanized north-Italian rite with a very distinct *ordo scrutiniorum*. He took care to describe this *ordo*. One anomaly in his sequence of topics even reflects a provisional scrutiny in this *ordo* supplied for people who could not attend the regular scrutiny meetings.

---

cration of the font), they come far closer to describing Text 45 than do manuscripts C and D of PRG CX, pointing to the fact that the omissions of Text 45 were not haphazard, but based on a specific liturgical book. See the *apparatus criticus* in Vogel and Elze, *Le Pontifical*, II, pp. 167–72.

[44]"Hic deponuntur acoliti cereos duos quas tenere videntur intro fontes (*sic*) in ipsa aqua . . . et insufflat sacerdus (*sic*) ter vitibus in aqua." (A. Dumas, *Liber Sacramentorum Gellonensis: Textus*, p. 335, nr. 2317 f).

[45]See J. Deshusses, *Le Sacramentaire Grégorien* I, p. 188, nr. 374e and the *app. criticus*.

A second authoritative model, Charlemagne's questionnaire (Text 14), was adapted in the archdiocese of Sens in order to serve as an instruction for its clergy, who knew a visit by an archdeacon twice a year to "scrutinize" sponsors before Easter and Pentecost baptism (Text 17). Elsewhere (Liège?) Charlemagne's questionnaire was adapted for a diocesan statute addressed to clergy: Bishop "Waltcaud" (Text 14A) changed it so that it describes a liturgical sequence (non-paschal). Texts 34 and 35 show how the questionnaire was adapted for clergy in a missionary area.

Finally, Hrabanus Maurus was a widely respected churchman in his own day, and it is not surprising that many composers of baptismal instructions would simply extract his chapters on baptism in his broadly circulated *De institutione clericorum*. While five Texts consist of little more than extracts from Hrabanus, here again it was seen that the composers of Texts 45 and 47 did not want simply a briefer version of Hrabanus. Their selection of passages and re-arrangements reflect features of specific liturgical books.

What is the significance of the fact that the composers sought to make their instructions reflect local liturgical practice? Why did they take the trouble to rearrange their models? It would have been much simpler for Bishop "Waltcaud" to have repeated verbatim Charlemagne's questionnaire when he used it to address the priests of his diocese. The key to understanding the Carolingian Reform seems to lie in the *care* the composers took. It is this which needs to be explained.

This care was shown in Chapter 5 in adaptations of an easily dismissed florilegium based on John the Deacon. In this chapter also, composers' changes from their models seem to have been due to their presence in a specific locality and direct knowledge of the people for whom they were writing. It is being seen that the success of the Carolingian Reform was dependent on local initiative. No Aachen-issued set of texts could achieve a revolution in the education of the clergy such as was needed. According to the manuscript evidence, only individual dioceses could assess the needs of their clergy, locate the resources for instructing them, and make the arrangements for producing books or establishing schooling, as was possible; but furthermore, it is being shown that the texts of instruction themselves were overseen by diocesan bishops and their assistants, who composed or edited them in accordance with local liturgical books. In terms of the Carolingian Reform, this changes past notions of the Reform as a quest for unity through standardized religious practice,[46] because local initiative allows for a variety of practice preferred in different areas.

The adaptations from certain authoritative models looked at in this chapter reflect differences in the celebration of baptism mostly due to rural parish

---

[46]See R. E. Sullivan, "The Carolingian Age: Reflections on its Place in the History of the Middle Ages" in *Speculum* 64 (1989), pp. 274–76.

conditions, where the Roman scrutinies were not done and "daily" baptisms (the expression is in Text 8.1) required a "short" *ordo* of baptism. These were adaptations of the Roman rite. But how far did liturgical diversity go? Was the Carolingian Reform at all concerned with eliminating non-Roman, long-indigenous rites? Now evidence for the persistence of these will be shown. Some Carolingian baptismal instructions barely stifle, or openly teach, non-Roman forms of baptism.

7

The Persistence of Indigenous Rites of Baptism

In this chapter three baptismal instructions that describe features of three different indigenous, non-Roman rites of baptism will be examined. Their existence is significant because of their creation and copying during the Carolingian period when, it has been thought, indigenous rites were eliminated.[1]

Text 7

Text 7 is anonymous and is entire only in a thirteenth-century manuscript from Spain (El Escorial, Real Bibl. de S. Lorenz. f. iv. 9), but the first nine lines survive in a ninth-century codex from Reichenau (St. Paul im Lavanttal 5/1). Its description of the ceremonies of baptism has some Roman features, but there are oddities.

First, the anonymous composer sets out four grades of coming to the faith: "We recognize that everyone who presses forward to receive the faith of the sacrament is first a catechumen. Then he is made a competent or an elect; after that a *fidelis*; and finally, a Christian" (see Chart G1). This is a variation of Isidore's three grades of catechumens, competents, and baptized.

The variation is not original with the author of Text 7. The Spanish monk, Beatus of Liébana, describes these four grades in the Prologue to Book II of his *Commentary on the Apocalypse*, written between 776 and 786: "When anyone who is still a pagan comes to the faith, when he has been instructed so that he believes, he is called a catechumen. When rightly he has believed and he demands to be baptized, he is named a competent. When, indeed, he has been dipped in the water of baptism he is called a *fidelis*. When truly he is chrismated with chrism, that is, with an anointing, he is called a Christian."[2]

---

[1]See A. Angenendt, *Kaiserherrschaft und Königstaufe*, pp. 32–45, and "Die Liturgie und die Organisation," pp. 172–74, citing the teaching of Vogel, Klauser, and others. Also see R. E. Sullivan, "The Carolingian Age," p. 293 and pp. 276 f., note 19, citing the influential work of Josef Jungmann and many others.

[2]"Quum aliquis iam paganus ad fidem venit, quum instruitur ut credat, caticuminus dicitur. Quum recte crediderit et baptizari se postulat, competens nominatur. Quum vero in aqua baptismi tinguitur, fidelis dicitur. Quum vero crismatur a crisma, id est unctione, dicitur Christianus . . ." (ed. H. A. Sanders, *Beati in Apocalipsin Libri Duodecim*, Rome, 1930, p. 124).

The author of Text 7 undoubtedly borrowed Beatus' schema. Then he elaborated: "For when anyone, converted from paganism, receives the Creed and is made a hearer of the word of God, he is named a catechumen.... Then, after his recognition of the faith, when he has registered his name and, associated among the number of the elect, demands the waters of the font, he will be an elect or competent. Indeed, he is called a competent from seeking (*petendo*), just as before he was called a catechumen from hearing. After this, when he is signed with the sacrament of baptism, he is called a *fidelis*. Finally, when he is anointed with chrism, he is marked out with the title Christian."[3]

If the author of Text 7 was familiar with Beatus' *Commentary*, this is one indication of the Spanish origin of Text 7, because Beatus' work was apparently unknown outside of Spain in the Carolingian period.[4] Another indication is the author's distinction between a catechumen and a competent in the above passage, which in three respects is very puzzling in comparison with OR XI and the Reginensis: 1) the first event he associates with the catechumen is the reception of the Creed; 2) the catechumen is anointed *before* he becomes a competent (see Chart G1); and 3) the enrollment ("nomen dederit") is associated with the competent or elect, not the catechumen. In the Roman *ordo*, it may be recalled, the delivery of the Creed does not take place among the initial ceremonies for the making of a catechumen, but a week later, at the *aurium apertio*; there is no anointing, that is, use of oil, on the candidates until the very day of baptism; and the registering of the candidates' names comes at the very beginning of the catechumenate. A delivery of the Creed and an anointing at the catechumen stage, and a name-giving associated with the competent stage, however, can be explained by recourse to Spanish liturgical books and descriptions of baptism.

Regarding the sources for the celebration of baptism in Spain, no liturgical book with an *ordo* of baptism survives before the León Antiphonary and the *Liber Ordinum* (*LO*), represented in eleventh-century manuscripts. The *LO* contains two *ordines* for baptism, one entitled "quolibet tempore" (for any time), the other for the Paschal Vigil. The latter goes back to the seventh century; "quolibet tempore" may be later.[5] As for descriptions of baptism in non-liturgical books, the most influential were those of Isidore of Seville (d. 636) and Ildefonsus of Toledo (d. 667).

The *De cognitione baptismi* of Ildefonsus gives a detailed description of the

---

[3]Vol. II, pp. 220 f.

[4]According to Sanders, *Beati*, p. xii. The twenty-four manuscripts he used to edit Beatus' Commentary are all post ninth-century and Spanish. Also W. Heil, "Der Adoptianismus," p. 102, says Beatus' works were not known in France in Alcuin's time.

[5]See Férotin, *Le Liber Ordinum*, p. xxi. Férotin says the León Antiphonary also reflects the liturgy at the time of King Wamba (second half of the seventh century) (p. xxxii).

ceremonies.[6] The first ceremonies of the catechumenate—the leading of the infants over goatskin rugs as a sign of penance; exsufflation with an exorcism; and an anointing of their ears and mouth while a priest says the words, "Effeta, be opened," take place only one week before Easter, on the same day as the delivery of the Creed.[7]

The *De cognitione baptismi* is a very complete exposition on the entire process of coming to the faith. Almost certainly, if there had been any earlier ceremonies for the catechumen in Toledo, Ildefonsus would have mentioned them. In the *LO* as well, which was originally compiled for Toledo, a rubric indicates that the Effeta ceremony is done on Palm Sunday, one week before Easter, and there are no ceremonies for the catechumen before this day, on which day also the Creed is delivered.[8]

The León Antiphonary shows some effort to lengthen the catechumenate.[9] It has an invitation to enroll and the initial ceremonies for the making of a catechumen (the same as in the Roman tradition) on the fourth Sunday of Lent, that is, two weeks before Palm Sunday and the delivery of the Creed. This invitation to enroll, however, is to be repeated on the fifth Sunday of Lent, and exorcisms are to be offered daily up to Palm Sunday. Thus it appears that these ceremonies were not considered mandatory, but only for those infants who were able to attend.

In sum, the day of the delivery of the Creed, Palm Sunday, essentially marked the beginning of the catechumenate in Spain, at least in some areas, and can explain why the author of Text 7 associates the delivery of the Creed with the beginning of the first stage of the catechumenate. Likewise, the early anointing of the catechumen corresponds to the Effeta anointing of the nose and ears with oil in Ildefonsus and other Spanish sources.

Finally, Spanish sources can explain why our author associated the enrollment ceremony with the competent stage. The term "competent" had long ago lost its original meaning as an advanced stage of the catechumen. In different liturgical books it is used at different places in the text. In the León Antiphonary there is a particularly impressive enrollment ceremony in which a deacon proclaims three times that any one who wishes to be baptized at Easter should register his or her name. At the end of the ceremony the candidates who have given their names are addressed with the words, "Competentes, orate . . ." for the first time. Probably the author of Text 7 associated "competentes" with its liturgical usage.[10]

---

[6]*PL* 96: 111–72. (Also edited by J. Campos Ruiz, *San Ildefonso de Toledo*, Madrid, 1971, pp. 236–378.)

[7]*Cap.* XXI–XXXI; *PL* 96:120–25.

[8]See Férotin, *Le Liber Ordinum*, *Cap.* LXXI, coll. 178–87.

[9]As Martin of Braga had tried to do at the Second Council of Braga in 572. See J. Vives, *Concilios*, p. 84, canon VIIII.

[10]See Chapter 6, note 16, for the same definition of a competent in Text 38.

More Spanish features of Text 7 are found in its description of the post-baptismal ceremonies. The author states: "After this [the immersion], he is anointed with the sacrament of chrism so that he is called a Christian. For Christ is interpreted "anointed" from this [word chrism]. Through the priest's imposition of hands the Holy Spirit invoked upon him flows down, and by these four grades he is a member of the body of Christ . . . ."[11]

What the author describes—a single chrismation immediately after the font, directly followed by an imposition of hands and invocation of the Holy Spirit, all performed by one minister who is a priest (*sacerdos*)—stands in stark contrast to the post-baptismal procedure in the Roman rite. That has *two* post-baptismal chrismations, the first administered by a priest, the second by the bishop to impart the Holy Spirit. It had long been established that only bishops might impart the Holy Spirit when they signed the neophytes with chrism, and only bishops might sign the *forehead* with chrism.[12]

A single chrismation, however, followed by the imposition of hands and invocation of the Holy Spirit by a priest is precisely what one finds in the *LO*'s *ordo* for baptism "quolibet tempore." After the infant is raised from the font, the rubrics state: "The priest (*sacerdos*) anoints him with chrism, making the sign of the cross on his forehead alone (*in sola fronte*). . . . Then he lays his *hands* upon him and says, 'God, . . . we ask and we seek that you pour forth upon these thy servants thy Holy Spirit. Amen. The Spirit of wisdom and understanding. Amen. The Spirit of counsel and fortitude. Amen. The Spirit of knowledge and piety. . . .'"[13]

Especially striking is the choice of the term *sacerdos* in Text 7 for the minister of confirmation, the same term used in the *ordo* "quolibet tempore." Although *sacerdos* could refer to a priest of episcopal rank, it is generally agreed that the *sacerdos* referred to in the *ordo* "quolibet tempore" must mean a presbyter and not a bishop, since this *ordo* is for "anytime" baptisms, when, as J. D. C. Fisher says, "bishops could hardly be available."[14] Dom Férotin believes that the *ordo* "quolibet tempore" is evidence that in Spain simple priests were confirming.[15]

The Second Council of Seville of 619, presided over by Isidore, forbade

---

[11]Vol. II, p. 222.

[12] See *Ep.* 25, 3 of Pope Innocent I of 416 in *PL* 20: 554 and see note 16 in this chapter.

[13]". . . et crismat eum sacerdos, faciens signum crucis in sola fronte, dicens: . . . Hoc peracto, item imponit ei manus impositionem [Silos 3 has: imponit ei manus sacerdos (see *Liber Ordinum Sacerdotal (Cod. Silos, Arch. monástico, 3)*, ed. by J. Janini, Abadia de Silos, 1981 (Studia Silensia VII), p. 57, nr. 24.)], ita: 'Deus, qui . . . petimus ac rogamus, ut infundas super his famulis tuis Spiritum Sanctum tuum. Amen. Spiritum sapientie et intellectus. Amen. Spiritum consilii et fortitudinis. Amen. Spiritum scientie et pietatis . . .'" (Férotin, *Le Liber Ordinum*, coll. 33 f.).

[14]J. D. C. Fisher, *Christian Initiation*, p. 96.

[15]Férotin, *Le Liber Ordinum*, col. 34, note 1.

presbyters to consecrate chrism or to sign with chrism the foreheads of the baptized—a clear indication, says Fisher, that they had been doing so.[16]

Férotin is not certain of the date of the *ordo* "quolibet tempore," but it is no earlier than the second half of the seventh century. There is, however, no actual proof of the on-going use of this *ordo*, that is, of simple priests performing confirmations in Spain, between the seventh century and the eleventh century, the time of the earliest manuscript of the *LO*.[17]

Also, in Text 7 the plural "hands" instead of "hand" is used to describe the hand-laying of the *sacerdos* during the act of confirmation. The plural expression is difficult to find in liturgical books in the west except in Spain, and it appears in the *ordo* "quolibet tempore."[18]

There are at least four other cases of identical expressions in Text 7 and the *ordo* "quolibet tempore" that do not appear to be in any other western *ordo*. There is almost no doubt that Text 7, with its single chrismation followed by an imposition of hands (plural) for the bestowing of the Holy Spirit, performed by the priest (*sacerdos*), and with expressions found nowhere else but in the *ordo* "quolibet tempore," is evidence of the circulation of this *ordo* in the Carolingian period—the first positive evidence of the practice of simple priests performing the entire rite of baptism in Spain, at least in some areas, after the seventh-century reforms legislated by Isidore.[19]

Text 7 has to have been written before the Reichenau manuscript was compiled in the second third of the ninth century. If the author used Beatus'

---

[16]See J. D. C. Fisher, *Christian Initiation*, p. 93. Fisher believes Isidore was attempting to bring the Spanish rite into closer conformity with the Roman. That simple priests in some areas were performing chrismations that originally belonged to the bishop is known from a letter of Pope Gregory I to Sardinia; see Ep. XXVI in *CCSL* CXL, IV, 26, pp. 245 f., lines 40–46.

[17]Férotin does say he has collected thirty-two references to a "Liber Ordinum" or similarly entitled book in Spanish sources dating between 633 and 1073 (p. xvi), so that the *ordo* "quolibet tempore" may well have been in use all this time, but any actual proof of its use is lacking.

[18]Only one manuscript of the *LO*, Silos 3, has the plural "hands" (see note 13). This confirmation prayer is unknown anywhere in the west outside of the *ordo* "quolibet tempore," according to Fisher, *Christian Initiation*, p. 98. Also in this *ordo* other hand-laying references are in the plural. In each case the rubrics or prayers containing "hands" (plural) appear to be unique to this *ordo*. One, a prayer for the blessing of the font, has the exact phrase, "per impositionem manuum," found in Text 7.

[19]In regard to the chrismation and hand-laying in the *ordo* "quolibet tempore," W. C. Bishop remarked over eighty years ago, "Dom Férotin has one of his concise and useful notes on the custom of *priests* administering confirmation: it would be interesting if we had some evidence as to the actual practice of the Spanish church in later times. We suppose that the evidence of the manuscript [of the *ordo* "quolibet tempore"] may be accepted as conclusive evidence of the survival of the custom down to the middle of the eleventh century." (*The Mozarabic and Ambrosian Rites*, Alcuin Club Tracts XV, London, 1924, p. 14).

Commentary on the Apocalypse he would have to have written Text 7 after 786. There are other reasons, however, to argue that Text 7 was written in Spain around the turn of the ninth century, at a time when the liturgy was open to Romanization due to a desire on the part of many orthodox Spanish to align themselves more closely with the Roman rite.

One is the inclusion and even emphasis in Text 7 of the ceremony of the giving of salt. Spain alone did not traditionally observe this ceremony. Ildefonsus acknowledged that some places did, but that there was no scriptural ground for it, and so no obligation to do so.[20]

Neither the *LO* nor the León Antiphonary has any mention of salt. Although Isidore does speak of it, Férotin believes that Isidore was only describing a custom that was instituted by the fathers, and that salt was never the custom in Spain as it was in the rest of the west.[21] Following the four stages of becoming a Christian, salt, however, is the only pre-baptismal ceremony our author specifically identifies and explains. Also, at another point he says the church has four sacraments: "salt, baptism, chrism, and the Body and Blood,"[22] adding salt to Isidore's oft-quoted definition of the sacraments of the church.[23]

Another interesting feature in Text 7 is the allowance for either a single or a triple immersion. This was a far more controversial issue than salt, vis-à-vis Spain's orthodoxy in western eyes. Spain practiced a single immersion, contrary to the Roman practice of a triple immersion.[24]

The allowance in Text 7 of one immersion would be astonishing if it was

---

[20]"Ii in nonnullis locis, ut refertur, sales accipiunt. . . . Quia vero ut catechumenis in adipiscendo fidei sacramento tradantur, evidenti sanctae Scripturae nullo documento monstratur, ideo nihil offici ubi non fit." (*De cognitione baptismi*, cap. xxvi [*PL* 96: 122 f.]).

[21]Férotin, *Le Liber Ordinum*, col. 25, note.

[22]Vol. II, p. 223.

[23]"Sunt autem sacramenta baptismum et chrisma, corpus et sanguis." *Origines* VI.xix.39, ed. W. M. Lindsay, *Isidori*.

[24]Single immersion had been introduced innocently in order to avoid any suggestion of Arianism: three separate immersions while reciting, "I baptize you in the name of the Father (dip) and of the Son (dip) and of the Holy Spirit (dip)" might imply a lack of complete unicity in the Trinity—that the Father, Son, and Holy Spirit could in some way be different from one another and therefore not equal, as the Arians held. In the late sixth century Pope Gregory I wrote a letter to Leander of Seville allowing the practice of either a single or a triple immersion, even recommending a single immersion to help fight Arianism in Spain, "for," he said, "differing customs within the one faith of the church can do no harm." In the early seventh century Isidore quoted Pope Gregory's letter when he legislated a single immersion in the Fourth Council of Toledo of 633, canon 6: "De babtismi [*sic*] autem sacramento propter quod in Spaniis quidam sacerdotes trinam, quidam simplam mersionem faciunt. . . . Beatae igitur memoriae Gregorius Romanae ecclesiae pontifex, . . . efflagitante sanctissimo Leandro episcopo de hac Spaniae diversitate . . . ait . . . quia in una fide nicil [*sic*] officit sanctae ecclesiae consuetudo diversa." (J. Vives, *Concilios*, p. 191.)

written outside of Spain. Alcuin, in a letter of warning to monks in Septimania (along the Spanish March) in 798, went so far as to suggest that the letter of Pope Gregory allowing a single immersion was a forgery, and insisted they follow the Roman practice of triple immersion.[25]

Rather, the allowance for a triple immersion and emphatic approval of salt in a *Spanish* baptismal instruction correspond to changes in the Spanish liturgy around the turn of the ninth century. Many Spaniards opposing Adoptianism, like Beatus of Liébana, were sensitive to the accusation of unorthodoxy against them by the Frankish reformers, and wished to show their unity with Rome in their liturgical practices. Also, Carolingian reformers were influencing the Spanish liturgy. It is known that circa 800 in the Narbonnaise or Septimanian region (an area stretching along the Mediterranean from the Rhone south to the Pyrenees, which was held by the Visigoths from the fifth to the eighth century) the Visigothic liturgy was being combined with Romano-Frankish liturgical books. Anscari Mundó attributes this largely to the activity of Benedict of Aniane (circa 750–821) in Septimania.[26] The Visigothic Benedict worked closely with the Carolingian court and was responsible for the supplement (between 810 and 815) to the Gregorian Sacramentary Charlemagne received from Pope Hadrian.[27] Benedict was given a copy of the Gellone Sacramentary[28]—a Franco-Roman type written in the north of France (790–800), and knew other eighth-century-type Gelasian Sacramentaries, because he used a revised one in his supplement.[29] These books undoubtedly had an influence on the Visigothic liturgists when they arrived in Septimania. M. S. Gros reconstructs from later manuscripts a baptismal *ordo* he believes was written circa 800 in Narbonne. Its creator combined features of the Roman *ordo* (that can be found in *OR* XI, the Reginensis, *OR* L, and the Gregorian Supplement) with Spanish features in the León Antiphonary and the *LO*. The author of Text 7 may have known and used a liturgical book in Spain that incorporated the ceremony of giving of salt and a rubric specifying three immersions. Both of these Romanizations appear in Gros' *ordo* of Narbonne.[30]

Finally, no less than twenty-seven lines of Text 7 are taken up with explaining why heretics returning to the church are not to be rebaptized. Such a

---

[25]*MGH Epp.* IV, *Ep.* 137, p. 215.

[26]A. Mundó, "Sur quelques manuscrits liturgiques languedociens de l'époque carolingienne (vers 800)" in *Cahiers de Fanjeaux* 17 (1982), p. 93.

[27]See J. Deshusses, *Le Sacramentaire Grégorien* I, p. 68.

[28]Mundó, op. cit., p. 88.

[29]See Deshusses, op. cit., pp. 68 f. and Mundó, op. cit., pp. 89 f. For the history of the Gellone Sacramentary see Deshusses, *Liber Sacramentorum Gellonensis: Introductio, Tabulae et Indices CCSL* CLIXA, Turnhout, 1981, pp. xviii–xxiii.

[30]M. S. Gros, "El Antiguo Ordo Bautismal Catalano-Narbonense," pp. 45, 58. See pp. 38–42 for his connection of this *ordo* with the Carolingian Reform.

disproportionate concern with this subject corresponds to Spain's wrenching troubles with Adoptianism at the end of the eighth and beginning of the ninth century. What was seen as heresy in the eyes of Charlemagne and his leading bishops and abbots was being defended and taught by Elipandus, Archbishop of Toledo, and Felix of Urgel in the last decade of the eighth century. The Council of Frankfurt convoked by Charlemagne in 794 condemned Elipandus and the Spanish bishops who sided with him. Alcuin wrote seven books "Contra Felicem," and in 799 Pope Leo III anathematized Felix. Felix recanted, but Elipandus never did.[31]

Our author was obviously influenced by the events going on around him.[32] Perhaps people were fearful that their baptisms were invalid if the minister had been one who sided with Elipandus. Our author's sensitivity to the needs of Spanish priests is apparent. He warns them that heretics are not to be rebaptized, but to be received back with chrism. This is well-attested in Spain.[33]

In conclusion, certain features of Text 7 prove that it is Spanish and probably written around the turn of the ninth century. Someone, perhaps in the area of Narbonne or Urgel, wrote a clerical instruction on baptism in the didactic genre associated with the Carolingian Reform. He spoke to a specific, local situation. The clergy to whom he wrote did not know a catechumenate with ceremonies before the time of the delivery of the Creed; they knew an anointing in the Effeta ceremony; and they were accustomed to performing the entire rite of baptism, including confirmation. It is little short of astonishing the way it has been possible to see even the variants of a single manuscript (cod. Silos 3) of the *ordo* "quolibet tempore" reflected in the cursory lines of our didactic tract. Roman practice had in no way completely replaced distinctive Spanish practices at the turn of the ninth century, according to Text 7.

Text 33 (Maxentius)

Maxentius, Archbishop of Aquileia (811–circa 826) wrote Text 33 in reply to Charlemagne's baptismal questionnaire. In his conclusion he expresses emphatically how he follows the tradition of the Apostles, the canonical regulations of the fathers, and the decrees of the most sacred documents of the Roman church in his belief, practice, and teaching. This is true as far as his explanations go, taken mostly from a patristic florilegium. Even his order of

---

[31]W. Heil, "Der Adoptianismus," pp. 99–108.

[32]From his monastery in Aniane Benedict had vigorously attacked Felix.

[33]Isidore says that heretics receive the chrism and the imposition of a hand in *De ecclesiasticis officiis* II, cap. XXV. 9 (*CCSL* CXIII, p. 106). Also Ildefonsus, following Isidore, says that heretics baptized in the name of the Trinity are not to be rebaptized, "but to be cleansed by chrism alone and the laying on of a hand." (*De cognitione baptismi*, cap. CXXI (*PL* 96: 161). In the *LO* there is a rite for reconciling an Arian which includes a chrismation (cf. Férotin, *Le Liber Ordinum*, col. 100).

topics does not, at least at first glance, appear to contradict the Roman *ordo* (see Chart G2).

H. Boone Porter pointed out some time ago that all the archbishops who responded to Charlemagne's questionnaire avoided any overt references to distinct local usages.[34] He was able to show, however, that Maxentius, while many of his words and phrases are found in the Reginensis, by a few expressions and the absence of certain topics, described a north-Italian baptismal *ordo*. Porter presented three arguments. First, Maxentius gave an exposition on the Creed that is also found in OR XI and the Reginensis (given to the catechumens at the *traditio symboli*), but Porter noted that a baptismal *ordo* of Aquileia, written either by Lupus I of Aquileia (mid-ninth century) or Lupus II (mid-tenth century) also has this same exposition on the Creed.[35]

Maxentius, in fact, borrowed it from Lupus' source, not the Reginensis or OR XI, because his version begins with a phrase found in Lupus' *ordo*, but not in the Reginensis and OR XI.[36] Porter concluded from this that Maxentius must have known a north-Italian formulation of the *ordo scrutiniorum* also known by Lupus.

Second, Porter pointed out that Maxentius failed to answer Charlemagne's question, "Why is the nose touched?" and suggested it was because Maxentius knew only an *anointing* of the nose and ears with oil, different from the Roman touching of the nose and ears with the priest's spittle.[37] The use of oil for the nose and ears is described in northern Italy in a sixth-century source, the *Tractates* on baptism of Ps.-Maximus of Turin.[38] Maxentius also failed to answer Charlemagne's question as to why the breast and back are

---

[34]H. Boone Porter, "Maxentius of Aquileia and the North Italian Baptismal Rites" in *Ephemerides Liturgicae*, 69 (1955), p. 6.

[35]The *ordo* of Lupus of Aquileia was published by M. B. De Rubeis, *Dissertationes duae* . . . , Venice, 1754, pp. 228–46. See Gamber, *CLLA*, nr. 294, p. 189. De Rubeis used a fourteenth-century manuscript from Cividale (Cividale, Museo archeologico nazionale, Cod. LXXXVII), which he believes is a copy of an *ordo scrutiniorum* from the time of Lupus I, Partriarch of Aquileia, circa 870.

[36]Maxentius: "Ratio igitur symboli huius omni brevitate connexa est . . ." Lupus: "Idcirco huius symboli ratio omni brevitate connexa est . . ." (Porter, "Maxentius," pp. 6 f.) (I have not yet been able to consult De Rubeis' *Duae Dissertationes* . . . , but a close comparison of the exposition on the Creed in Maxentius with the exposition on the Creed in the Reginensis and OR XI shows three places where Maxentius differs from both the Reginensis and OR XI (in all of its manuscripts). It would be interesting to know if Lupus' *ordo* had Maxentius' variations. They are : (1) the omission of the word "ipsius" by Maxentius in "Hic ascensio *ipsius* super caelos"; (2) "postremum" by Maxentius in "Hic postremo ecclesiae vocatio . . . "; and (3) the inclusion of a phrase of the Creed, "ac vita aeterna" by Maxentius in ". . . peccatorum remissio et carnis resurrectio [*ac vita aeterna*] perducetur." Vol. II, p. 465.

[37]Porter, "Maxentius," p. 7.

[38]Cf. *PL* 57: 773A and 774B.

anointed. This ceremony was not done at least in some places in northern Italy.[39]

Third, Porter pointed out that Maxentius said nothing about episcopal confirmation, but did say that the gift of the Holy Spirit is given in the one post-baptismal chrismation. It could be argued that Charlemagne did not ask about a second post-baptismal chrismation by the bishop, and that is why Maxentius was silent, but Porter was right in noting that Maxentius attributed to the one post-baptismal chrismation the "fullest infusion of the Holy Spirit."[40] J. D. C. Fisher has pointed out that the Milanese and other north-Italian *ordines* of baptism since the time of Ps.-Maximus of Turin (sixth century) have only one post-baptismal chrismation.[41] Ps.-Maximus,[42] the Sacramentary of Biasca,[43] the Sacramentary of Bergamo,[44] the *Manuale Ambrosianum*,[45] and the *Ordo* of Beroldus[46] all have only one post-baptismal chrismation. (None of them mentions the gift of the Holy Spirit.)

Beyond the three observations of Porter there are other signs that point to the use of a distinct north-Italian baptismal rite by Maxentius, whatever efforts he took to mute his differences with the Roman tradition.

Maxentius must have known the *pedilavium* or footwashing ceremony, which comes after the one post-baptismal chrismation in almost all the north-Italian sources beginning with Ambrose of Milan. He said nothing about it, almost undoubtedly because this much beloved ceremony in northern Italy stood in blatant contrast to the Roman rite. One must note, however, the extremely odd position of the topic Creed ("[De symbolo]" on Chart G2) in Text 33. Maxentius placed it *after* the post-baptismal chrismation and veiling and before the Eucharist, exactly where the *pedilavium* takes place in

---

[39]Neither the north-Italian "Order of Scrutinies" published by C. Lambot (*North Italian Services*), nor the twelfth-century Milanese *ordo* of Beroldus (ed. M. Magistretti, *Beroldus*) mention it.

[40]". . . sancti spiritus largissima infusione." Vol. II , p. 464.

[41]Fisher believes the spiritual seal which followed the first post-baptismal chrismation for Ambrose in the fourth century dropped out, and the one chrismation, whether performed by a bishop or a simple priest, came to constitute confirmation in northern Italy and imparted the gift of the Holy Spirit. Cf. *Christian Initiation*, pp. 38 and 45.

[42]Dom B. Capelle, "Les 'Tractatus De Baptismo' Attribués à Saint Maxime de Turin" *RB* XLV (1933), p. 115, dates the *Tractates* to the sixth century.

[43]Milan, Bibl. Ambros. Cod. A 24 bis inf., s. IX, Biasca (Gamber, *CLLA*, nr. 515, p. 266). For information on its date, which Gamber and others believe is tenth-century, see Fisher, *Christian Initiation*, pp. 39 f. Fisher describes the post-baptismal ceremonies of Biasca, op. cit., p. 44.

[44]Bergamo, Bibl. di S. Alessandro in Colonna, Cod. Sacramentorum Bergomensis, s. IX[2/2] (B. Bischoff), northern Italy (Gamber, CLLA, nr. 505, p. 264). Ed. A. Paredi, *Sacramentarium Bergomense* (Monumenta Bergomensia VI), Bergamo, 1962, p. 166.

[45]Milan, Bibl. Ambros. Cod. T 103 sup., s. X/XI, Milan (Gamber, *CLLA* nr. 580, p. 283), ed. M. Magistretti, *Manuale Ambrosianum*, pars altera, p. 209.

[46]M. Magistretti, ed., *Beroldus*, pp. 112–14.

the north-Italian *ordines*. The topic of the Creed is so obviously out of place that it almost draws attention to itself. For this topic Maxentius described the delivery of the Creed and gave the same exposition on the Creed as in the Reginensis. Was Maxentius trying to counter any possible criticisms from Charlemagne's court? If Maxentius thought Charlemagne wrote his questionnaire to check to see which of his archbishops were teaching non-Roman usages, the first thing he knew Charlemagne would have looked for in a response from northern Italy was whether a foot-washing was described—a benchmark of non-conformity with Rome.[47]

At exactly the place in his description where the non-Roman *pedilavium* would occur, Maxentius put the most Roman of expositions on the Creed, as if to say, just at the place where they would look for his lack of conformity, "I follow the Roman rite." Ironically, the foot-washing ceremony was a profession of faith according to Ambrose, for it recalled Jesus' words to Peter, "If I do not wash you, you have no part in me," and Peter's response, "Lord, not my feet only, but also my hands and my head" (Jn. 13: 8–9). Maxentius' over-done remarks about his following apostolic tradition and the decrees of the bishops of Rome become humorous in light of the actual baptismal instruction he sent Charlemagne.

Maxentius may have had a twinkle in his eye when he placed the topic of the Creed where the *pedilavium* occurs and when he gave an exaggerated testimony to his Romanity. On the other hand, to write his response to Charlemagne he may well have used a Romanized north-Italian *ordo* that had eliminated the foot-washing. It is certainly hard to ignore the many phrases he borrowed directly from a liturgical source. He had an *ordo* under his eyes. Which *ordo* was it? One example of his using phrases from the liturgy occurs where he quoted the words the priest says when he gives salt to the catechumens. The words are almost, but not quite, the same as in *OR* XI and the Reginensis. There are small differences, and two of these differences are also found in the north-Italian *Manuale Ambrosianum*.[48]

Maxentius placed the topic of salt ("[De sale]") after the first topic on catechumens and competents, and before the topic on exorcism and exsufflation, unlike Amalarius, Theodulf, and Leidrad.[49] In a fragment of a

---

[47]In his conclusion he says to Charlemagne and the experts at the court who would read his treatise: Nec non et sanctae sedis apostolicae venerabilium romanae ecclesiae catholicorum pontificum decreta, purissima fidei sinceritate sequimur sacratissima documenta." Vol. II, p. 466.

[48]Maxentius: "Accipe salem sapientiae propitiatus tibi in vitam aeternam" Vol. II, p. 463. Reginensis: "Accipe, ille, sal sapiencie propiciatur in vitam aeternam" (Mohlberg, *Sacramentarium Gelasianum*, p. 43, nr. 289). The *Manuale Ambrosianum*, like Maxentius, omits "ille" and has "tibi." (Magistretti, *Manuale Ambrosianum*, pars altera, p. 469.)

[49]Texts 54.1, 28, 30, and 50 are the only other of our Texts with salt before exorcism/exsufflation.

Romanized north-Italian *ordo* of baptism (it is a condensed, non-Paschal *ordo*) edited by Dom Lambot,[50] the giving of salt takes place before a clearly described exsufflation and .exorcism.[51] Thus, Maxentius' order of salt before exsufflation reflects actual liturgical practice in northern Italy.

Finally, one can note Maxentius' inclusion of the topic competents ("[De catecumino sive competente]"), since it is the only topic he included about which Charlemagne did not ask. For Maxentius, competents were identical with catechumens.[52] This conforms perfectly with what one finds in the north-Italian baptismal rites, where "competentes" is used from the very first week in Lent to refer to the catechumens.[53]

In conclusion, as Porter pointed out, if one looks beneath the surface of Maxentius's exposition to Charlemagne, north-Italian features are everywhere evident. It may well be that Maxentius, following a Romanized north-Italian *ordo*, sincerely thought this was the Roman rite of baptism. It has been shown in Chapter 4 that the "Roman *ordo*" included a variety of rites.

Text 49

Text 49 consists of two brief questions. In six of its eight manuscripts it is part of a larger clerical *interrogatio*.[54]

The *ordo* of baptism it describes, if brief, is distinctive (see Chart G3). In response to the question, "How do you baptize?" the priest says, "In the name of the Holy Trinity I make a triple immersion in the basin (*conca*) of the font. [I anoint him] with oil and chrism. I wash his feet following the Lord's example. I dress him in a white garment in the custom of priests. I give him the Lord's Body and Blood, because the Lord said, ..."[55]

---

[50]It comes before the *Ordo scrutiniorum*, which has been compared to Text 38 (see Chapter 6), in the same manuscript.

[51]In Milan, Bibl. Ambros. T 27 sup., s. XI, the first three folios are lost, so that the actual words for the giving of salt are not included. But a rubric on folio 5 for baptizing a sick person ("infirmus") says "follow the above *ordo* up to the giving of salt." All that exists of the "above *ordo*" (ff. 3–5) does not include salt, but does include a major exorcism ceremony with multiple exsufflations, so that salt must come before exorcism/exsufflation. Cf. C. Lambot, *North Italian Services*, p. 6.

[52]"Qui [catecumeni] ideo conpetentes dicuntur, id est poscentes dei gratiam . . ." Vol. II, p. 463.

[53]See, for example, Lambot, *North Italian Services*, p. 8. The same feature is in the north-Italian Text 38, discussed in Chapter 6.

[54]It contains all of the following questions: "Tell me, why is a priest consecrated (ordained)?" "Tell me, why do you baptize?" "How do you baptize?" "Why do you say Mass?" "How do you say Mass?" "How do you offer the sacrifice?" Some of the six manuscripts have more questions preceding or following these, but they are not the same in each manuscript. Two manuscripts (L, P16) have only the first part of Text 49, inserted within another baptismal instruction.

[55]See vol. II, p. 576.

The *pedilavium*, or foot-washing ceremony, is a feature known only in the baptismal rites of northern Italy, southern Gaul, and perhaps Ireland, as witnessed in a number of Milanese rites of baptism, the *Missale Gothicum*, the *Missale Gallicanum Vetus* (circa 700), the Bobbio Missal (eighth century), and the Stowe Missal (circa 800). Caesarius of Arles (d. 542)[56] and Ps.-Maximus of Turin[57] also refer to it. No other of our Texts contains explicit mention of the foot-washing.[58] Despite the non-Romanity of the *pedilavium*,[59] there are eight known manuscripts of Text 49. It circulated with very popular canon law material.[60]

Can this response of a priest as to how he baptizes really have described the actual *ordo* of baptism priests reading Text 49 should follow, consisting simply of an immersion in water in the name of the Trinity, an anointing, a footwashing, a white robe, and reception of the Eucharist? Or should one see Text 49, part of a didactic *interrogatio sacerdotalis*, as merely a model response that applied everywhere and nowhere? Perhaps this is how Text 49 was taken by some, but an indication that it described baptism in some areas is found in St. Gall, Stiftsbibl. Cod. sang. 40 (S1). In this codex an editor of Text 49 omitted the foot-washing and emphasized the use of the Trinitarian formula in the immersion by adding, "that is, of the Father, and of the Son, and of the Holy Spirit." It does not seem he would have concerned himself with these changes unless he regarded Text 49, even in an instruction-reader for priests, as an accurate reflection of what priests did. He was working in the Swiss area. Minus

---

[56]G. Morin, ed., *Sancti Caesarii Arelatensis Sermones*, Sermo CCIV, 3 (*CCSL* CIV, p. 821) and Sermo LXIV, 2 (*CCSL* CIII, p. 276).

[57]*PL* 57: 779B.

[58]Text 1 and Text 50 may suggest it, and Text 33 and Text 6 may have suppressed its mention.

[59]Another interesting feature is that the priest says he anoints the baptized person with oil *and* chrism. The *post*-baptismal anointings, whether one (non-Roman) or two, were done with chrism, not oil. Perhaps the phrase is an attempt to indicate that the priest performs the only post-baptismal anointing the neophyte will receive, without a bishop's chrismation.

[60]In A11 the six questions given in note 54 immediately follow a series of excerpts from the *Collectio Sangermanensis* on the clerical grades, also in question-response form. Cf. R. Reynolds, "The 'De officiis vii graduum:' Its Origins and Early Medieval Development" in *Mediaeval Studies* 34, 1972, p. 137, and on the *Collectio Sangermanensis* see H. Mordek, *Kirchenrecht und Reform im Frankenreich: Die Collectio Vetus Gallica, Die älteste systematische Kanonensammlung des fränkischen Gallien: Studien und Edition* (Beiträge zur Geschichte und Quellenkunde des Mittelalters 1), Berlin/New York, 1975, pp. 144–47. In A13, following our six questions are more questions and responses, some of which are similar and in part identical with the text of the *Collectio Sangermanensis*. They are based on Isidore and of a type commonly found in paracanonical material. Thus, the context of Text 49 in A13 as well as in A11 shows the association of Text 49 with canonical material at least in southern France, and may explain why there are so many manuscripts of Text 49.

the *pedilavium*, the order of triple immersion; presbyteral chrismation; white vestments; and Eucharist, without any reference to episcopal confirmation, is the same as Text 33 (Maxentius), of north-Italian origin.

Again, in Laon, Bibl. mun. 288 (L), an early ninth-century manuscript from northeastern France, Text 49 lacks the second question and response referring to the *pedilavium*. The *pedilavium* was not celebrated in northeastern France.

The *apparatus* in the Editions indicates the great number of variant readings to which Text 49 was subjected, indicative of its having been much-copied and altered for different areas down to the very end of the ninth century, despite its distinct differences from the Roman rite.[61]

In conclusion, it has been shown that blatantly non-Roman elements of the baptismal rite, such as the foot-washing, no salt, single immersion, and presbyteral confirmation persisted. They were not combatted by composers of baptismal instructions, but taught to Spanish, southern Gallican, or north-Italian clerics. Texts 7, 33, and 49 attest this, but they also show that Romanity was having its effect on indigenous rites. An *ordo* close to a Romanized Spanish rite of Narbonne influenced the Spanish composer of Text 7; Maxentius (Text 33) in Aquileia had under his eyes a Romanized north-Italian rite; and some manuscripts of Text 49 omitted the non-Roman *pedilavium*. The desire for Romanity is associated with the Carolingian kings, but the Roman liturgy had been influencing western liturgies for centuries. (In fact, all the "indigenous" rites are to some extent Roman.) Texts 7, 33, and 49 only emphasize that consideration of the local liturgical usage, whether that meant a Gallican or a Romanized sacramentary book, guided the composers of baptismal instructions for the clergy.

These three Texts are important, in one regard, for liturgical historians. In another regard, they are important for raising the question of the chief aims of the Carolingian Reform. The reform legislation demanding liturgical conformity according to the Roman rite, if that had meant a single *ordo*, would have conflicted, according to our Texts, with the legislation demanding clerical educational reform. It seems from the Texts that the education of the clergy could not be effective if the clergy were all given a single text describing the same *ordo* of baptism. When it came to the task of actually composing clerical instructions, the composers picked up the liturgical books in use in their area, not some newly imported sacramentary. The reason liturgical regionalism persisted during the Carolingian period may be due, in part, to composers' use of the liturgical books that were at hand locally, and to a natural link in the minds of the composers between the effective instruction of the clergy on baptism and sensitivity to their liturgical preferences. Is it too bold to propose that the goal of educating the clergy actually encouraged the maintaining of

---

[61]See the edition for the dates and places of origin of the manuscripts of Text 49. Vol. II, p. 576.

diverse sacramentary books, and thus the diverse celebration of baptism? In other words, the effective education of the clergy simultaneously discouraged liturgical conformity.

Key to this hypothesis is acknowledgment that the Carolingian Reform was a locally implemented phenomenon. That is the major conclusion of the past four chapters dealing with the Texts as quasi-liturgical expositions. In Chapters Five through Eight a full range of the celebration of baptism across the Carolingian Empire, from Amiens, where some form of *OR* XI was observed (Text 30 by Jesse), to southern France, where the Old Gallican *pedilavium* persisted (Text 49) has been seen. An analysis of the selection and arrangement of topics led to knowledge of the liturgy itself—controversy over salt, spittle, barefeet, and washing of feet. It has been shown that the didactic tracts hold more than appears on the surface. Even though many of them are little more than redactions of one of a few authoritative models, such as a florilegium based on John the Deacon, or Alcuin's *ordo*, or Charlemagne's questionnaire, nevertheless their variations are significant. They reflect a composer's familiarity with a baptismal rite that conflicted with his model. He rearranged his model to suit better his liturgical experience of baptism. In some cases it was even possible to identify the specific liturgical book familiar to the composer. It was remarkable how his changes from his model did reflect the distinctive features of a specific liturgical book. It demonstrated a care on the part of the composers that one would not suspect in mere redactions of popular models. The crucial question became, then, *why* they took the trouble to change their models.

The answer seemed to be, time and again, that the composer was someone who knew the clergy for whom he was writing and the particular liturgy familiar to them. He composed his baptismal instruction with full knowledge of his recipients and of their needs. To recall some examples, Jesse, writing to his clergy in the diocese of Amiens, described a distinct variation of OR XI found nowhere else but in his treatise from Amiens (Text 30). An anonymous composer of a variation of Leidrad of Lyons' treatise made his instruction suitable for a rural parish priest probably somewhere in the archdiocese of Lyons (Text 26). The composer of Text 2 altered a florilegium based on John the Deacon so that it would describe a "quolibet tempore" rite. He added instruction on the devil's works and pomps, and more instruction on the Eucharist, perhaps thinking of some rural parish priest who often baptized people with no prior catechetical instruction. In two manuscripts of Text 3 a canon about returning the Creed on Holy Thursday was omitted. Someone, probably at Tours, took the trouble to omit this irrelevant canon that would have confused pastors in the Tours area. Alcuin's *ordo* (Text 9) was found to describe very closely the rite of baptism in the Sacramentary of St. Martin of Tours. In Text 38 Alcuin's *ordo* was transformed so that it would describe a north-Italian *ordo* of scrutinies. The composer was from northern Italy. His local knowledge of baptism was revealed in his incorporation of a provisional scrutiny used in a church where not everyone attended the full series of scrutinies. Text 17, written by a bishop in the archdiocese of Sens, revealed distinctive features of baptism observed in his own diocese, such as the biannual visit of an archdeacon to examine sponsors, and the use of oil, not spittle, in the effeta ceremony. Bishop "Waltcaud" of Liège (Text 14A) transformed Charlemagne's questionnaire into a description of a "quolibet tempore" rite for the clergy of his diocese. Texts 34 and 35, from the missionary area of Mondsee and Freising, were compiled with the needs of clergy in a missionary situation in mind. Finally, the Spanish composer of Text 7 included the topic of heretics returning to the church, sensitive to the needs of Spanish clergy dealing with Adoptianists.

The Texts examined in Chapters 4 through 7 brought the local scriptorium's personnel into focus in a way that has not been appreciated before. They would not have bothered to rearrange their models if they had not known their recipients and had had no concern for the effective reception of these instructions. It is here, in the minutiae of variant forms of a didactic florilegium, that one finds the key to the Carolingian Reform. Aachen did not, and could not, direct the educational reform of the clergy. A single program issuing from Aachen could not have met the diverse needs of the clergy in different dioceses. The local character of the Reform seen in our Texts cannot help but change past notions of Romanity, centralism, and liturgical conformity as the achievements, or even the chief aims, of the Reform.

In Chapters 4 through 7 one reason the tracts differ from one another has been seen. The composers were familiar with different baptismal rites, which they wished to describe. More reasons why the tracts differ from one another are found by looking at their explanations, that is, what each composer chose to say about the various topics of baptism. The next chapter will explore this aspect of the Texts.

8

Carolingian Interpretation of the Ceremonies of Baptism

It was said that the Carolingian baptismal instructions have been ignored, in part, because they are not obvious sources of information for historians, liturgiologists, or theologians. They were deemed to be unoriginal and repetitive didactic tracts, concerned above all with the definition of words pertaining to baptism.[1]

When their explanations are compared carefully, however, three features emerge that are very surprising in light of what has traditionally been thought to characterize the Carolingian baptismal literature as a whole. While it is not feasible to compare fully in this chapter all of the Texts, to illustrate these features five Texts will be compared on their explanation of "catechumen and catechesis."[2]

Bishop Jesse of Amiens (Text 30) says that catechumen is a Greek word. In Latin it means hearer (*auditor*) or one who is instructed (*instructus*), because a catechumen hears the doctrine of the faith and is instructed how he ought to approach holy baptism.[3] (To explain the time and order in which a catechumen is made, Jesse supplies a paraphrase of a Roman *ordo* of the enrollment and scrutinies, which was examined in Chapter 4. Then Jesse continues:) Even after he professes his faith, the catechumen does not yet merit to receive the body and blood of Christ, because he has not yet been reborn in the water of baptism. Whence Blessed Augustine says in a sermon on the words of the Lord to Nicodemus: "'Unless anyone is born again he cannot see the kingdom of God'" (Jn. 3:3). All catechumens are like the Jews to whom Jesus did not yet trust himself (cf. Jn. 2:24). If we ask a catechumen, Do you believe in Christ? he says I believe, and signs himself and does not blush at the cross. If we ask him, Do you eat the flesh of the Son of man and drink his blood? he does not know what we are saying, because Jesus has not yet trusted himself to him." So much for Augustine, says Jesse.

To catechize means to teach or to cast out (*castigare*), whence the Apostle: "Let him who is catechized share all good things with him who catechizes"

---

[1]Introduction, p. 8.

[2]I have partly translated directly, partly paraphrased, and partly summarized what follows. See their editions in volume II for the Latin text.

[3]A variation of Isidore, *Origines* VII.xiv.7. (For all the following references to Isidore's *Origines*, see the edition of Lindsay.)

(Gal. 6:6). This shows that he catechizes who teaches and he is catechized who learns.

First, Jesse simply defines the Greek word catechumen, giving a variation of Isidore's definition. Following this elementary definition (in question-response form), in contrast he gives a very long, detailed paraphrase of an *ordo scrutiniorum*, containing words such as "acolitus," "electi," "candelabris," and "turibilis," with almost no glosses.[4]

After this, Jesse refers to Augustine by name and quotes Augustine's comparison of a catechumen to the Jews in Jn. 2:24. Jesse defines the verb to catechize[5] by giving two synonyms and then quoting an example of its use in Scripture. Jesse uses the Galatians passage, however, simply to demonstrate the active and passive meaning of the verb.

What is one to make of this explanation of catechumen and catechesis? On the one hand, the instruction is elementary to the point that Jesse becomes a grammarian. On the other hand, there is the *ordo scrutiniorum* and Augustine's analogy, which assumes his readers have good familiarity with the second chapter of John's Gospel.

Jesse himself pinpoints the difficulty of instructing his clergy in the preface of his work. He begins:

"To the sacred priests and to all those of our diocese worthily serving Christ, Jesse, humble bishop, sends greetings . . .". [Jesse explains that his absence from his diocese forces him to write rather than speak to them.] "I know that many of you know well the mysteries [of baptism], but . . . it seemed more convenient to write to all than to certain unlearned ones. Thus I ask you who are more capacious in mind to instruct and exhort those who are less intelligent in a spirit of gentleness, so that attentively they ask about the things in it [Jesse's letter] which they do not know."

Jesse's words are a precious glimpse of his efforts to promote clerical instruction in his diocese and the problem he faced. A disparate clergy explains why there is such a broad range of sophistication in his explanation. The "certain unlearned ones" are ordained priests, because he includes them with those priests who "know well" the mysteries of baptism: "many of you know well . . . But it seemed best to write to all . . ." Jesse's instruction gives one some idea of what he expected his clergy to be capable of explaining. At the same time, he was clearly striving to raise the level of intelligence of his priests, hoping even those of lesser capacity would absorb at least a percentage of what he wrote.

His treatise is almost a school text. Five of his topics are in question-response form, probably taken from an earlier clerical instruction on baptism

---

[4]After "susceptores viri vel feminae" he does say, "id est, patrini vel matrinae."
[5]He does this under the topic "De exsufflatione."

in question-response form, and revealing his intent that his diocesan letter teach, not simply admonish or legislate. In fact, Jesse's text is meant to be studied. It is not at all merely a written version of what he would have delivered orally, had he been present. One of the most striking features of his whole instruction is the large number of scriptural quotations. Some of his explanations are little more than a string of biblical passages. Perhaps some of his clergy were familiar with the *ordo scrutiniorum* he described, but even for his priests who would never use it in their rural parishes, it was useful for broadening their general knowledge of the priestly office.

Amalarius of Metz, Archbishop of Trier (Text 23), another leading bishop of the Carolingian Reform, chose different things to say about catechumen and catechesis: Everyone, Amalarius explains, is born under the yoke of sin, as the Psalmist states: "Behold I was conceived in iniquity and in sins my mother conceived me." (Ps. 51:5) This is because of the disobedience of the first man. We cannot be re-formed to God's image except through baptism, nor can we enter the kingdom of heaven "unless we are reborn from water and the Spirit" (Jn. 3:5). Before baptism we walk about "in the desires of the flesh" (Eph. 2:3) living according to "the old man" (Eph. 4:22). For all these reasons one must be instructed by doctors of the church so that he sees his present state and future state through grace after baptism, and leaves his false gods for the one true God. When he has been thus instructed he becomes a catechumen, that is, one who is instructed or a hearer. Augustine in his book *De fide et operibus* says those who seek baptism must be catechized so that they not only hear what they should believe but also how to live in order to receive eternal life. Concerning which instruction, you can find it in Augustine's *De caticizandis rudibus.* Over the little ones (*parvulos*) we say a prayer that they will be freed from blindness of heart and loosed from Satan's bonds,[6] and, with time, will be able to recognize what should be denounced and what believed.

Amalarius immediately makes a connection between the catechumen and sin. Until they are baptized, catechumens live according to "the desires of the flesh." Three other scriptural references emphasize the point. To explain catechize as meaning instruct, he refers the reader to Augustine's *De caticizandis rudibus*, but for infants, he explains, to catechize means to exorcise.

Amalarius has a somewhat different emphasis than Jesse. Jesse does define catechize as to instruct or to cast out. Under the topic of exorcism he says that "the infant is exorcized or catechized," but he focuses more on catechize as meaning to instruct, as his comment on the Galatians' passage attests.

Amalarius expects his readers to have access to a copy of Augustine's *De*

[6]Cf. the prayer for the making of a catechumen in the Reginensis Gelasian Sacramentary, ed. Mohlberg, *Sacramentarium Gelasianum*, pp. 42 f., nr. 285.

caticizandis rudibus and to be able to read it. Or perhaps he only refers them to the Doctor and the title to instruct his readers that Augustine wrote such a work. He gives his readers a theological reason for the catechumenate. He begins, not with an Isidorian definition, but with the Psalmist and three passages from the New Testament, to explain the necessity of baptism.

Like Jesse, some of Amalarius' explanation for the catechumen is common, while some is unique. He alone refers to the liturgical prayer of exorcism said over the infants.

Yet another leading bishop of the Reform, Theodulf of Orléans (Text 16), chose to say still different things about the catechumen: Infants, says Theodulf, are made catechumens to observe an ancient custom. For, those believers who came to the Apostles for baptism were instructed and taught by them and then were baptized. Whence the Apostle says, "Or are you ignorant, brothers, that all of us who have been baptized into Christ Jesus were baptized into his death?" (Rm. 6:3) These words show that they were not ignorant of the mysteries of baptism when they were baptized. Also the Lord said, "Go, teach all nations, baptizing them . . ." (Mt. 28:19), not "Go, baptize. . . ," so that we should know that first we ought to instruct, then baptize. Therefore, infants are made hearers and catechumens, not because they can be taught at their ages, but so that ancient custom is observed. Catechumen means a hearer or one being instructed. What was once taught through Moses, "Hear, O Israel, the Lord your God is one God" (Dt. 6:4), the catechumen now hears through a priest, so that abandoning the worship of creatures he worships the one Creator.[7] Catechumens believe in Christ, but still carry their sins. They are like those who believed in Jesus, but "Jesus did not trust himself to them" (Jn. 2:24).[8] All those taught and baptized by John [the Baptist] were a type [*typum*] of catechumen,[9] because his baptism could not delete sins.

Theodulf emphasizes the purpose of making one a catechumen to observe tradition. He also stresses the necessity of being instructed before being baptized, a sensitive issue under Charlemagne, who demanded mass baptisms of the heathen he conquered.[10] His scriptural support from Rm. 6:3 is unique, using Paul's words, "Or are you ignorant, brothers, that we who have been baptized . . ." to prove that the first Christians were not ignorant, but were taught, before they were baptized. On the other hand, the use of Mt. 28:19 to defend instruction before baptism occurs in other baptismal instructions. He quotes Isidore's definition of a catechumen (a hearer or one being instructed), as

---

[7]Cf. Isidore, *De ecclesiasticis officiis* II.xxi.1 (*CCSL* CXIII, p. 96; for all further references to Isidore's *De eccl. off.*, see *CCSL* CXIII).

[8]Jesse refers to the Jn. 2:24 passage via Augustine. A florilegium containing Augustine may have been their source.

[9]Cf. Isidore, *De eccl. off.* II.xxi.2.

[10]See Introduction, p. 3.

does Jesse and Amalarius; but he also (following Isidore) compares them to the Jews baptized by John the Baptist, which Jesse and Amalarius do not.

A fourth leading bishop of the Reform, Leidrad of Lyons (Text 25), gave Isidore's definition of a catechumen as one who is instructed, and defined catechize only as to instruct. Then, in a variation of Isidore, he compared the catechumens to the Israelites Moses instructed about observing the Passover ("the sacrifice of the lamb and its blood") before they crossed the Red Sea. Isidore simply compared the catechumens to Moses instructing the Israelites with "Hear, O Israel . . ." (Dt. 6:4). Leidrad, by adding that Moses instructed them about the lamb and its blood, connects the catechumenate with preparation for the Eucharist. This was partially found in Jesse, for whom catechumens are those not worthy to receive the Eucharist. It is a different emphasis from that of Amalarius or Theodulf. Leidrad says nothing else about catechumen or catechize.

Text 50 is a sort of condensed version of a compendium on the ecclesiastical offices in question-response form.[11] Regarding catechumen and catechize, one reads: Question. Why are the names of the catechumens written down by an acolyte? Response. Clearly, that what is written may be fulfilled: "Your eyes saw me yet unformed, and in your book all [the days made for me] were written" (Ps. 139:16), and "Rejoice because your names are written in heaven" (Lk. 10:20). Whence blessed Augustine says: See, beloved, you who offer your profession in an angelical court. The names of those professing their faith are written in the book of life not by any man, but by a superior heavenly power.[12] Question. Why, after their names are written down, are the catechumens signed? Response. So they can say: "The light of your face is signed upon us, Lord" (Ps. 4:7) and because the doorposts of the Israelites were signed with the blood of lambs before they crossed the Red Sea (cf. Gen. 12:7), which signifies baptism. Question. What is to catechize? Response. Catechize is a Greek word which means to teach, to imbue, to instruct, and a catechumen is one who is instructed or a hearer or a listener (*instructus, audiens, vel auditor*).

---

[11]Traces of this are evident in, for example, the large number of scriptural citations; the citing of Augustine (three times) and Bede; the lack of connection between the salt given to the catechumens and the salt ordered to be used in the Law, due to the omission of some explanation; and the inclusion of more unusual topics such as the significance of Holy Thursday for consecrating the chrism, the blessing of the font, and the removal of the head cloth after seven days, which are found in comprehensive treatments of the ecclesiastical offices such as Amalarius' *Liber officialis*. Perhaps Text 50 was intended for a schoolroom, as a quiz or study guide in connection with the study of some major work on the ecclesiastical offices. Despite saying very little on some topics, a complete exposition on an Apostles'-type Creed takes up one fourth of the work.

[12]It is from a Ps.-Augustinian sermon *De symbolo* (PL 40:637).

Augustine says that the catechumen, as much as he progresses, still carries the load of his iniquities until he is renewed through the water.

This composer emphasizes the liturgical significance of the catechumen. The catechumen is one who is enrolled and signed, the first step in the progress toward baptism. The composer has the same reference as Leidrad to the Israelites and the blood of lambs, but Leidrad uses the Passover as a type of the Eucharist; this composer sees the Passover event in relation to the signing of the doorposts as a type of the signing of the catechumens. He gives the enrollment ceremony added significance by explaining it as a fulfillment of God's own words. By quoting or referring to Scripture four times and Augustine twice, he broadens the readers' knowledge. The pedagogical flavor of the tract comes out not only in the question-response format, but in a small point of diction: "audiens vel auditor.[13]" Giving both forms of "hearer" reveals the composer's consideration of his reader, whom he wished to be literate, not merely aware of what catechumen meant. The catechumen is connected with a still sinful state, but this is not the emphasis, as it is with Amalarius. Amalarius also connects the catechumen with a liturgical event, but it is the exorcism prayer, not the enrollment and signing.

To summarize, first, one feature of the five texts is that together they present a very diverse picture of what should be emphasized, or said at all, about the catechumen. Jesse is thinking of a participant in a Roman *ordo* of scrutinies celebrated in his diocese. Amalarius is thinking of one in a state of sin. Theodulf is thinking of one who must be instructed before he receives baptism. Leidrad is thinking of one who is being prepared to participate in the Eucharist. The composer of Text 50 is thinking of one who symbolizes the heavenly call.

A second feature is their pedagogical nature, their interest in defining terms and familiarizing the reader with Scripture and the fathers. Jesse has approximately thirty-eight scriptural quotations in his treatise, yet only four of them are specifically on baptism. Fifteen mention salt or ears or odor or catechize or some other word related to baptism. The remainder have nothing to do with baptism. Sometimes they simply complete, amplify, or illustrate a thought, as, for example, where Jesse says: "For rightly [the devil] is exsufflated and cast out, 'as if dust in the face of the wind'" (cf. Vulg. Ps. 1:4, Ps. 17:43, or Ps. 34:5). Such use of Scripture reflects Jesse's own almost subconscious training perhaps, but he wishes his readers to have this same familiarity with Scripture. At other times, scriptural exegesis takes over as the main point of what is said under a topic. When Jesse compares the priest touching the nose and ears with saliva to Jesus healing the man born blind with mud made from his spittle, he uses the opportunity to digress on the

---

[13]Isidore uses *auditor* in *Origines* VII.xiv.7; *audiens* in *De ecclesiasticis officiis* II.xxi.1.

incarnation of the Word: The Word descended and mixed with the world as the spittle mixed with the mud. Jesse then quotes Jn. 1:14, "And the Word was made flesh and dwelt among us." One could dismiss this kind of explanation as wildly distorted interpretation of the ceremony of the touching of the nose and ears, or one could credit Jesse for having seized the moment to teach his clergy some fundamental theology derived from the Bible.

Theodulf has approximately eighty scriptural quotations in his treatise. He used Zach. 3:2 to illustrate exorcism, but actually proceeds to gloss, not the pertinent word "rebuke," but the word "Jerusalem," and brings in another quote from Isaiah to explain Jerusalem meaning vision of peace. In short, Theodulf took the opportunity the Zacharia passage presented to give his readers further exegesis that has nothing to do with the subject at hand. Under the topic of Creed, expanding on the teaching that the Creed is the "abbreviated word" of Isaiah, he uses the occasion to instruct his readers on the greatest commandment. This, he says, is also an abbreviation of the entire Law and the prophets, and then presents Mt. 22:37 ("Love the Lord your God with all your heart, mind, and strength, and your neighbor as yourself"). On another topic, Theodulf uses Scripture to illustrate an etymological digression on the word "renounce" (*abrenuntio*). The root, he explains, is *nuntio*, and sometimes *renunciare* means to announce, as in the Psalms, "I will tell and announce" ("Narrabo et renuntiabo"). But, he concludes, *abrenuntiare* always means to renounce. It is almost as if Theodulf, by this clarification of *renuntio* and *abrenuntio*, was in a classroom answering the query of some observant student.

Apart from their use of the Bible, there are many other signs of these five composers' efforts to heighten the intellectual level of their readers generally, not only on baptism. One is citing patristic authorities and their works. Amalarius cites the letter of Augustine to Bishop Boniface on infant baptism. Theodulf introduces his readers to Clemens Prudentius, "a most learned and most Christian poet," and his work, the *Psychomachia*, from which he gives a definition of pomp. Such a reference (in fact, two manuscripts of Theodulf's treatise omit the section entirely) was far more information than was necessary for the cleric in order to explain baptism. So also is Theodulf's long digression on the symbolism of the number seven and on the seven gifts of the Holy Spirit.

A third characteristic of the five Texts is that while the authors may use some of the same sources, they edit them, giving different variations of Isidore, for example, or different interpretations of scriptural passages.

These three characteristics are illustrative of the baptismal literature as a whole. Regarding its diversity, it is true that one can study sub-groups of the tracts and find great commonality. Thirteen Texts, for example, are little more than minor variations of Alcuin's *ordo* (Text 9); four Texts are variations of John the Deacon; five Texts are similarly extracted forms of Hrabanus Maurus' chapters on baptism in his *De institutione clericorum*. If, however, one read all of the Texts, one would find a significant amount of variety in what the composers may have chosen to say, or to add, or to emphasize about any one topic. To give an illustration, here is what other baptismal instructions, beyond the five looked at above, say about catechumen and catechesis.

In Texts 1–5 Isidore is quoted at varying lengths that the catechumen is a pagan convert who wishes to leave idolatry and be instructed, while Text 9 offers no Isidorian definition of the word, but only that a pagan coming to baptism is made a catechumen so that he renounces the evil spirit and his pomps. In Texts 15, 15A, and 28 there is no mention of any renunciation or exorcistic purpose to being made a catechumen. In Text 17 one is made a cate-chumen in preparation for receiving the Eucharist. It is explained that now the sponsor of an infant does the learning, and to catechize is defined as to ad-monish or to sign. In Text 18, Isidore's "gentilis" (gentile convert) is glossed as related to "genitus" (begotten; not yet instructed). In Text 33 the free will and the confession of the catechumen, who is an infant or a youth, is taught, and Rm. 10:10 is quoted. In Text 34 (a florilegium) sentences of Niceta of Remesiana are added to the definitions of Isidore and Alcuin. Texts 34–36 in-clude a long excerpt from Augustine's *De catecizandis rudibus*. In Text 44 (ex-tracted from Hrabanus Maurus) catechumens are compared to deaf and mute people and to the paralytic in the Gospel, healed through the faith of others. Text 51 has a long extract from Augustine on John's story of Jesus healing the man born blind (Jn. 9).

Regarding their pedagogical nature, the *general* education of the cleric is as much, if not a greater, concern than his baptismal expertise. When viewed as a whole, the baptismal instructions are, in fact, much more than instructions on baptism. The examples are endless of a concern to educate the cleric *gener-ally*. This may mean his familiarity with Scripture and patristic works, his knowledge of Greek words, and his allegorical sensibility; or it may mean his capability simply to read Latin and understand the meaning of basic words. One example of the concern to teach vocabulary is Text 58. This anonymous instruction is made up largely of extracts from Isidore. Under the topic of scrutiny, which Isidore fails to define, its composer gives a list of no less that fifteen synonyms for the verb to scrutinize. Also, he gives the meaning of devil in Hebrew. The definition (*deorsum fluens*; falling downward), from Jerome, probably came from a florilegium or glossary well known to this edu-cator. Three other baptismal instructions that devolved from glosses on the prayers of baptism to mere vocabulary lists will be discussed shortly.

Further examples of the desire to make the baptismal instructions more than instructions on baptism are the many variations of Alcuin's *ordo* (Text 9). If one wished to point to a Text that is *not* concerned with the general educa-tion of the cleric but is narrowly confined to what order and why each of the necessary baptismal ceremonies was done, with no adornment of definitions or Scripture, the closest one might come is Text 9 (although it does have "id est . . ." twice, and one quotation from Scripture). Thirteen Texts, however, show the desire to supplement Text 9 with very basic instruction about the meaning of words that occur in the baptismal rite. Most of them contain every word of Text 9, but two additions in Text 41 are the explanation of the devil's pomps ("his boastings and his demands") in Old High German, and an exposition on a Nicene-type Creed. Added in Text 53 are an Isidorian definition of the catechumen and the symbol, the example of Jesus healing the man born blind, a definition of the word scrutiny, an exposition on an Apostles'-type Creed, and definitions of the devil's works and pomps. Added in Text 52 are definitions for every catechumenate topic, and a detailed exposition of the words of the three-fold interrogation of faith at the moment of baptism. In Text 12 scriptural quotations are added; in Text 19 Isidorian definitions of the words baptism and catechumen, and a definition of *abrenuntio* are supplied. Texts 10, 27, 55, and 42 combine the sentences of Text 9 with other explanation, in florilegium-fashion. These examples show that Text 9, lacking almost any Isidorian-type definition of words, was frequently considered to be insufficient without supplementation or at least an opportunity to provide further elementary instruction.

A third feature of the Texts as a whole is the extensive editing applied to their sources. Isidore is almost never quoted exactly. The baptismal literature has been called repetitive, and it appears so until one carefully compares the Texts with their sources. Maybe they are not significant changes theologically, but why, nevertheless, do they exist? The composers took time and trouble to make these changes.

The same care the composers took to alter their models' sequence of topics is also shown in their selection, amplification, and rewording of their sources. Their care can be shown in countless small ways. When they copied Augustine or Gregory or Isidore, they did not do so blindly. The composer of Text 6, for instance, quoted Ambrose, but stopped abruptly where Ambrose begins to speak of the spiritual seal (episcopal confirmation). Text 6 is from northern Italy, where the episcopal confirmation is thought to have dropped out since the time of Ps.-Maximus of Turin in the mid-sixth century.[14] In Text 7, salt is added to Isidore's list of the sacraments of the church. Text 7, from Spain,

[14]Ambrose says, "The church, having put on these garments through the laver of regeneration says in the Song of Songs..." Text 6 states: "The church, having put on these garments through the laver of regeneration, after the sacrament of baptism is done it is necessary that the regenerated are confirmed with the reception of the Lord's Body and Blood." The awkwardness of the sentence indicates that the composer simply cut out a whole section of Ambrose that speaks of the "spiritual seal" of the Holy Spirit. J. D. C. Fisher has noted that the liturgical books from northern Italy from the ninth through twelfth centuries do not describe any episcopal hand-laying or second chrismation for imparting the seven-form grace of the Holy Spirit. See *Christian Initiation*, p. 44. This is not conclusive, however. In some areas of northern Italy influenced by Romanizations, episcopal confirmation may have been celebrated. See the analysis of Text 2 on pp. 75 f.

where giving salt to the catechumens was not the custom, was written where the liturgy was being influenced by Romanizations. In Text 58 Isidore's simple "tinction" is changed to "three-fold tinction.[15]" Perhaps the composer was aware of Alcuin's wrath regarding the Spanish practice of single immersion. Three Texts (4, 8, 21) contain Isidore's teaching on three kinds of baptism: water, blood, and tears, but the composer of Text 57 altered Isidore, specifically stating that there are two kinds of baptism, and omitting tears. Two Texts say that only priests are allowed to baptize, except in danger of death when any cleric or lay person can validly baptize. In Text 21, however, it says that if necessity demands, *deacons* may baptize, and it says nothing about lay people. Text 21 is part of the *Collectio Sangermanensis*, and this may explain its interest in the canonical privileges of a deacon vis-à-vis a priest.

These characteristics of the baptismal literature as a whole may appear surprising to anyone who thought the Carolingian liturgical expositions as a genre had little to offer as merely repetitive, didactic florilegia. They are that, in part, but they are also diverse in their explanations; shaped to different levels of sophistication in their pedagogy; and, finally, their patristic sources have been selected and edited with care. How are these features to be explained?

First, why do the Texts say different things? One reason that they can have different explanations must relate to the overriding purpose of the Carolingian baptismal literature. What was, in fact, the usefulness to a cleric of a baptismal instruction such as Text 9 (translated in Chapter 6) or the many Texts which, in quasi-expository fashion, provide some brief explanation of a series of topics pertaining to the ceremonies of baptism? What, after all, were they to do with this information? Viewed as a whole, it could be said that it matters less *what* the Texts say about each topic than that they say *something*. By providing the cleric with an orderly "memo" on baptism, they might be useful in preparation for an examination by his bishop or an archdeacon. Or, they might function simply as a vehicle for basic education. These brief Texts are not identical in what they say about any topic; one gives an Isidorian definition, another gives an example from Scripture; but it does not seem to matter, as long as *something* is said. There is no one "right" answer to "What is a scrutiny?" nor one necessary point that must be made regarding the catechumen.

This characteristic of the Carolingian baptismal instructions, which stands out only when they are compared as a whole, must be taken into consideration when reflecting on their role or function in the context of the Carolingian Reform. That a cleric be literate about baptism, that he could describe *an ordo* and give *a* Latin synonym for Greek words like catechumen and

---

[15]"In ipsa *terna* tinctione reddimur pulchri . . . ." Vol. II, p. 623.

symbol and say *one* reason why he puts salt on the catechumen's tongue, is more important than which *ordo*, which synonym, or which reason. Jesse describes one Roman *ordo* of scrutinies; Amalarius another; Leidrad no Roman *ordo* at all. One Text gives an exposition on a Nicene-type Creed, while another on the Apostles' Creed. One Text says pomps in Greek means public ostentation; another says it means funeral obsequies. The diverse nature of the explanations sheds an important light on the priority of the Carolingian Reform: make the clergy literate about baptism, let them be able to know something; less important is any consensus or fixed canon of teaching.

This does not mean that any one composer did not care what he selected to say. He may have had great interest in stressing a certain point about the catechumen, or salt, or exsufflation. The point is that it seems he could say what he wished, while respecting some set of ordered topics.[16]

If one looks for the ninth-century theology of baptism, it would seem that no consensus was achieved on the purpose, necessity, and effect of the individual ceremonies. A separate study is necessary to give full attention to the Carolingian theology of baptism expressed in the Texts. Carolingians have been accused of holding a primitive, magical view of the material elements of the water, oil, salt, and consecrated bread, and of being overly preoccupied with the exorcisms to remove evil spirits.[17] There is no indication in the Carolingian baptismal instructions, however, of an attempt to correct the notion that the material elements worked their effect apart from prayer that the Holy Spirit would operate through them; and there is less concern with the devil or evil spirits than might be thought. In some Texts the topic of exorcism is omitted entirely. Their teaching on the reception of the Holy Spirit is one example of how unrigid they were about the purpose and effect of the individual ceremonies. The reception of the Holy Spirit was not confined to a single ceremony or moment in all of the Texts, but can be found in different Texts occurring in the pre-baptismal exsufflation, the anointing of the breast and back, and even the touching of the nose and ears (Text 50), as well as in the font itself and in the post-baptismal anointing and the episcopal hand-laying. In contrast to what has been written about the popular ninth-century idea of baptism, if the population absorbed through their parish priests what the priests were taught in the baptismal instructions, their desire for baptism was due to a variety of joyful promises it held out, including membership in a royal and priestly family, participation in the Eucharist, and hope of eternal life with the white-robed saints in the heavenly kingdom. All that can be stressed here is that there were many different explanations or emphases

---

[16]The repeated appearance of such phrases as "per ordinem" (Text 14; Charlemagne's questionnaire); "eodemque ordine" (Text 30; Jesse); "Ordo vel brevis explanation de caticizandis rudibus" (Texts 34–36); "*Primus* paganus catecuminus fit . . ." (Text 9) show the importance given to an ordered set of topics.

[17]See A. Angenendt, "Die Liturgie und die Organisation," pp. 186–91.

regarding the theological import of any ceremony, and no sense of one "correct" explanation.

Second, why are the Texts as a whole overwhelmingly pedagogical, sometimes to the point where the general education of the cleric takes over baptismal instruction? The pedagogical emphasis shows that the baptismal instructions are a distinct genre of literature that their composers understood had a special role in the context of the Carolingian Reform. The Carolingian baptismal instructions were vehicles for the education of the clergy. How often, in fact, were they the prime vehicle? Baptism was the first and most fundamental teaching office of the priest, and at least a minimum knowledge of baptism was necessary for him to be ordained and to remain in office.

When the baptismal instructions function as elementary school texts—exam aides, study guides, even Latin primers—the actual challenge of the Carolingian Reform is being seen. Individuals responsible for composing the instructions sometimes faced a fundamental problem of minimal literacy. The composers addressed their needs, as well as those who were more learned. Our tracts are a living witness of Jesse's disparate clergy.

Why was it so disparate? How had it come about that there were ordained priests who were barely literate? Some idea of the complexity of the situation that led to uneducated clergy who served the public can be gained from reading Imbart de la Tour. It was related to nomination and appointment procedures, the system of proprietary churches, endowments of churches to abbeys or cathedrals by lay lords, the appointment of ill-trained men to private chapels, which then became parish churches with the expansion of parishes and the need for smaller churches within them.[18] It is understandably difficult to give any historical weight to an anonymous, didactic, quasi-liturgical gloss, or a florilegium of patristic definitions, unless one reads such literature knowing that it is anchored in the reality of the ninth century with its proprietary churches and expanding rural parishes. Then it is astonishing the way the baptismal tracts attest to the scene of the illiterate cleric himself who was the butt of all the legislative concern. The tracts show he really existed, he was at large, teaching and ministering to even more ignorant people who formed their entire understanding of Christianity through him.

Finally, what does it mean that the composers were not content to use their sources without adding to them, rearranging them, rephrasing them, or otherwise editing them? The composers were not disinterested copyists, but reflected on their sources and were concerned to make alterations. This care was seen, for example, in Text 6, when its composer omitted Ambrose's words on the spiritual seal of confirmation. Why this concern, if baptismal instruction was only a vehicle for the general education of the clergy? It can

---

[18]Cf. Imbart de la Tour, *Les paroisses rurales du IVe au XIe siècle*, Paris, 1900, especially pp. 173–233.

be explained in two ways, perhaps. One is the idea that education is more effective when the text is relevant to the learner. Another is that the composer had personal knowledge of the clergy for whom he wrote and the liturgy they celebrated. Text 6 was composed for clergy in northern Italy who did not observe episcopal confirmation. The evidence points to the composer taking pains to describe the rite of baptism in use locally. It also becomes much more understandable why the composers adjusted their models if they *knew* the clergy. The editing of sources indicates that the education of the clergy was a local process of bishops and perhaps others (archdeacons, school masters) discerning their own clergy's needs and fashioning appropriate texts of instruction. It is easy to forget that the local bishop usually had personal knowledge of all his priests, as did his archdeacon and other assistants. The human dimension of the Carolingian Reform to educate the clergy cannot be overlooked when trying to explain how the Reform did succeed historically in changing the conscientiousness of clergy about their own education. Personal knowledge of the clergy must help to explain the two seemingly contrary conclusions of the manuscript evidence: one, the care taken by the composers to describe specific liturgical books or rites of baptism and to edit their sources; and two, the priority of the general education of the clergy over the subject of baptism, which was only a vehicle, if a prime vehicle, for their general education.

Among our Texts four represent a different type of baptismal instruction. They consist of glosses on the words of the baptismal rite. A momentary look at these Texts vividly illustrates, in one case, the care taken over a baptismal instruction in a local scriptorium, and in another case how the general education of the clergy took over the whole purpose of the baptismal instruction.

The four Texts will be considered from lengthiest to briefest. First, the composer of Text 31 glossed a series of fifteen prayers from the rite, providing the entire text of each prayer and inserting after every sentence or phrase a synonymous phrase. Second, the composer of Text 43 did not write out the full text of any prayer. Rather, he listed a large number of words that can be found in ten different prayers of the rite. The words, each followed by a synonymous word or phrase, are listed without distinction as to prayer, but in the same order, word-for-word and prayer-for-prayer, that they are found in the rite. Third, in the same manner, the composer of Text 24 listed a series of words that can be found in fourteen different prayers of the rite. This Text has a far smaller selection of words from each prayer, however, than Text 43. Finally, Text 11 is the briefest of all the glosses. Although its composer glossed a list of words that come from sixteen different prayers of the rite, sometimes there are only one or two words from any one prayer.

Many, but not all, of the words that the four composers glossed are the same. Also, the gloss itself, or interpretation, may be different. One reason for the variety of words glossed is that the composers used different sacramentaries with different prayers. Almost all of the prayers can be found in the Reginensis Gelasian Sacramentary (described in Chapter 3). In two Texts, however, two prayers glossed in each are not found in the Reginensis, but only in Gelasian of the eighth-century-type sacramentaries.

The first prayer in Text 31 that is not in the Reginensis begins, "Deus inmortale presidium omnium postulantium."[19] The second prayer, or, more accurately, proclamation, of Text 31 not found in the Reginensis is: "And I anoint you with the oil of salvation."[20]

It is not necessarily surprising that at least two of the four Texts were composed from Gallicanized sacramentaries. The composers worked, it seems, from the sacramentaries available to them. What is most interesting to find, however, is that one copyist of Text 43 (there are seven known manuscripts of Text 43), which has no words necessarily from a Gallicanized sacramentary, went out of his way to include in his copy parts of Text 31, the parts glossing words found only in Gallicanized sacramentaries. Exactly in the same place where Text 31 has the prayer "Deus inmortale presidium," the copyist of the "Paris version" of Text 43[21] inserted this prayer and its glosses from Text 31. He then continued to copy the remainder of Text 43 unaltered. When he was through, however, he again turned to Text 31 and borrowed its last section that begins with an excerpt from Text 49 (see Chapter 7) and concludes with the gloss of the proclamation, "And I anoint you with the oil of salvation."

In short, the copyist of the "Paris version" of Text 43 had both Texts 43 and 31 under his eyes and was fully conscious of their differences. As his primary model he followed the briefer Text 43, not altering it, but only supplementing it with material in parallel places in Text 31. It seems that the reason he borrowed from Text 31 was in order to include specific items from a Gallicanized sacramentary in his version of Text 43.

The image of a Carolingian compiler with several texts spread before him, halting in his task to select a few specific items not in his primary model but in another baptismal gloss, is a provocative one. Why did he do this, unless these were prayers familiar to those for whom he was writing? The "Paris version" of Text 43 is an impressive attestation of the care that some redactors of baptismal instructions took to make these instructions applicable to a specific group of clergy.

Yet, lists of words taken from the baptismal rite were in some cases copied simply to teach Latin vocabulary, not to understand the meaning of specific prayers. In Text 31 the complete prayer texts are given along with their phrase-by-phrase interpretation. In Texts 43, 24, and 11, however, there is no way of telling from these glossaries which prayers they interpret. Since they do not provide the prayer context, one would expect to find them associated

---

[19]See Chapter 6, note 40, on this prayer.
[20]"Et ego te linio oleo salutis."
[21]See the variations of P16 in vol. II, p. 555, *app. crit.*

in their manuscripts with an *ordo* of baptism that does provide the prayers. The one known manuscript of Text 24, however, has no baptismal *ordo*. Of the seven manuscripts of Text 43, only one (Me) has a baptismal *ordo* preceding Text 43, but a comparison of this *ordo* with the words glossed in Text 43 shows that the *ordo* bears no association with the exposition of prayers that follows it. Only four of the ten prayers glossed in Text 43 are found in the *ordo*. The two earliest manuscripts of Text 11 do not contain any *ordo* of baptism.

This suggests that the glosses had a function other than liturgical commentary. The brief lists of words could have been intended simply as primers for clerics who needed to be taught to read Latin or to expand their vocabulary. For example, Text 31, unlike Texts 43, 24, and 11, has:

> (Prayer text) Deus Abraham, Deus Isac (*sic*), Deus Iacob, Deus qui Moysi famulo tuo in monte Sinai aparuisti et filius (*sic*) israhel de terra aegipti eduxisti *diputans* (*sic*) aeis (*sic*) angelum pietatis tue qui costodiret (*sic*) eos die ac nocte.

> (Explanation) Idem, Tu, Deus, qui eduxisti filius (*sic*) israhel de eagipto (*sic*) et *misisti* tuum angelum qui costodised (*sic*) illum . . .

The composer of Text 31 correctly interpreted *deputans* in the prayer as *misisti*, for in the prayer *deputans* has the sense of sending. In Text 11, however, the interpretation of the word *deputans* is *adnumerans*. The composer of Text 11, perhaps unaware of the prayer context of *deputans*, explained it according to his own understanding, not as "sending" but as "reckoning," or "considering," or "counting as" (*adnumerans*).

Another example concerns the word "inminere."[22] In the prayer the sense of the word is "to be imminent," "to approach," "to be about to happen." The composers of Texts 43 and 24 accurately interpreted *inminere* in its prayer sense as *appropinquere* or *supervenire*. The composer of Text 11, however, interpreted *inminere* as *adcrescere et exaltare* (to increase and to exalt). The explanation is no longer appropriate for the prayer.

The reason for these two misinterpretations was the disassociation of the glosses from the prayer texts. The brief glossary lists were an end in themselves. They served simply to educate the cleric in a general way, not to explain a specific prayer of baptism.

What can be learned about the nature of the Reform from this chapter? The diverse explanations indicate that the Carolingian Reform was not programmatic as to texts. The choice of texts used to educate the clergy, at least on baptism, was left up to the bishops and those they commissioned to compose

---

[22]In the exorcism prayer "Nec te latet, satanas. . . ." Cf. Molhberg, *Sacramentarium Gelasianum*, p. 67, nr. 419.

baptismal instructions. No legislation prescribes a baptismal treatise that all the clergy should know. Is it an aspect of the Carolingian Reform that deserves much more attention. Is it curious that such an ambitious body of legislation for reform in regard to clerical education was negligent in regard to stipulating specific commentaries that all the clergy should learn? The evidence of the Texts says that the education of the clergy, not theological and liturgical unity, was the uppermost aim of the Reform.

What do the various interpretations of baptism mean in relation to the idea of unity? On the one hand, there was a lack of unity on the teaching of baptism across Carolingian Europe. Furthermore, it was perpetuated by some of the very leaders of the Reform, Bishops Jesse, Theodulf, Amalarius, and Leidrad, who made no effort to insist on a common understanding of the purpose and importance of each of the ceremonies. This is not a question of unity regarding essential beliefs of the faith, but wherever room for interpretation was permissible, there was a wide latitude of explanations. There was no one answer, for example, to when baptism originated or why salt was given to the catechumens. The Carolingian Reform was concerned not with systematic theology, but with morality; not with formulas, but with literacy. The goal of the Reform could not be effectively accomplished by imposing standard teaching texts, because the diversity and needs of the clergy was too great. The choice of texts had to be left up to those who implemented the Reform at the local level.

On the other hand, a second fact that can be learned about the Carolingian Reform from this chapter is that, while current scholarship is demonstrating the large amount of diversity rather than unity that prevailed during the period of the Carolingian Reform, especially in the area of the liturgy, the corpus of Carolingian baptismal instructions must have created a certain kind of unity that did not exist before the Carolingian Reform. The Carolingian baptismal instructions were a new genre of literature that belonged distinctly to the Reform. The reception of these instructions by so many priests must have promoted a common sense among the clergy that they were part of a single great endeavor to raise them up as teachers and moral examples to the people. It is hard to imagine any parish priest being untouched by a new self-consciousness about his education during this period. The tracts illustrate in a way no Reform laws can a unity of endeavor. A barely literate cleric and an erudite bishop struggled together over the same baptismal texts, one composing, the other digesting. Unity was created during the Carolingian Reform in this sense: there was a broad recognition of a common goal and a sharing of ideas from high to low, from composers to readers, from Jesse's more learned to less learned.

A final task before concluding this study is to show that what has just been said about the concern of the composers extended also to those who compiled the manuscripts.

9

The Baptismal Instructions and Their Manuscripts

It is necessary to keep in mind the context of the tracts in their collection volumes and to remember that they are only one text amid a vast amount of other material copied for the instruction of the clergy. It was shown that the purpose of such texts as canon law collections, penitentials, sermons, acts of councils, and liturgical *ordines* was transformed in these volumes. Here they served to educate the cleric in the broadest sense. It is conceivable that the baptismal tracts were copied in manuscripts far away from their place of origin for their pedagogical value, without regard for the rite they describe.

It must be seen if a manuscript's area of circulation and intended recipient correspond with the contents of the Text(s) in it. Did the manuscript compilers know what was in the tracts and care whether they were suitable for the recipients of their volumes? Are our Texts true indicators of the continued diversity of the liturgy throughout the Carolingian period? To a large degree, the implementation of the Reform really lay in the hands of the manuscript compilers, who selected, copied, and disseminated the books that were to bring about reform. In concluding Part II, it is necessary now to show the correlation between the *contents* of the instructions and the intended destinations of the volumes in which they were copied.

First, the large number of *different* baptismal instructions is noteworthy. The compilers of our collection volumes did not all settle on one or a very few baptismal expositions, but in sixty-five ninth-century manuscripts there are sixty-four *different* Carolingian baptismal instructions. (Many of the manuscripts contain more than one baptismal instruction.) Certainly, some Texts did attain a more popular status than others. Text 9, associated with Alcuin, is in seventeen of our ninth-century manuscripts; Text 16, by Theodulf of Orléans, is in nine; and Text 23, by Amalarius of Metz, is in seven. That, however, makes it all the more remarkable that in sixty-five manuscripts from the ninth century there are sixty-four *different* baptismal instructions.

One way to explain this variety is that even in volumes intended for the education of a cleric in the broadest sense, the Carolingian baptismal instructions reflect the preferences, concerns, or needs of the specific area in which they were copied. The manuscript compilers were as selective in copying baptismal instructions as the authors were in composing them. This explanation is supported by the numerous cases of a correlation between a Text and its manuscript.

Table 1 shows the date, place of origin, and hypothesized purpose or intended destination of each volume,[1] and then the Text(s) contained in it. Some examples of correlation are the following:

Albi, Bibl. mun. 38 bis (Al1), an instruction-reader for priests from southern France, contains Text 49, an extremely brief and simple description answering a question for a priest as to how he baptizes. It includes the *pedilavium*, the foot-washing ceremony long indigenous to southern Gaul.[2]

Albi, Bibl. mun. 42 (Al2), probably a schoolbook for an episcopal school, from southern France, contains Theodulf (Text 16). Theodulf was a Visigoth, and it has been shown above that his description of baptism has at least one Spanish symptom.[3] Clerics in the Visigothic region (the Narbonnaise) might have had a special interest in Theodulf's instruction if that is the area in which Albi 42 was written. Also, the great reformer Benedict of Aniane, near Narbonne, was a Visigoth. He received many liturgical texts from northern France (including the Gellone Sacramentary)[4] and his monastery may have procured a copy of Theodulf's baptismal instruction. Theodulf's fame as a teacher and theologian in his own day would explain his treatise being used in a bishop's school.

Albi, Bibl. mun. 43 (Al3), an instruction-reader for priests from southern France, contains Text 49. This Text is thus again (see Albi 38 bis) in a manuscript meant for simple priests and from a region where the *pedilavium* was celebrated. Furthermore, Albi 43 also contains Text 26, the anonymous variation of Text 25 (Leidrad of Lyons), which condenses and rearranges his topics to conform to a "quolibet tempore" *ordo* for rural parish priests, perhaps in Leidrad's own diocese.[5]

Angers, Bibl. mun. 277 (An) is a monastic schoolbook from the region of Lyons which contains a group of three Texts: 15A, 27, and 23 (Amalarius). This same combination also appears in another manuscript from the area of Lyons, Paris, BN lat. 10741 (P10), which is probably an instruction-reader for priests. Amalarius was one of the leading intellectual figures of his day and his baptismal treatise answering Charlemagne's questionnaire is lengthy

---

[1]The reader will recall that they were judged to be one of four kinds of books on the basis of their other contents, without consideration of the baptismal Text(s) selected for copying in each.

[2]See Chapter 7, pp. 111 f.

[3]See Chapter 4, p. 63.

[4]See Chapter 7, note 28.

[5]In regard to the possibility that Albi 43 was written in the Visigothic area of southern France, Leidrad of Lyons was intimately connected with Visigothic manuscripts. See R. Reynolds, "The 'Isidorian' *Epistula ad Leudefredum*: An Early Medieval Epitome of the Clerical Duties" in *Medieval Studies* XLI (1979), p. 277 and note 136.

and fairly sophisticated. When Agobard, Archbishop of Lyons, was removed from his see in 835 for disloyalty to Louis the Pious, Amalarius was elected to take his place. He was a zealous reformer and educator during his short term (835–838) in Lyons.[6] His enthusiasm to share his works and to see to the education of the clergy would have extended to the production of both schoolbooks and instruction-readers for priests in which his own baptismal instruction would be used. Both Angers 277 and Paris, BN lat. 10741 are dated after 835. Angers 277 is almost undoubtedly a *monastic* schoolbook. This would indicate the close cooperation of the Bishop of Lyons and monasteries in the education of the secular clergy.

The two other Texts grouped with Amalarius' Text are also related to Charlemagne's questionnaire, which may explain the association of all three. Text 15A is a variation of Magnus of Sens' response to Charlemagne, and Text 27 is a variation of Alcuin's *ordo* (Text 9), associated with Charlemagne's questionnaire (see Chapter 6). Text 27 has a long addition on the renunciation of Satan. The Council of Tours of 813 placed a special emphasis on the renunciation[7] and perhaps Text 27 originated in the area of Tours where this Council's decrees were made known. Another possibility, however, is that Text 27 originated in the area of Lyons, where Angers 277 originated. Leidrad of Lyons wrote at length on the renunciation in a second letter to Charlemagne after Charlemagne had read his baptismal response and told Leidrad he had not said enough on the renunciation of the devil. If the composer of Text 27 knew Leidrad, he might have taken Charlemagne's reprimand of Leidrad to heart.

El Escorial, Real Bibl. de S. Lor. L. III. 8 (Es1), a bishop's pastoral manual, contains Text 3, one of the four florilegia based on John the Deacon, and which was probably intended for a schoolroom. In the El Escorial L. III. 8 copy of Text 3, however, the *capitulum* from the Council of Laodicea on returning the Creed on Holy Thursday is lacking, an especially appropriate omission for a volume intended to serve as a bishop's pastoral guide.[8] Raymund Kottje has written that El Escorial L. III. 8 was a collection volume

---

[6]Eleanor Duckett creates the scene: "With great delight Amalarius entered his cathedral in this same year of 835. He remembered Leidrad, once archbishop here, and his work for the school of chant, a school now respected far and wide. Here was a wonderful opportunity, given by kindness of fortune, to put into practice his own corpus of chanted texts, his Antiphonary, and also to spread the teaching, the original thought, of his own *Liber officialis*. . . . He lost no time. Hardly had he appeared before his clergy as their father in God when he summoned them to meet in assembly—assistant bishops, archdeacons, priests, and minor ministers. Before them he held up both his works, and then he proceeded to lecture to them for three entire days upon the interpretation of the Mass and upon the system of chant. . . . Finally he arranged for the making of copies of his books." (*Carolingian Portraits: A Study in the Ninth Century*, Ann Arbor, 1962, p. 110.)

[7]See Chapter 1, note 9.

[8]See Chapter 5, pp. 76 f.

for pastoral care compiled at Senlis and very closely connected with Bishop Herpuin of Senlis (c. 840–870).[9]

Florence, Bibl. Med. Laurenz. Ash. 1923 (F2), a schoolbook written at Corbie at the very beginning of the ninth century, and St. Gall, Stiftsbibl. Cod. sang. 124 (S2), another schoolbook (monastic) written in the area of St.-Amand circa 804–820, contain Text 30 by Jesse of Amiens. Corbie and St.-Amand both lay in Jesse's diocese of Amiens (within the archdiocese of Rheims). The fact that two schoolbooks from these famed monastic centers contain Jesse's instruction, at least one compiled almost if not the very year Jesse wrote Text 30 to his priests, indicates cooperation between these monasteries with their schools and scriptoria and the bishop of Amiens. The large number of our volumes that were intended as schoolbooks was noted, the implication being that clerical educational reform was taken up in the schools with which bishops had close connections. The fact that a monk at Corbie would have included Jesse's instruction for diocesan priests, which includes a detailed description of a local variation of the Roman *ordo* of baptism, in a schoolbook, suggests that secular clergy were being trained at Corbie at Jesse's request, or that the scriptorium at Corbie was cooperating with Jesse in producing schoolbooks for the cathedral school at Amiens.

Laon, Bibl. mun. 288 (L), an instruction-reader for priests from eastern France ("Laon not certain"), contains Text 31, glosses on the prayers of baptism. Because the full text of the prayers are given, it is possible to identify some sacramentary books that have its same series of prayers. They include the Sacramentary of St. Martin of Tours; the Sacramentary of Senlis (written at Paris); the Sacramentary of St. Denis (written at St.-Amand); and perhaps a sacramentary represented by Brussels, Bibl. Roy. 11196–11197. The origin of Laon 288 in eastern France and perhaps Laon is interesting in that Laon was in the same archdiocese (of Rheims) as Senlis and St.-Amand. It seems that the compiler of Laon 288 chose Text 31 because it reflected the sacramentary in use in his area. Furthermore, inserted into Text 31 is Text 49, the brief, simple interrogation of a priest, but only its first part. Omitted is the part that describes the *pedilavium*, never a custom in northeastern France.

Munich, Clm 6325 (Mu3), from Freising, and Vienna, ÖNB 1370 (Vi6), from Mondsee, two instruction-readers for priests, contain, respectively, Text 35 and Text 34 (an abbreviated version of Text 35). These instructions, beginning with a long section, "De caticizandis rudibus," correspond to the needs of priests in a missionary area. Mondsee and Freising were in the diocese of Salzburg. Arno of Salzburg may have solicited the help of these scriptoria in producing instruction-readers for priests in the missionary area of Bavaria.[10]

---

[9]R. Kottje, "Zur Herkunft," pp. 623 f. See also Chapter 2, note 12.

[10]Or, on the possibility that Mondsee was preparing monk-priests for the parishes it acquired in the Avar district, see Chapter 2, note 33.

St. Paul im Lavanttal, Stiftsbibl. 5/1 (Sp1), a schoolbook from Reichenau, contains only the first nine lines of Text 7 followed by six other complete Texts. Text 7, which originated in Spain, probably traveled to the Reichenau area with works of Isidore. Reginbert, librarian at Reichenau, compiled St. Paul 5/1 with the help of a student.[11] The student copied Book II of Isidore's *Differentiarum* and began to copy Text 7 (which begins, "Dispositis nonnullis Differentiarum sententiis . . ."), but he stopped halfway down the page. On the next (recto) folio, in Reginbert's own hand, begins a collection of six baptismal instructions. One can envision Reginbert stopping the student and supplying baptismal instruction better suited to the clergy of northern Italy. At least two of the Texts Reginbert copied (Texts 1 and 6) were composed in the north-Italian area.

St. Paul 5/1 was intended as a schoolbook, but Reginbert's care to reject baptismal instruction that would have puzzled priests in northern Italy suggests that Reichenau was involved in the education of the secular clergy, perhaps at the request of the archbishop of Mainz, in whose far-flung jurisdiction Reichenau lay. Another of the Texts Reginbert included was Text 44, consisting of extracts from the *De institutione clericorum* of Hrabanus Maurus. Hrabanus wrote his work while he was instructor at the monastery school of Fulda, but for the education of the clergy, not monks. A copy of it was given to the archbishop of Mainz when he came to Fulda in 819.[12] By the time Hrabanus himself became archbishop of Mainz in 847, the *De institutione clericorum* was one of the most widespread manuals of instruction for the secular clergy.[13]

Munich, Clm 14410 (Mu8), probably a bishop's pastoral manual from northern Italy or Bavaria, contains Text 33 by Archbishop Maxentius of Aquileia. It was shown that Maxentius' response to Charlemagne did not succeed in muting distinctive features of the north-Italian rite.[14] This codex also contains Text 38, which it was shown describes an *ordo scrutiniorum* of some north-Italian bishop's city.[15]

Troyes, Bibl. mun. 804 (Tr1) is a bishop's reference work from the Loire area. It contains Text 16 by Theodulf of Orléans addressed to his Metropolitan, Magnus of Sens, and, immediately following Text 16, a reply to Magnus from another suffragan bishop of Sens. Both bishops include numerous

---

[11]Reginbert knew other Spanish texts at Reichenau: Karlsruhe, Bad. Landesbibl. Aug. XVIII, written in his own hand, contains a collection of creed material of largely Spanish origin according to K. Künstle, *Eine Bibliothek der Symbole* (Forschungen zur Christlichen Litteratur- und Dogmengeschichte 1), Mainz, 1900, pp. 3–5.

[12]See Chapter 2, p. 32.

[13]Cf. J. B. Mullinger, *The Schools of Charles the Great and the Restoration of Education in the Ninth Century*, London, 1877, pp. 142 f.

[14]Cf. Chapter 7, pp. 107–111.

[15]Cf. Chapter 6, pp. 84–87.

remarks reflecting local custom in their dioceses. The "Loire area" includes part of the archdiocese of Sens. Also, Theodulf was abbot of Fleury-sur-Loire.

There are also many examples on Table 1 of no obvious correlation between the place of origin or intended use of a codex and the baptismal Text(s) in it. The fact, nevertheless, that a correlation can be seen in some cases indicates that even where no correlation is obvious, the manuscript compiler probably had a very specific reason for selecting the Text(s) that he did. Even though baptismal instructions usually take up only a tiny proportion of the volumes, and even though the manuscript compilers intended their material as tools to teach Latin, increase vocabulary, and raise the level of scriptural knowledge, it is also possible to say that they chose their material with care, with a sensitivity to local rites of baptism and to the specific needs of the clergy of the dioceses in which they worked.

Because the contents of the Texts do correlate with the place of origin and intended purpose of the volumes in which they circulated, they are accurate evidence of what local parishes were teaching their clergy and how baptism was being celebrated.

This finding has two important consequences for Carolingian studies. One relates to the history of the liturgy. One of the results of this study has been to turn up further evidence for the diversity of the liturgy in the Carolingian period. Liturgical diversity has already been well attested.[16] The evidence rests on liturgical books themselves. More and more diverse ones, or fragments of them, have been discovered and dated to the ninth century. Differing liturgical books, however, are not necessarily the best evidence of widespread liturgical diversity, or popular liturgical diversity. It is one thing to do a systematic study of the extant liturgical books and conclude that there was diversity in liturgical practice because the books are different. One is still left wondering, in many cases, if these books were used outside of the single monastic community that owned them. When, however, such differences as the liturgical books hold are echoed in instructions for parish priests, that is, for those who were to teach the people, then one can truly be amazed at the amount of liturgical diversity. Our genre of literature is evidence of another kind than liturgical books that liturgical diversity was not confined within the walls of monastic or canonical communities, but characterized public worship in the Carolingian empire. The Carolingian baptismal instructions are in some ways better evidence of the real state of liturgical diversity than many sacramentaries or missals intended for cloister use. We have shown that even though the baptismal instructions were not meant to be carried to the font, they are quasi-liturgical expositions mirroring locally familiar rites of baptism.

---

[16]Cf. R. E. Sullivan's comments and bibliography in "The Carolingian Age," pp. 293 f. and F. Paxton, *Christianizing Death*, pp. 93 f. and 156 f.

Second, the conclusion of this chapter has consequences for other genres of literature in Carolingian collection volumes. Works that in other books may have been used differently, in our volumes were copied for pedagogical purposes. Capitularies, canon-law collections, penitentials, *ordines*, sermons, paschal calendars, and *interrogationes sacerdotales* were copied together to make textbooks from which clerics could learn—learn to read, learn how to conduct their offices, learn how to teach and explain the sacraments and the faith, and learn how to live an exemplary moral life. If it is repeatedly the case, for example, that the penitentials are in volumes primarily intended to sharpen clerics' general knowledge rather than for actual use in a confessional, must the theory be re-examined that a large number of variant penitentials continued actually to be applied in the ninth century despite their discouragement in ecclesiastical reform legislation? Non-Roman penitentials continued to be copied, but is this because they were excellent mind-broadening tools, allowing consideration for so many more diverse crimes, conditions, circumstances and penances than Halitgar's Penitential, rather than because a priest actually found them necessary when hearing confessions?

Or again, there are sixteen different diocesan capitularies in our manuscripts. Because of their didactic intent in their written form, however, there need be little relation between the specific crimes, abuses, or negligences discussed in the capitularies and the real-life problems in the area where and when the capitularies were copied. In other words, it might be false to assume that the cleric who received Theodulf's Capitulary went into taverns and kept a mistress and charged a fee for baptisms, rather than that he was meant to read the capitulary simply to be educated generally on what was demanded of the clerical life, with no assumption that the capitulary was actually accusing him of any of these crimes. Can capitularies copied in our volumes have any value for assessing the real degree of problems, such as clerical illiteracy or immorality, or the real extent of reform in specific areas?

Or again, thirteen of our manuscripts contain twelve different canon-law collections. The following list shows the name of the collection beside the intended destination of its manuscript:

Al1	instruction-reader for priests	Collectio Vetus Gallica
Al3	instruction-reader for priests	Dacheriana
Co1	bishop's reference work	Dionysio-Hadriana
Fr	bishop's reference work	Dionysio-Hadriana
Lg	instruction-reader for priests	"Collection of Laon (Cambrai)"
Mi	bishop's pastoral manual	"Collection in Two Books;" and a Collection based on the Quadripartitus
Mu9	instruction-reader for priests	Collectio Sangermanensis excerpt and the "Collection in 53 Titles"

No	bishop's reference work	Dionysio-Hadriana and Concordance of Canons of Cresconius
P3	instruction-reader for priests	An interpretation of the D-H
P10	instruction-reader for priests	Dacheriana
P15	bishop's reference work?	Collectio Sangermanensis
V3	schoolbook	A version of the D-H (excerpt)
Vi6	instruction-reader for priests	Collectio Hibernensis fragment

It is tempting to conclude from this that the Dionysio-Hadriana, supposedly imposed everywhere by Charlemagne as the official body of canon law, in fact had limited success, especially in the kinds of books intended for the parish priest. Maybe so, but do the various other canonical collections really witness that a large diversity in church law regulated Carolingian society? Might the copying of diverse canon law collections be due to their pedagogical value? They may have been copied to teach priests anything from the definition of a canon-law collection to the Nicene Creed. Heavily supplemented with moral, doctrinal, and liturgical instruction, the canonical collections may sometimes even have been copied for this instruction alone. The *Collectio Sangermanensis*, for example, contains Texts 20, 21, and 22, and other chapters besides those on baptism are pure pedagogy. All twenty-one Books of the *Collectio* begin with an Isidorian-type instruction in question-response form. Some Books contain three or more entirely didactic chapters. The first nine chapters of Book XII on the church consist of question-response instruction on the meaning and origin of terms such as "basilica," "synagogue," "altar," "picture," and "font." The *Collectio Sangermanensis* was used, if not originally compiled, as a vehicle for improving the educational level of the clergy.

Despite such cautionary queries, there is always the possibility that the specific text was selected for study because it was the text used and preferred, or answering the real needs, in the area where it was copied. That this, in fact, was the case is supported by the evidence of the Carolingian baptismal instructions. In this chapter the correlation of the Texts and their manuscripts was shown. Presumably the care of the manuscript compilers was not confined to baptismal instructions, but they also selected the penitential, capitulary, and canon-law collection according to what was in use locally.

What has been found regarding the Carolingian Reform in the light of the Carolingian baptismal instructions and their manuscripts may now be summarized.

PART III: CONCLUSION

10

The Carolingian Reform in Light of the Baptismal Instructions and Their Manuscripts

What the Carolingian baptismal instructions in their manuscript context illustrate is that the principal aim of the Carolingian Reform in the eyes of the Carolingians was the education of the clergy. It is for this reason that the Carolingian Reform is famous in the history of Western Europe. If it had been concerned only with imposing a set of norms for the life of the church, of standardizing the liturgy, of establishing a single monastic rule, the Carolingian Reform could be said to have failed. What it succeeded in doing was reviving a love of learning and a widespread view that literacy and knowledge were necessary and praiseworthy. A sense was achieved that every cleric, down to the rural parish priest, should have a basic education. This meant that a system of education was recognized as necessary that reached the grass-roots level of society. Schools had to be accessible throughout the dioceses, books had to become available to parish priests.

The manuscripts examined in this study show, for one, the extent to which the implementation of the Reform was an archdiocesan and diocesan undertaking. The four kinds of books in which the baptismal instructions circulated point to the crucial role of individual bishops and the resources available to them in their own dioceses.

First, the books we have labeled instruction-readers for priests show almost no standardization in their collection of works. An exception proves the point: Out of eighteen different instruction-readers, nine contain the mass exposition, "Dominus vobiscum. Salutat sacerdos. . . ." (Four of these nine also contain a different mass exposition not found in any other instruction-reader.) Dom Wilmart believes "Dominus vobiscum" was composed in response to Charlemagne's legislation of 789 and 802 demanding that priests know and understand the Roman mass prayers. (The text explains the Canon of the mass of the Gregorian Sacramentary word for word in the form of a gloss.) Wilmart says it was composed for priests of little intelligence.[1]

If "Dominus vobiscum" was so widely copied, why did there not come to be one official commentary on the Nicene Creed or one standard exposition on the clerical grades or the Lord's Prayer? Because "Dominus vobiscum" did

---

[1]See vol. II, pp. 126 f. under "Expositions on the Mass."

achieve this status,[2] it seems other works could have. There are only a few cases, however, in which two instruction-readers have one or more same works in common, and sometimes this may be because they originated in the same area. Albi, Bibl. mun. 43 (Al3), for example, probably from southern France, has the Lyonese *Collectio Dacheriana* also found in Paris, BN lat. 10741 (P10), from the area of Lyons.[3]

The instruction-readers make it evident that there was no standard set of works that every priest received. These books were products of the Carolingian dioceses, containing what was felt suitable for clergy in a specific location. In some areas priests were expected to be able to understand and benefit from such works as the *De essentia divinitatis* (a commentary on the Trinity), whereas priests in other areas were given simpler works to read. Perhaps the popularity of the mass commentary "Dominus vobiscum" was due only to its eminent suitability for priests of little intelligence.

Second, the manuscripts we have labeled schoolbooks also indicate the nature of the Reform as an individual diocesan and archdiocesan undertaking, in the following way. Some of the baptismal instructions consistently appear in the same kind of book. For example, all three ninth-century manuscripts of Jesse's Text 30 are schoolbooks; all five ninth-century manuscripts of Text 49 are instruction-readers; both of the two ninth-century manuscripts of Text 5 are schoolbooks; and the same is true of the two ninth-century manuscripts of Text 10, the two of Text 14, and the two of Text 19. Another interesting feature, however, is that of the twenty-four baptismal instructions that have more than one ninth-century witness, fifteen or perhaps sixteen[4] are in both a schoolbook and an instruction-reader. In seven cases the schoolbook and the instruction-reader containing the same Text are from the relatively same area and time period. Text 23, for example, is in an instruction-reader from the area of Lyons (Paris, BN lat. 10741, s. $IX^{3/3}$) and in a monastic schoolbook from the area of Lyons (Angers, Bibl. mun. 277, s. $IX^{3/4}$). Text 1 is in an instruction-reader from Switzerland (St. Gall, Stiftsbibl. Cod. sang. 40, s. $IX^{2/3 \text{ and } 3/3}$) and in a schoolbook from Reichenau (St. Paul im Lavanttal, Stiftsbibl. 5/1, s. $IX^{3/3}$). Text 16 is in an instruction-reader from northeastern France (Leningrad, RNB Q. V. I no. 34, s. $IX^{ex.}$), and in an episcopal schoolbook from northeastern France or Lotharingia (Munich, Clm 14532, s. $IX^{ex.}$). Texts 42 and 60 are in an instruction-reader from Mainz (Sélestat, Bibl. mun. 132, s. $IX^{ca. med.}$) and in a monastic schoolbook from Lorsch (in the diocese of Mainz)

---

[2] It is not because of the attribution of "Dominus vobiscum" to a famous authority. R. Reynolds has found only three manuscripts in which it bears an attribution. Cf. "Pseudonymous Liturgica in Early Medieval Canon Law Collections" in *Fälschungen im Mittelalter*, Teil II, Hannover, 1988, p. 71.

[3] For which works are found more than once among our sixty-five ninth-century manuscripts, see vol. II, "A Topical Survey," pp. 126–148.

[4] P51 is not determinable. See Table 1.

(Vat. Pal. lat. 485, s. IX, ca. 860–875). It was pointed out that Amalarius, when Archbishop of Lyons, could have had his instruction (Text 23) copied both for the students at his cathedral school and the diocesan priests whom he would examine. Jesse, as Bishop of Amiens, addressed his instruction to his clergy, but it was immediately being read in schoolbooks in monastic schools in his diocese. A schoolbook from Reichenau (Sp1) contains Text 44, a variation of the description of baptism in the *De institutione clericorum* of Hrabanus Maurus. Reichenau, it was said, belonged to the far-flung archdiocese of Mainz where Hrabanus was archbishop from 847–856. Reichenau was perhaps serving its archdiocese's needs by training secular clergy.

Instruction-readers and schoolbooks from the same diocese or archdiocese could share the same Texts because of a close cooperation in the education of the secular clergy between famous monastic centers with schools and scriptoria (Lorsch, Reichenau, Corbie) and the bishop of the diocese in which they lay. Schoolbooks with the same Texts as instruction-readers from the same area could indicate that the bishop was employing the monastic schools in his diocese to help prepare secular clergy.

Some abbots were not loathe to have "externi" in their schools. One of Benedict of Aniane's reforms at the Council of Aachen of 816 was to forbid this.[5] Theodulf's first diocesan capitulary states that if any priest wants to send his nephew or any relative to school, he should send him to one of the monasteries over which Theodulf had control in his diocese.[6] It is surprising that even our tiny sampling of schoolbooks is able to reflect this cooperation of the bishop or archbishop and the monastic schools in his jurisdiction.

It is possible that some monastic schools, independently of a bishop's request, wished to give monks in their schools priestly training, in order that they might serve as monk-priests in parishes owned by the monastery.[7] One example of the interest of a famous abbey school in training secular clergy is the appearance, in a monastic schoolbook from Lorsch dated 860–875 (V3), of Text 14A, a diocesan statute of Bishop "Waltcaud" to parish priests briefly outlining a "quolibet tempore" *ordo* of baptism. Lorsch did, in fact, have a serious interest in training secular clergy in the latter ninth century. Its land holdings, over entire villages, continued to grow throughout the ninth century, and parish priests were needed to serve the people on these lands.[8]

Nevertheless, the phenomenon of baptismal instructions for the secular clergy being copied into books intended for use in a monastic schoolroom cannot be due entirely to monasteries wishing to staff parish churches they

---

[5]"Ut schola in monasterio non habeatur nisi eorum qui oblati sunt." (*MGH LL.* I, p. 202.) See Chapter 2, p. 33.

[6]Quoted in Chapter 2, note 36.

[7]See Chapter 2, pp. 33 f.

[8]See Chapter 2, p. 30.

owned. Theodulf's capitulary, just referred to, makes this clear. Nor can it be argued that all Carolingian baptismal instructions penetrated monastic schoolbooks by happenstance—for example, because they were part of a collection of form letters, or because of their author. Seven schoolbooks contain only one Carolingian baptismal instruction, Text 9, associated with Alcuin.[9] The interest is in works of Alcuin, not baptismal instruction *per se*. But all of these seven are episcopal, not monastic, schoolbooks. Four out of five of the monastic schoolbooks on Table 1 contain more than one baptismal instruction. In these cases providing baptismal instruction is definitely part of the purpose of the monastic schoolbook.

In sum, bishops were having an important impact on the curriculum of studies in some monastic schools. When Text 30 by Bishop Jesse of Amiens is found in three monastic schoolbooks (two from his own diocese), it suggests that monastic schoolbooks were absorbing the interests and goals of the bishops implementing the reforms.

As to the third kind of book, bishop's pastoral manuals, these contain items that would be necessary for a bishop in order to issue pastoral legislation and instruction for his clergy. The selection of diocesan statutes, sermons, canon-law collections, and much else in them reflect the priorities and concerns of a specific bishop for his clergy—what he felt they needed to hear, and the level of learning he expected of them. Bishops' manuals contain texts that did not always originate in the bishop's own area. There was extensive borrowing and copying among bishops across Carolingian Europe. It is also a fact, however, that a large amount of re-editing of texts happened with this copying.[10] It shows that bishops were putting these texts to use locally, not only collecting them for private interest or historic preservation.

Finally, the books we have labeled bishops' reference works also point to the crucial role of individual bishops in clerical educational reform. Troyes, Bibl. mun. 804 (Tr1), for example, with its nine expositions on the Creed, four on the Lord's Prayer, two on the mass, etc., probably served as a resource volume for those commissioned to compile instruction-readers for priests. Paris, BN lat. 12444 (P15), consisting only of the *Collectio Sangermanensis*, may have served as a "reference room only" exemplar from which parts of the *Collectio* might be copied into an instruction-reader. Munich, Clm 14508 (Mu9), for example, contains a long extract from it.

In sum, the evidence of the four kinds of books signifies that the Carolingian Reform must be studied, and its success evaluated, on the basis of individual dioceses. Individual bishops are the key to understanding the success of the Reform, as they were able to implement it in their particular sees. The Carolingian Reform had encouragement from the royal palace, but

---

[9]Vi3, Mu4, P18, Tr2, Mu12, Mu13, V5.
[10]See, for example, P. Brommer's *app. crit.* in his *Capitula episcoporum*.

in its actual implementation, it may only be possible to speak accurately of the "Sens' Reform under Magnus," or the "Lyonese Reform under Leidrad."

It has actually been possible to reconstruct all the stages of the implementation of the Reform in one archdiocese. A group of related Texts (Texts 14–19) show how Charlemagne depended on the hierarchical structure within each archdiocese to disseminate his reforms. First, ca. 812 Charlemagne issued a questionnaire to his archbishops (Text 14) asking how they and their suffragan bishops were teaching their priests and the people about baptism. Magnus, Archbishop of Sens, distributed the questionnaire to his suffragan bishops, soliciting their answers. The bishops responded (Theodulf's Text 16) to Magnus, and Magnus then composed his response to Charlemagne (Text 15) from their answers. Following the five regional reform councils of 813[11] Magnus made the councils' decisions known to his diocesan bishops. The bishops in turn called local synods and reiterated the decisions. One major concern was clerics' knowledge of baptism, and a suffragan bishop of Magnus dutifully taught his priests on this topic (Text 18). The clerics in the villages belonging to Sens, told to become knowledgeable on baptism, were given instructions in question-response form (Texts 17 and 19). Texts 17, 18, and 19 were reworked, but they were originally suffragans' responses to Magnus, as is clear by the passages in them identical to Magnus' "composite" response to Charlemagne.[12]

The procedure which can be documented for Sens probably occurred in other archdioceses as well. (Other of our anonymous Texts have passages identical to passages in archbishops' responses.) The example of Sens is importance evidence of Charlemagne's reliance on the archdiocesan unit as the means by which imperial reforms issued from Aachen actually were carried into effect at the grass-roots level of society. The case of Sens corroborates the evidence that the Reform relied ultimately on local bishops commissioning assistants to compile appropriate instructions for their own priests.

A further step that is needed is to fit the evidence of the four kinds of books into the scene of parish churches and rural clergy in the ninth century. The instruction-readers and the schoolbooks give particular cause for reflection. The bishops faced a two-pronged challenge regarding the education of the clergy. One was providing remedial education for those who were already ordained and serving in parishes. Another was providing adequate training for future parish priests. If the Reform had equal impact everywhere at the same time, instruction-readers should have disappeared after the first generation of clergy subjected to the Reform. But they do not disappear. Of our eighteen volumes labeled as instruction-readers, only five date to the first third of the ninth century, and three even date to the end of the century. Either

---

[11]See Chapter 6, p. 88.
[12]See S. A. Keefe, "An Unknown Response," pp. 54–64.

the Reform began belatedly in many areas, or the system of lay ownership of churches continued to feed unfit clergy into the priesthood. Our Texts raise crucial questions about the true feasibility of the educational reform of the clergy if an equal effort was not made to eliminate lay involvment in clerical appointments.

According to Imbart de la Tour, Charlemagne strove to create an equalibrium between the powers of the lay lords and the rights of the church in the parishes. It was the patronage system over centuries that was responsible for an uneducated clergy. Lay lords possessed land and built private churches, appointing one of their serfs or tenants as priest. The local bishop ordained him, presumably without much fuss, because he would only be serving a private church. It often happened, however, that these private churches on the lord's land became parish churches as the need for them arose with an increasing population. Two images of parish churches must be kept in mind. One was the public church, founded in a public *vicus*, or market town, autonomous, not in a domain, endowed by the inhabitants of the town, in the care of an archpriest or priest elected by the inhabitants, and who was under the jurisdiction of a bishop. The other was the private church, founded in a *villa* (domain or personal property) of a lay lord or bishop or monastery, over which the owner of the land had certain rights. He could sell it, pledge it, or give it as a benefice.[13]

Imbart de la Tour says that by the Carolingian period many of these churches were baptismal churches and were already, or were becoming, parish churches. They might have been owned by a community or a single person, by a monastery or by the king, by a bishop or a layman.[14] In the eighth century the right of lords to possess private churches, that is, rural churches, whether oratories or larger churches, including baptismal churches, was well established.[15] The lord had the right of presentation and bishops could not refuse his candidate without reason.[16] Ninth-century legislation did insist that the assent of the diocesan bishop was necessary before priests could be installed in a private church, and these priests must receive from him their letters of ordination, appear at his synods, and render account of their ministry to him.[17] Many lay lords, however, apparently ignored the rights of the bishop. Agobard of Lyons (d. 840) attacked the abuses of the proprietary church system and saw in it the abasement of the priestly office.[18] His objections, however, did not prevail, and after 840 the institution of privately owned parish churches under the government of a bishop, long recognized in

[13]Imbart de la Tour, *Les paroisses rurales*, p. 173.

[14]*Ibid.*, p. 200.

[15]*Ibid.*, p. 215.

[16]*Ibid.*, p. 217.

[17]*Ibid.*, p. 218.

[18]*Ibid.*, pp. 221 f.

law and custom, was maintained.[19] Archbishop Hincmar of Rheims (845–852) recognized the right of lords to choose the priests of churches belonging to them and to present them for ordination. The bishop could refuse to ordain those chosen by simony, or who were "illiterate or incapable."[20] The words give one suspicion that the presentation of ignorant, unfit candidates was still a reality in the mid-ninth century.

The instruction-readers, which date from the very beginning to the very end of the ninth century, correspond with Imbart de la Tour's negative assessment of the progress of free churches. In fact, it was the seignorial system and proprietary churches that prevailed, and with them, as historians of the much later Gregorian Reform know, the ignorance of many clergymen.[21] The specific scriptoria where our instruction-readers were copied is known in only four cases (Me, 820-40, at Fulda; Mu3, s. $IX^{1/2}$, at Freising; Sch, s. $IX^{med.}$, at Mainz; and Vi6, s. $IX^{1/4-2/4}$, at Mondsee). These centers at these times, then, perhaps designated a scribe or group of scribes to help their bishop produce remedial instructions for parish priests in their area. Only identification of more manuscripts as instruction-readers will allow a clearer picture of the ongoing struggle to educate priests outside of schoolrooms.

As for the schoolbooks, they show that at least a percentage of priests were being trained. It is here, in the schoolbooks, that the second prong of the Reform is seen, the effort to establish a system of schooling for all those aiming for an ecclesiastical career. The *monastic* schoolbooks are the very evidence historians need to verify the close cooperation of bishops and the monasteries in their dioceses in the schooling of the secular clergy. Famous Carolingian masters, their manuscripts, and their schools have received or are receiving attention, but literary elites and famed centers of learning have been kept separate from the education of the secular clergy. A whole aspect of the greatest of the Carolingian schools and scriptoria, their service to the needs of their dioceses, has received no thorough investigation. Yet our "schoolbooks" indicate that this aspect may be their most significant lasting legacy. The enduring effect of the Carolingian Reform was an upgrading of expectations for the secular clergy, and centers like Corbie, Laon, Tours, Fulda, Reichenau, and St. Gall, because of their resources, played a critical role in that accomplishment.

What really was the condition of the church in the Carolingian countryside? Who was the priest, what was his education, and how well did he perform his ministry? In short, how did the people of the ninth century experience the church? Even if a full answer can never be had, one can come much closer to the reality of the Carolingian Reform by identifying, from

---

[19]*Ibid.*, p. 223.

[20]*Ibid.*, p. 224.

[21](I do not wish to exclude the problem of unfit bishops, as well.)

diocese to diocese, the four kinds of books intended to serve the education of parish priests.

The manuscript evidence for the local nature of the Carolingian Reform is corroborated by the baptismal tracts themselves. First, by comparing their sequences of topics with popular models of baptismal instruction, it was seen why there were so many different baptismal instructions. Composers altered their models to conform their instructions better to local rites of baptism. It was actually possible to identify some specific sacramentary books or *ordines* that they followed. They could not have done this, and would have had no reason to do so, unless the Reform was a locally implemented effort involving composers who *knew* the recipients of their instructions and the rite of baptism familiar to them.

Out of this there is more to be learned about the nature of the Carolingian Reform. If it was a local, rather than an Aachen-implemented enterprise, that fact eliminates conformity, or standardization, as one of the main objectives of the Reform.

It is often said that one of the accomplishments of the Carolingian Reform was the standardization of the liturgy according to the Roman rite.[22] Regarding baptism, some, but by no means all, of the Carolingian reform legislation suggests that it should be celebrated according to the Roman *ordo*. The wording is less than specific: "Let them observe *catholic* baptism;" "Let them baptize according to the Roman *custom*;" "It ought to be done according to the *ordo* of the Roman *tradition*." In one document, the mass and the divine office should be celebrated according to the Roman *ordo*, but this is not said about the *baptisterium*.[23]

Those composers who believed they described the Roman *ordo* of baptism had differences from one another. Compared to OR XI and the Reginensis it was found that Jesse (Text 30) copied the rubrics of an *ordo* of baptism that was not OR XI, as liturgical historians have said. Amalarius (Text 23) stated three times, "just as we find written in the Roman *ordo*." Whatever *ordo* he had under his eyes was not OR XI. Theodulf (Text 16) also differed from OR XI. He gave the impression that the scrutinies were somewhat archaic, but a custom the church tried to preserve during Lent. Unlike Amalarius, he never referred to the "Roman *ordo*." Leidrad (Text 25) did not use the term "Roman," and was almost apologetic about the word "scrutiny."

These Texts show that the Roman *ordo* of baptism was not a single text, such as OR XI or the Reginensis, which had acquired some sort of official recognition. The "Roman *ordo* of baptism" meant a type of rite, of which there could be numerous legitimate variations. The single most important feature of this type for some Carolingians seems to have been the observation of the

---

[22]See Chapter 7, note 1.
[23]See Chapter 4, note 1.

scrutinies during Lent in preparation for Easter baptism. For Amalarius, to celebrate baptism "according to the Roman *ordo*" was to celebrate the scrutinies. Gallicanized manuscripts (Andrieu's "B" collection) of OR XI continue only through the scrutinies. Even in the Carolingian reform legislation one *capitulum* states that to baptize according to the Roman *ordo* means to observe the scrutinies.[24] To the extent that bishops like Jesse and Amalarius tried to observe the *ordo* of scrutinies, the evidence points to the lack of any single Roman *ordo* to which they all conformed. OR XI must now be seen as just one among many variations of the Roman *ordo*, perhaps far less significant than OR L, or variations closer to OR L than to OR XI.[25]

Also, Charlemagne's baptismal questionnaire is no evidence of his desire to impose a single celebration of baptism. His questions do not follow the outline of Text 9 (associated with Alcuin) or any liturgical *ordo*. He never uses the word "Roman," and he omits the topics of triple immersion and a second post-baptismal chrismation (episcopal confirmation), two chief features of the Roman rite in contrast to the Spanish custom of a single immersion and the Old Gallican and north-Italian custom of only one post-baptismal chrismation. Charlemagne simply asks the archbishops to describe the ceremonies "per ordinem." Baptism must be done "ordinabiliter" he decrees after the five councils of 813. Charlemagne must have recognized that there was necessary variety within what could be described as the Roman rite of baptism. It ranged from Alcuin's *ordo* for a *paganus* done in a single session (Text 9), to OR XI in a cathedral setting with seven scrutinies during the weeks of Lent and a bishop and many lesser grades of clerics in attendance, to the supplement of the Gregorian Sacramentary by Benedict of Aniane, which provides essentially an *ordo ad infirmum* from an eighth-century-type Gelasian sacramentary. In sum, there is no evidence that Charlemagne held up one *ordo* he wished to see celebrated throughout his realm. Considering what Carolingians themselves, from Alcuin to Archbishop Maxentius of Aquileia, considered was "the Roman *ordo*" of baptism, the term must be understood very broadly.

Certainly one of the most remarkable finds of this study is the lack of standardization of the celebration of baptism across Carolingian Europe throughout the entire ninth century. Even Text 49 with its blatantly non-Roman *pedilavium* is in a manuscript written in the last quarter of the ninth century and in one dated s. IX–X. Text 49 circulated in southern France where the *pedilavium* was indigenous. Other Texts also describe features of baptism of different geographical areas. Text 7 describes a Spanish *ordo* of baptism. It is

---

[24]*Ibid.*

[25]The prevalence of features of OR L is interesting because OR L was the hybridization that finally did become, although not until the twelfth century, the generally recognized Roman *ordo* of baptism. Features of OR L are found in Texts 30, 23, 26, 32, 50, 8.1, 38, 41, 52, 51, 15, 55, 12, 47, and 11.

the first evidence for the use of the "quolibet tempore" *ordo* of the Spanish *Liber Ordinum* in the Carolingian period, attesting to the continued practice in Spain of simple priests confirming. Maxentius of Aquileia (Text 33) emphatically tells Charlemagne that he follows the Roman tradition, yet his description reveals a number of north-Italian peculiarities. It may reflect the same *ordo* that served Lupus of Aquileia (mid-ninth century). Text 38 describes almost perfectly the north-Italian *ordo* of scrutinies published by Lambot. It is the first evidence of the use of the *ordo* in the ninth century.

Other Texts describe a shortened *ordo* of baptism without the Roman series of scrutinies. Their composers were describing a "quolibet tempore" type of rite. Their features often come close to rites for a *paganus* or *infirmum* in the liturgical books.[26] All these Texts differ from one another because of the specific liturgical books their composers had in mind. It was sometimes possible to point to a specific sacramentary containing one or more of their features. Often it was not possible to find in any known sacramentary a feature described in one of the Texts.[27] The Texts are evidence of a great number of liturgical books now lost. They dispel the idea of any one paradigmatic *ordo* recognized across the empire and the idea of a Carolingian fixation for one correct rite. They attest to the ongoing variety of the celebration of baptism.

Rather than Romanity, conformity, or standardization, the Carolingian Reform was about the education of the clergy. This was emphatically brought out by examining a second aspect of the contents of the tracts, their explanations for each topic or ceremony of baptism. Three features of the Texts as a whole are one, the diverse nature of the explanations, two, the pedagogical aim of their composers to the point that the general education of the cleric often received priority over his knowledge of baptism, and three, the prodigious editing of their sources.

The diverse nature of the explanations showed that the baptismal literature as a whole was not intended to promote uniformity of thought and teaching on baptism. The Carolingian clergy were not taught to be concerned with rigid sets of prayers, precise formulas, or exact moments or amounts of spiritual grace in these instructions. There was a great variety of teaching on the purpose or effect of the individual ceremonies. Some Texts were copied more frequently than others perhaps (according to the extant manuscripts),

---

[26]See pp. 156–58.

[27]Still not found in liturgical books are: in Text 30, the invocation of the Holy Spirit with the touching of the nose; in Text 23, the prayer for the touching of the ears, its formula "Contradic Satanae?," its version of the three-fold profession of faith, and its use of the word "linteo" for the headcloth; a liturgical formula renouncing pomps before works, as suggested in Text 54.1; in Text 50, an episcopal insufflation of the neophytes when being confirmed, and a rubric directing the neophytes to wear their head covering (not their albs) for seven days; and in Text 47, an invocation of the Trinity with the prebaptismal anointing of the breast (if this is what Hrabanus Maurus meant).

but the Reform was not programmatic as to texts of baptismal instruction. There was no one officially promulgated baptismal commentary, and composers freely adapted whatever models and sources they chose.

The overriding pedagogical aim of the Texts showed that the composers understood this genre of literature had a special function. Baptismal instructions were a vehicle for educating the clergy in the broadest sense. Whether it was to be introduced to Prudentius' *Psychomachia* or to learn one meaning of "inminere," the desire to make the cleric literate or expand his general knowledge was the chief concern of the composers. The glosses that devolved into mere vocabulary lists showed the true challenge of the Reform in some areas. One interesting aspect of the overwhelmingly pedagogical nature of the Texts is that, because there was no pressure on the composers to offer a standard theology of baptism, the Texts provide opportunity to study the variety of thought on baptism in the ninth century. Theology interweaves the Texts unsystematically and often accidentally, but in the course of an exposition on the Creed, or exegesis of a scriptural passage, differences in the understanding of baptism are revealed.

The third feature of the Texts as a whole, the prodigious editing of their sources, showed that in the eyes of the Carolingians the education of the clergy could not succeed with standardized texts of instruction. The Reform was not and could not have been implemented from Aachen by the commissioning of "official" commentaries. The true character of the Reform lies in the differences between the Texts and any one model. The goal of the Reform was to make effective pastors. A great variety of instruction was the key to reaching every local priest, the success of whose education would directly effect his parishioners. The composers were not content simply to reiterate Isidore, Alcuin, and Ambrose, but selected their sources and edited them with care. The image of the editor of the "Paris version" of Text 43 halting in his task to include some specific items taken from another Text in front of him, Text 31, is impressive when it is known that those items are only found in Gallicanized sacramentaries. It showed that the redactors, working in their local scriptoria, knew the particular clergy for whom they were writing.

The next study demanded by this present one is the study of personal relationships to track down, as far as possible, the specific people— bishops, abbots, scribes, and who they knew. More can be done to link people and places, beginning with the essential work of Bernhard Bischoff on Carolingian scriptoria. Our Texts prove that it is a worthwhile endeavor. Perhaps the most valuable result of this study is the encouragement the Texts give to pursuing work on individual libraries, scriptoria, schools, and human careers.[28]

---

[28]For example, what was the effect on exchanges of texts due to the fact that Hildebald, Archbishop of Cologne (787–819) from 802 was simultaneously Abbot of Mondsee? (See G. Schmitz, "The Capitulary Legislation of Louis the Pious" in *Charlemagne's Heir*, ed. P. Godman and R. Collins, Oxford, 1990, p. 427, note 15.)

A final task of Part II was to show the correlation between the Texts and the area of circulation and intended recipient of their manuscripts. This has importance for other genres of literature. Presumably the care of the manuscript compilers was not confined to baptismal instructions, but they also selected the penitential, capitulary, and canon law collection according to what was in use locally. If this is correct, then the Reform era must indeed be re-defined. The diversity in our manuscripts in their selection of material, if it reflects the actual ongoing application of this material, is astonishing in the face of what traditionally has been thought to characterize the Carolingian Reform. Consider also that this diversity of Creeds, canon-law collections, penitentials, etc., has been found in a study of only sixty-five manuscripts. Even this sampling, however, reflects an extraordinary *lack* of standardization across Carolingian Europe throughout the time when it has been thought that standardization was the achievement of the reformers.

What has been seen through the window of the Carolingian baptismal instructions is that the Carolingian Reform accepted a wide diversity of liturgical books familiar to the clergy of individual areas; that its priority was clerical education, not conformity to a single rite; that it was implemented by individual bishops and therefore unequally, depending on local initiative and resources; and that it must be evaluated on the basis of individual archdioceses and dioceses where the archbishop and bishop had the help of the monastic schools and scriptoria to accomplish their goals. The formation of society which the Carolingians, lay and church magnates, envisioned could only be brought about through education. There was oral instruction through regional councils, diocesan synods, *missi*, sermons, visitations and examinations, but the written text was considered vital. The Carolingians recognized that they could not bring a people together in a lasting bond merely through legislation. In the literary productivity of the Carolingians was the motivation, always, to build the City of God. The Carolingian endeavor, nonetheless, allowed for many rooms in the Father's mansion.

The Carolingian baptismal instructions have shown the Carolingians busily engaged in their building program. There is still more to be learned in the further study of more Carolingian manuscripts. It has been seen that even didactic, quasi-liturgical texts have value for historians. In exploring the minutiae of an individual manuscript or the sequence of topics of a single baptismal instruction, our minds have been joined with a Carolingian engaged in the task of the Carolingian Reform. These pedagogical volumes and obscure, didactic baptismal tracts are the core of the historian's work. One cannot neglect any documents that are profoundly "living" in their reworking. These tell of resistance and cooperation, borrowing and independence, conformity and non-conformity, local sensitivities, preferences, needs—in short, everything between a common goal and its local implementation.

If importance is measured in terms of lasting impact, as John Contreni said of the School of Laon, the importance of the Carolingian Reform is attested by the numerous tenth-, eleventh-, and twelfth-century manuscripts containing Carolingian baptismal instructions. Much work remains to be done in assessing the long-range effects of the Carolingian Reform. A study is needed of our post ninth-century manuscripts. The evidence for the success of the Carolingian Reform and its historical value for the Christianization of Europe will lie in the continuing work of students and scholars on the living evidence of the manuscripts.

A Note on Baptismal Rites for an Infirmus or a Paganus

If the average rural pastor of the countryside obviously could not follow the rubrics of the paschal *ordo* of baptism in the sacramentaries, what *ordo* did he follow? After the paschal *ordo* of baptism in the Gelasian and most of the Gelasian of the eighth-century-type sacramentaries, there were additional *ordines* of baptism for a pagan (*paganus*) and for a sick person (*infirmus*). These covered situations where access to a cathedral city and a bishop, or attendance at a series of formal scrutinies, was impossible (the usual situation in rural areas and certainly in missionary regions)[1] and when there was danger of death and the baptism had to be done quickly.

It was seen that the early sixth-century description of adult baptism by John the Deacon of Rome mirrored some of the features of the *ordo* for a pagan in the Gelasian Sacramentary (Reginensis).[2] Perhaps, then, even in the early sixth century the *ordo* for a pagan was commonly used in the local parish churches around Rome for baptisms on one of many Sundays. Certainly by the late eighth century the *ordo* for a pagan had become the rite of baptism most people experienced.

Text 9, the description of baptism used if not composed by Alcuin, which was by far the most widely copied of all of our Texts, begins: "Primo *paganus* catechumenus fit." The *ordo* of baptism in the Sacramentary of St. Martin of Tours, which it was seen may have influenced Text 9, is a condensed version of a paschal *ordo*; that is, all of the ceremonies are done at a single session. (All of the rubrics referring to the separate meetings of the catechumens are absent, except for a remnant referring to Holy Saturday when the "Nec te latet" exorcism should be said.) In other words, the *ordo* is unlike the major Easter Vigil *ordo* in the eighth-century-type Gelasian sacramentaries, but like their *ordo ad infirmum*.

It was seen that chapters XXV–XXX of the *De institutione clericorum* I of Hraba- nus Maurus were also a popular model for Carolingian baptismal in-

---

[1] It was conceded that to observe the scrutiny would not be possible everywhere. The *Concordia Episcoporum* of 813, Cap. I, stated: "De scrutinio faciendo decrevimus, ut in episcopiis et ubi conventus est populi et clerici et possibilitas permittit, ibi celebretur." (*MGH Conc.* 2, p. 297).

[2] See Chapter 5, pp. 71–73.

structions (Texts 44–48). Like Text 9, these chapters describe an *ordo* for a pagan. Just as, however, Text 9 was copied to instruct priests who would be baptizing healthy infants (in Charlemagne's questionnaire [Text 14] and in Text 5, "Primo paganus" is changed to "Primo infans"), so the *ordo* for a pagan in Hrabanus Maurus and in the liturgical books, it may be assumed, was the usual rite of baptism. It suited the situation of the vast majority of the Frankish population which did not have ready access to a cathedral city and a bishop.

Other evidence that *ordines* for a pagan and for a sick person were used regularly by at least the ninth century to baptize healthy infants includes the following. Whereas the Reginensis *ordo* for the baptism of a sick catechumen[3] begins with a rubric stating that the priest says over the catechumen the prayers "written above," in the Gellone Sacramentary (an eighth-century-type Gelasian sacramentary) this *ordo* for an *infirmum* catechumen has been elaborated in far greater detail. Unlike the Reginensis, it presents in full all the prayer texts so that the reader does not have to "refer to the above *ordo*," and it provides explicit rubrics for the initial signing, giving of salt, and series of exorcisms said over the male, then female, catechumens.[4] The fact that the Gellone greatly expanded and clarified the Reginensis' *ordo* for an *infirmum* so that it could be used alone, without any reference to the Paschal *ordo*, suggests the increased use of the *ordo ad infirmum*.

Not only is the *ordo ad infirmum* almost never absent from the liturgical books, but there is evidence that it also circulated independently from the major Paschal *ordo*. Brussels, Bibl. Roy. 10127–10144 (s. VIII[ex], northeast France, or perhaps the area of Liège), is a codex its editors call a vade mecum of a rural priest who needed to have at hand all the texts indispensable to exercise his priestly ministry."[5] It contains canon law, penitential, and computational texts, various liturgical *ordines*, the Gregorian antiphonary, an *ordo* for a sick catechumen taken from an eighth-century-type Gelasian sacramentary,[6] various benedictions, and eleven Masses for great feast days and their seasons. The volume was carefully planned,[7] and the *ordo* for a sick person is the only *ordo* for baptism provided for the user of this book. Another "liber sacramentorum excarpsus" of Paris, BN lat. 2296 (St.-Amand, s. IX with some

---

[3]"Item ad succurrendum infirmum caticuminum," Mohlberg, *Sacramentarium Gelasianum*, pp. 94–97, nn. 602–16.

[4]Cf. A. Dumas, *Liber Sacramentorum Gellonensis: Textus*, pp. 339–47, nn. 2344–2386. At nr. 2366 an alternative to all the scrutiny prayers if the candidate is in extreme danger of dying is given (suggesting the *ordo* was used in less-than-emergency situations).

[5]C. Coebergh and P. de Puniet, "Liber Sacramentorum Excar[p]sus," p. 79.

[6]Ff. 115–121v., "Incipit ordo ad infirmum caticuminum faciendum." *Ibid.*, pp. 98–105.

[7]See the description by M. Andrieu, *Les Ordines* I, pp. 91–96.

s. X additions) provides for baptism only the prayers and rubrics for the cases of a sick, possessed, and pagan catechumen (Reginensis nn. 594-616).[8]

The *ordo* of baptism of the *Hadrianum Supplementum* that Benedict of Aniane supplied was taken from an eighth-century-type Gelasian sacramentary very close to Gellone's *ordo ad infirmum*.[9] Since the *Hadrianum* Charlemagne received from Rome did not provide a complete *ordo* of baptism, the *ordo* Benedict provided in the *Supplementum* must be considered the type most useful for baptisms in Frankish lands.

OR XXXI provides a rite "for those who come to baptism without the scrutiny," very similar to an *ordo ad infirmum*. It consists of a prayer for the making of a catechumen, giving of salt, delivery of the Creed, "Nec te latet" exorcism, "effeta," anointing of breast and back with the renunciation, and baptism.[10] Features of OR XXXI are found in some of our Texts, indicating the popular use of this *ordo* or one very similar to it.

The "quolibet tempore" *ordo* in the Spanish *Liber Ordinum* for simple priests comes before the major Paschal *ordo*. In fact, the Paschal *ordo* breaks off after two prayers and refers the user back to the "quolibet tempore" *ordo* for the remainder of the rite. J. D. C. Fisher comments that the Paschal *ordo* "was no longer regarded as the norm."[11]

By "norm" Fisher meant usual, not "normative" in the sense of "canonical," because the canonical norm for the celebration of baptism remained Easter and Pentecost, not "anytime." Recognition, nevertheless, of the taking over of "quolibet tempore" baptism is the legislation regarding Easter and Pentecost. The Constitution of Arno of Salzburg states that "*public* baptism" should take place on the two canonical days of Easter and Pentecost.[12] The word "publicum" indicates that baptism took place at other times, but that one should insure that there were some candidates at Easter and Pentecost so that some baptisms will always take place on these two liturgical feasts.

---

[8]Edited by C. Coebergh and P. de Puniet, "Liber Sacramentorum Romane Ecclesiae Ordine Excarpsus (Cod. Parisiensis, B.N. lat. 2296, s. IX–X)" in *CCCM* XLVII, 1977, pp. 159–64.

[9]9See A. Dumas, *Liber Sacramentorum Gellonensis: Introductio, Tabulae, et Indices*, p. xxxii (under "Le Pontifical, sections 345–512." Section 345 is the *ordo ad infirmum*).

[10]See M. Andrieu, *Les Ordines* III, pp. 504 f., nn. 99–107.

[11]J. D. C. Fisher, *Christian Initiation*, p. 99.

[12]See Chapter 4, note 1.

TABLE 1

Manuscript		Date & Place of Origin[1]	Approx. Size[2]
Al1	Albi, BM 38 bis	IX ca. med., prob. so. Fr.	235 x 167mm.
Al2	Albi, BM 42	IX ex., prob. so. Fr.	230 x 160mm.
Al3	Albi, BM 43	IX 4/4, prob. so. Fr.	197 x 163mm.
An	Angers, BM 277	IX 3/4, region of Lyons	170 x 115mm.
Au	Autun, BM 184	IX 2/3, west. Fr.	230 x 150mm.
B2	Bamberg, SB Lit. 131	IX 4/4 or IX/X, so. Ger.	198 x 129mm.
Co1	Cologne, DB CXV	IX 1/3, Cologne	355 x 240mm.[3]
Es1	Escorial, RB L. III. 8	860–70, Senlis	216 x 152mm.
F2	Florence, BML Ash. 1923	IX in., Corbie	160 x 100mm.
Fr	Freiburg, UB 8	IX 2/2, east. Fr.	305 x 265mm.
L	Laon, BM 288	IX 1/3, east. Fr. (Laon?)	210 x 140mm.
Lg	Leningrad, RNB Q.V.I.34	prob. IX ex., no.-east. Fr.	190 x 152mm.
Me	Merseburg, BD Hs. 136	820–40, Fulda	262 x 165mm.
Mi	Milan, BA A 46 inf.	IX 4/4, Rheims	292 x 248mm.
Mi2	Milan, BA L 28 sup.	IX 3/3, prob. no. It.	170 x 125mm.
Mc1	Montecassino, ADB 323	IX 2/2, cent. It.	250 x 180mm.
Mp1	Montpellier, BI Méd. 310	IX 2/3, west. Fr.	215 x 157mm.
Mp2	Montpellier, BI Méd. 387	IX 2/3, Fr.	137 x 116mm.
Mo	Monza, BC e-14/127	IX-X, no. It.	270 x 170mm.
Mu2	Munich, Clm 6324	IX 3–4/4, prob. Freising area	219 x 145mm.
Mu3	Munich, Clm 6325	IX 1/3, Freising	205 x 130mm.
Mu4	Munich, Clm 6407	ca. 800, Verona	240 x 145mm.
Mu7	Munich, Clm 13581	IX, west. Fr. mostly	285 x 192mm.
Mu8	Munich, Clm 14410	IX 1/3, no. It. or Bavaria	258 x 173mm.
Mu9	Munich, Clm 14508	IX 3/4, no.-east. Fr.	226 x 154mm.
Mu10	Munich, Clm 14532	IX ex., no.-east. Fr. or Lothar.	220 x 175mm.
Mu12	Munich, Clm 14727	817–847, Regensburg	194 x 133mm.
Mu13	Munich, Clm 14760	817–47, Regensburg	165 x 110mm.
Na	Naples, BN VI G 37	IX	195 x 170mm.
No	Novara, BC XXX	IX 2/2, prob. no. It.	457 x 305mm.
Or	Orléans, BM 116	IX 3/4, west. Fr.	190 x 138mm.
P3	Paris, BN lat. 1008	IX-X, Fr.	146 x 100mm.
P	Paris, BN lat. 1012	IX 1/3	194 x 129mm.
P5	Paris, BN lat. 1248	IX med., no. Fr.	162 x 107mm.
P51	Paris, BN lat. 1687	IX ex.	290 x 255mm.

approx. lines to a page[3a]	proposed intended destination of the ms[4a]	Texts contained in the ms
28	reader	49
26	schoolbk. (episc.)	16
20	reader	49, 26
20–21	schoolbk. (monast.)	15A, 27, 23
26	schoolbk.	11, 9, 10?
22	schoolbk. (episc.)	8, 1, 6, 5, 9
27 (double cols.)	bp.'s ref. work	9
24	bp.'s pastoral manual	3
24	schoolbk.	30
34 (double cols.)	bp.'s ref. work	23
20	reader	31, 49
23	reader	16
26	reader	43
33	bp.'s pastoral manual	60
18 (4–6 wds./line)	reader	3, 9
35	schoolbk. (monast.)	11, 12
21	bp.'s ref. work?	16, 43
15 (6 wds./line)	reader	39, 40
24	schoolbk.	19, 2, 39, 40
18	reader	35
18	reader	35
23	schoolbk.	9
27	schoolbk.	23
25	bp.'s pastoral manual	33, 37, 38
27	reader	20, 43, 3
20	schoolbk. (episc.)	16
17	schoolbk.	9
19	schoolbk.	9
?	schoolbk.	16
36	bp.'s ref. work	2
27–28, 18 (5 wds./line)	reader	28, 54, 13
20, 22	reader	49, 25
21 (4–6 wds./line)	reader	9, 51
18	reader	2, 11, 12
42	(not determinable)	15a

TABLE 1 *(cont.)*

Manuscript		Date & Place of Origin	Approx. Size
P61	Paris, BN lat. 2328	prob. IX 2/4, so. Fr.	288 x 175mm.
P10	Paris, BN lat. 10741	IX 3/3, area of Lyons	245 x 192mm.[4]
P12	Paris, BN lat. 12262	IX ca. med., Fr.	260 x 185mm.[4]
P13	Paris, BN lat. 12279	IX ex., no. Fr?	310 x 250mm.[4]
P15	Paris, BN lat. 12444	VIII–IX, prob. Fleury	295 x 190mm.[4]
P18	Paris, BN lat. 13373	IX in., Corbie	232 x 141mm.
S1	St. Gall, SB 40	IX 2&3/3, Switz.	295 x 213mm.[5]
S2	St. Gall, SB 124	804–20, area of St. Amand	252 x 152mm.[5]
S3	St. Gall, SB 222	IX 2/3 or 3/3, prob. east Fr.	178 x 125mm.[5]
S4	St. Gall, SB 235	ca. 800, St. Gall	275 x 175mm.
S5	St. Gall, SB 446	IX 3/3, St. Gall	250 x 185mm.
Sp1	St. Paul im Lavanttal 5/1	IX 2/3, Reichenau	220 x 115mm.
Sch	Sélestat, BM 132	IX med., Mainz	169 x 101mm.
Tr1	Troyes, BM 804	IX 2/4 or 2/3, Loire	250 x 200mm.
Tr2	Troyes, BM 1528	IX in., prob. Orléans	184 x 122mm.[6]
V2	Vatican Pal. lat. 278	IX 2/3 or med., no.-east. Fr.	203 x 178mm.
V3	Vatican Pal. lat. 485	860–875, Lorsch	268 x 178mm.
V4	Vatican Reg. lat. 69	IX 2/2, Tours?	185 x 120mm.
V5	Vatican Reg. lat. 272	IX ca. med., Rheims	255 x 180mm.
V6	Vatican Reg. lat. 284	IX 2/3, no. half of Fr.	260 x 184mm.
V7	Vatican Reg. lat. 571	IX 1/4, perh. Paris area	279 x 236mm.
Vd	Verdun, BM 27	IX 2/3, east. Fr.	136 x 100mm.
Vi3	Vienna, ÖNB 795	ca. 798, vicinity Salzburg	228 x 140mm.
Vi5	Vienna, ÖNB 823	IX 2/2, west. Ger. or east. Fr.	180 x 130mm.[7]
Vi6	Vienna, ÖNB 1370	IX 1–2/4, Mondsee	180 x 130mm.
W3	Wolfenbüttel, Helm. 532	ca. 820, prob. Salzburg	235 x 150mm.
Z1	Zürich, ZB Car. C. 102	IX 3/3, Switz.-no. Italy	279 x 187mm.
Z2	Zürich, ZB Rh. 95	IX/X, prob. so.-west. Ger.	197 x 135mm.

1. The date and place of origin refer to that part of the manuscript in which the baptismal instruction is contained in cases where the manuscript combines originally separate parts. P51 is one inserted folio.

2. The length is given first, then the width, and refers to the folio size, not to the cover size.

3. This information kindly supplied by the librarian of the Diöcesan Bibliothek, Cologne.

3a. Lines per page refer to the page(s) containing the baptismal instructions.

4a. "Reader" refers to an instruction-reader for priests. "Bp.'s ref. work" refers to a bishop's reference work or library volume (cf. Chapter Two).

approx. lines to a page	proposed intended destination of the ms.	Texts contained in the ms.
34 (double cols.)	schoolbk.	54.1
25, 26	reader	15A, 27, 23
33	bp.'s ref. work	25
47 (dense)	schoolbk. (episc.)	16
29	bp.'s ref. work?	20, 21, 22
24	schoolbk.	9
30, 23, 33	reader	49, 8.1, 1, 9
28, 26	schoolbk. (monast.)	30
19–21	bp.'s pastoral manual	9
36	schoolbk.	1,6
27	schoolbk. (episc.)	60, 9, 9, 23
28	schoolbk.	7, 14, 1, 6, 5, 9, 44
18 (4 wds./line)	reader	42, 60
39	bp.'s ref. work	16, 17
21 (5–6 wds./line)	schoolbk.	9
25	bp.'s pastoral manual?	16
29	schoolbk. (monast.)	30, 42, 60, 14A
26, 25	schoolbk.	3, 10
27	schoolbk.	9
22	bp.'s ref. work	16, 23
27	(not determinable)	18
16 (4–6 wds./line)	schoolbk.	19, 24
30	schoolbk.	9
24	schoolbk.	1, 9, 55
18	reader	34
25	schoolbk. (episc.)	39
22, 24	schoolbk.	2, 14, 23
19	schoolbk. (monast.)	3, 43

4. This information kindly supplied by Jacqueline Sclafer, Conservateur en chef, Cabinet des manuscrits, Bibliothèque nationale, Paris.

5. This information kindly supplied by Prof. Dr. P. Ochsenbein, Stiftsbibliothekar, Stiftsbibliothek St. Gallen.

6. This information kindly supplied by Mde. A. Plassard, Conservateur, Bibliothèque municipale de Troyes.

7. This information kindly supplied by Dr. Eva Irblich, Deputy-Keeper, Handschriften- und Inkunabelsammlung, Österreichische Nationalbibliothek, Vienna.

CHART A1

Ordo XI

Third Week in Lent
> Wednesday: enrollment:
>> sign of cross;
>> prayers "for the making of a catechumen" with
>> imposition of hand(s);
>> salt.
>
>> 1st scrutiny: 6 different exorcism
>> prayers with genuflections & signings.
>
> Saturday: 2nd scrutiny (same as 1st).

Fourth Week in Lent
> Optional Day: 3rd scrutiny (same as 1st) and
>> the *aurium apertio:*
>
>>> *traditio evangeliorum*
>>> *traditio symboli* (in Greek & Latin)
>>> *traditio orationis dominicae.*

Fifth Week in Lent
> Optional Days: 4th & 5th scrutinies (same as 1st).

Sixth Week in Lent
> Optional Day: 6th scrutiny (same as 1st).
>
> Holy Saturday: 7th scrutiny: "Ordo qualiter
> catecizantur:"
>
>> sign of cross on forehead;
>> exorcism prayer, "Nec te latet, Satanas...";
>> nose & ears touched with spittle & "effeta" said;
>> *redditio symboli* (chanting of Creed by priest
>> while circulating and imposing a hand over the
>> infants.
>
>> blessing of the font;
>> baptism;
>
>> anointing on top of head with chrism by priest;
>> reception of *stola, casula, crismale,* & ten
>> coins from bishop;
>> vesting in white robes;
>> episcopal confirmation with chrism on forehead;
>> first reception of the Eucharist at the Vigil Mass.

CHART A2

Reginensis Gelasian Sacramentary

Third Week in Lent
Optional day: enrollment:
prayers "for the making of a catechumen;"
salt;
exorcism prayers of the 1st scrutiny;

Aurium apertio:

traditio evangeliorum;
traditio symboli (Nicene, in Greek & Latin);
traditio orationis dominicae.

Holy Saturday
exorcism, `Nec te latet, Satanas . . ." with
imposition of hand;
nose & ears touched with spittle, & 'effeta'
said;
breast and back (between shoulder blades)
touched with oil and
renunciation of Satan, his works, and pomps;
return of the Creed (*redditio symboli*) (priest says while
imposing a hand);

blessing of the font;
3-fold interrogation of faith;
baptism with 3 immersions;

anointing of top of head with chrism by
priest;
confirmation by the bishop with imposition
of hand and chrism on forehead;
(Easter Vigil Mass continues).

CHART A3

Ordo Romanus L

Third Week in Lent
    Wednesday: enrollment:
            renunciation of Satan, his works & pomps;
            3-fold profession of faith;
            exsufflation 3 times in face with exorcism,
            "Exi, inmunde spiritus . . .";
            prayers "for the making of a catechumen"
            with sign of cross by priest on forehead
            and imposition of hand;
            salt.

            1st scrutiny: 6 exorcism prayers with
            genuflections and signings, as in *Ordo* XI.

    Saturday: 2nd scrutiny.

Fourth Week in Lent
    Optional Day: 3rd scrutiny and *aurium apertio:*
            traditio evangeliorum;
            traditio symboli (Nicene Creed in Greek & Latin);
            traditio orationis dominicae.

Fifth Week in Lent
    Optional Days: 4th and 5th scrutinies.

Sixth Week in Lent
    Optional Day: 6th scrutiny.

    Holy Saturday: *Ordo* for catechizing:
            redditio of the Lord's Prayer & Creed;
            exorcism prayer, "Nec te latet . . .";
            nose and ears touched with spittle & "Effeta" said;
            breast and back anointed with oil in the form of a
            cross while renouncing Satan, his works & pomps;
            priest recites Creed over infants.
            blessing of font;
            (in Gallican mss: renunciation of Satan, his
            works and pomps);
            3-fold profession of faith;
            baptism;

            anointing top of head with chrism by priest;
            cappam placed on head (or in some mss reception
            of *stola, chrismale,* and ten coins from bishop);
            vesting in white robes;
            episcopal confirmation with imposition of a hand
            and chrism on forehead;
            first reception of Eucharist at Easter Vigil Mass.

CHART A4

PRG CVII

Ordo for baptizing infants:
  renunciation of Satan, his works and pomps;
  3-fold profession of faith;
  exsufflation 3 times in face with words of
  exorcism;
  prayers "for the making of a catechumen"
  with sign of cross on forehead and imposition of hand by priest;
  salt;
  exorcism prayers (same 6 as in *Ordo* XI).

(*Ordo* for catechizing continues immediately:)
  exorcism, "Nec te latet, Satanas . . .";
  nose and ears touched with spittle and "Effeta"
  said;
  prayer, "Deus, inmortale presidium . . .";
  breast and back (between shoulder blades)
  anointed with oil in form of a cross while
  renouncing Satan, his works and pomps.

  blessing of font;
  baptism;

  anointing with chrism on top of head by priest;
  white *mitra* placed on head with, "Accipe
  vestem sanctam candidam . . .";
  vesting in white robes;
  first reception of the Eucharist at Mass;
  episcopal confirmation with imposition of hand
  and chrism on forehead, if a bishop is present.

CHART B1

TEXT 30 (Jesse)

De caticumino (including an *ordo* of the catechumen with 6 scrutinies and an *aurium apertio*).

De competente

De sale

[Quod] exorcizatur sive catecizatur infans.

De exsufflatione.

[De caticizare.]*

[De naribus et auribus tanguntur de saliva.]

De unctione pectoris et scapularum ex oleo.

De abrenuntiatione et pompa diaboli

[De albis vestibus]

[De novo nomine 'Christianus.']

De symbolo.

De trina mersione.

De unctione capitis.

De velamine capitis.

De confirmatione episcopi.

De confirmatione corporis et sanguinis Christi.

*Wherever brackets appear on the Charts, I have supplied a topic heading from words in the Text for topics not given a title in the Text.

CHART B2

TEXT 23 (Amalarius)

De catecumino.
De scrutinio.
Cur in fronte faciamus signum.
Quali signo signemos nos.
Cur septies scrutinium agatur.
De genuflexione.
De oratione dominica.
De symbolo [apostolorum].
De exorcizatione.
De exsufflatione.
De sale.
Quando fiat novissimum scrutinium.
De tactu narium et aurium [de sputo].
De unctione scapulae et pectoris [et de oleo].
De abrenuntiatione [et operibus et pompis].
[Reddunt patrini et matrinae orationem
dominicam et symbolum].

Recapitulatio (the topics are recapitulated in this order:
        [catecuminus;
        sal;
        adiuratio diaboli et signum crucis;
        genuflexio;
        traditio orationis dominicae;
        traditio symboli;
        nares et aures per sputum;
        pectus et scapulae;
        confessio fidei;
        baptismum].)

De unctione capitis.
De tegumento capitis [*linteo*].
De indumento [albis vestimentis].
De confirmatione corporis et sanguine domini.
De parvulis non intellegentibus et tamen fidem habentibus.
De parvulis non loquentibus.
De nostra credulitate.
[De qualiter nos et nostri suffraganei doceremus populum.]

CHART B3

TEXT 16 (Theodulf)

I.   Cur infans cathecuminus efficitur.*
II.   Quid sit cathecuminus.
III.   Cur exsufflatur.
IIII.   Cur exorcizatur.
V.   Cur cathecuminus accepit salem.
VI.   Quae sit interpretatio symboli secundum latinos.
VII.   De credulitate quomodo credendum sit in deum patrem omnipotentem et in iesum christum filium eius natum et passum et in spiritum sanctum, sanctam ecclesiam catholicam, et cetera quae secuntur in eodem symbolo.
          [De parvuli necdum ratione utentes.]
VIII.   De scrutinio.
VIIII.   Cur tanguntur de sputo nares et aures.
X.   Cur pectus oleo unguitur vel scapulae signantur vel liniuntur.
XI.   Quid sit abrenuntiatio.
XII.   De abrenuntiatione satane et omnibus operibus eius atque pompis vel quae opera diaboli et pompae.
          [Confessio fidei.]
XIII.   De sacramento baptismi.
XIIII.   Cur albis induitur vestibus.
XV.   Cur sacro chrismate caput perunguitur.
XVI.   Cur mistico tegitur velamine.
XVII.   Cur ab episcopo confirmatur per manus impositionem accipiat septiformis gratiae spiritum.
XVIII.   Cur corpore et sanguine dominico confirmetur.

* These titles, preceded by Roman numerals, are listed at the beginning of the treatise in most manuscripts.

CHART B4

TEXT 25 (Leidrad)

Cap. I.   De significationibus sacri baptismatis.
           [De caticumino.]
           [De exorcismo et exsufflatione.]
           [De sale.]
           [De competentibus.]
           [De scrutinio.]
Cap. II.   De tactu narium et aurium.
           [De unguntur in pectore et inter scapulas oleo.]
Cap. III. De abrenuntiatione satanae vel quae sint opera eius et pompae.
Cap. IIII. De symbolo.
Cap. V.   De credulitate.
Cap. VI.   De baptismo [et de trina mersione.]
Cap. VII. De sacra unctione [de chrismate presbiteri, impositione manus
           (manuum) confirmatione episcopi].
Cap. VIII. De vestimentis albis.
Cap. VIIII. De corpore dominico et sanguine.
Cap. X.   De infantibus vel his qui pro se respondere non possunt.
Cap. XI.   De disciplina vivendi et docendi.

CHART B5

TEXT 26

Qualiter catizizas infantem.

[De caticumino.]

[De exorcismo aut exsufflatione.]

[De conpetentibus.]

[De sale.]

[De tactu aurium.]

[De tactu narium.]

[De unctione pectus et inter scapulas.]

[De abrenuntiatione.]

[De operibus diaboli.]

[De pompis diaboli.]

[De baptismo (de fonte; aqua; renunciatione; professione fidei; trina mersione).]

[De unctione crismatis.]

[De vestibus albis.]

[De eucharistia.]

[De inpositione manum (*lege* manuum?).]

[De baptismo.]

[De differentia baptism[at]is et chrismate.]

CHART C1

John the Deacon

[De catecumenis.]
[De abrenuntiatione.]
[De catechesis per benedictionem imponentis manum.]
[De exsufflatione.]
[De exorcismo.]
[De salis acceptione.]
[frequens inpositio manus et tertio benedictio conditoris.]
[De symboli traditione.]
[De competentibus vel electis.]
[De scrutiniis.]
[De tactu aurium cum oleo.]
[De tactu narium cum oleo.]
[De pectoris unctione.]
[De nudis pedibus.]
[De trina mersione.]

([De albis vestibus.]) (mentioned 2ce)
[De unctione chrismatis.]
[De linteolo vel mystico velamine.]
[De albis vestibus.]
[De communicatione corporis et sanguinis.]

[De confessione parvulorum.]

CHART C2

Text 1

I.   De baptismi praecepto in evangelio.
II.   De interpretatione baptismi.
III.   De sacramento baptismi vel quod sit in verbo et aqua.
IIII.   De catechumenis et exorcismis.
V.   De sufflatione et exsufflatione.
VI.   De salis acceptione.
VII.   De competentibus.
VIII.   De scrutinio.
VIIII.   De cathacesis vel symboli traditione.
X.   De tactu cum sputo.
XI.   De tactu aurium.
XII.   De tactu naris.
XIII.   De unctione pectoris et scapulae.
XIIII.   De abrenuntiatione.
XV.   Utum pueri per se confessionem faciant.
XVI.   De trina mersione.
XVII.   De unctione chrismatis.
XVIII.   De linteolo.
XVIIII.   De albis vestibus.
XX.   De communicatione corporis Christi.
XXI.   De impositione manus pontificis.
XXII.   De pedum nuditate.

CHART C3

Text 2

De catecumenis.

De abrenuntiatione.

De opere diaboli.

De pompa.

De exsufflatione et exorcismo.

De salis acceptione.

De symbolo.

De eo quod neoffitorum aures sancto oleo a sacerdotibus liniantur.

De tactu narium.

De pectoris unctione.

De baptismo.

De trina mersione.

De oppressione diaboli in baptismate peccatique interfectione.

De albis vestibus.

De chrismatis unctione.

De mistico velamine.

De communicatione corporis et sanguinis domini.

De institutione sacrificii panis et calicis atque de praeceptis in ea non inmutandis.

De sacramento panis et calicis.

De eo quod panis corpus est et vinum sanguis uterque unitas ecclesiae.

De aquae et vini commixtionis significatione.

De inpositione manus pontificis.

CHART C4

Text 3

[I.   De tribus gradibus.]
II.   [De catecuminis.]
III.   De abrenuntiatione.
IIII.   De abrenuntiatione vel confessione parvulorum.
V.   De catacessi.
VI.   De exsufflatione et exorcismo.
VII.   De salis acceptione.

I.   De competentibus.
II.   De symbolo tradendo.
III.   De scrutinio.
IIII.   De tactu aurium [oleo].
V.   De tactu naris.
VI.   De pectoris unctione.
VII.   De pedum nuditate.
VIII.   De reddendo symbolo.

I.   De baptismo.
II.   De baptismatis praecepto evangelico.
III.   De lavacro aquae in verbo.
IIII.   De trina mersione.
V.   De opressione diaboli in baptismate peccatique interfectione.
VI.   De imitanda morte Christi in baptismate.
VII.   De resurrectione Christi imitatione.
VIII.   De unctione chrismate.
VIIII.   De linteolo.
X.   De albis vestibus.
XI.   De commutatione (communicatione) corporis Christi.
XII.   De inpositione manus pontificis.

I.   De institutione sacrificii panis et calicis atque de praeceptis in ea non
      inmutandis.
II.   De sacramento panis et calicis.
III.   De eo quod panis corpus est et vinum sanguis utraque unita ecclesiae.
IIII.   De aquae et vini commixtionis significatione.
V.   De communicatione corporis et sanguinis domini.

I.   De penitentibus.

CHART C5

Text 4

De catecuminis.

De exsufflatione.

De exorcismus (*sic*).

De salis acceptione.

De conpetentibus.

De symbolo.

De scrutinio.

De tactu aurium [oleo].

De tactu narium.

De pectoris unctione.

Signantur et scapulae . . .

De abrenuntiatione.

Quod parvuli per se abrenuntiare non possunt.

De baptismo.

Cur alio profitetur parvuli baptismum.

De tribus generibus baptismi.

Cur non nisi sacerdotibus liceat baptizare.

De trina mersione.

De albis vestibus.

De crismatis unctione.

De communicatione corporis et sanguinis domini.

De sacramento panis et calicis.

De impositione manus episcopi.

CHART D1

Text 9

caticuminus et renuntiatio

exsufflatio

exorcismus

sal

traditio symboli

scrutinia

nares

pectus

scapulae

trina mersio

alba vestimenta

caput, mysticum velamen

corpus et sanguis domini

impositio manus a summo sacerdote

CHART D2

Text 38

caticuminus

exorcismus

sal

competentes

caticizare

scrutinia

exsufflatio

traditio symboli

pectus

nares

scapulae

abrenuntiatio

interrogatio fidei ("iterum")

trina mersio

alba vestimenta

caput, mysticum velamen

corpus et sanguis domini

impositio manus a summo sacerdote

CHART E1

Text 14 (Charlemagne's Questionnaire)

caticuminus

scrutinium

symbolum

credulitas

abrenuntiatio

opera diaboli

pompae diaboli

insufflatio (exsufflatio)

exorcismus

sal

nares tanguntur

pectus unguatur

scapulae signentur

pectus et scapulae liniantur

alba vestimenta

caput perunguitur crismate

mysticum velamen

corpus et sanguis dominicus

CHART E2

Text 15 (Magnus of Sens)

baptismum et trina dimersio*

catechumenus

scrutinium

symbolum

qualiter credere in Deum patrem

abrenuntiatio et operibus et pompis

insufflantur

exorcismus

salem

tanguntur aures et nares de sputo et dicitur "effeta"

pectus unguitur

scapulae signantur

signatur iterum in pectoris et scapulae unctione

candidis induuntur vestimentis

sacro chrismate caput perunguitur

mystico velamine teguntur

manus impositio

corpore et sanguine domini communicantur

*Text 15 does not have titles. I use words from the Text to identify each of the topics.

CHART E3

Text 17

Cur . . . prius caticuminus efficitur

De scrutinio

De symbolo

De credulitate

De abrenuntiatione

[De operibus diaboli]

[De pompis diaboli]

De insufflatione

[De exorcismo]

Quod caticuminus accipere deceat (*sic*) salem

Nares et pectus et scapula signentur

De albis vestibus

[De sacro chrisma caput unguatur]

[De corpore et sanguine Christi]

[De trina mersione et invisibilem animam mundare quomodo potest]

CHART E4

Text 14A

qualiter presbiter scit vel intellegit*

caticuminus

exsufflatio

exorcismus

sal

nares tanguntur

pectus unguitur

scapulae signentur

pectus et scapulae liniantur

abrenuntiatio

opera

pompae

credulitas

alba vestimenta

caput perunguitur

mysticum velamen

corpus et sanguis domini

*The words are taken from Text 14A's series of questions.

CHART E5

Text 34

De caticizandis rudibus.

De catecuminis vel quid sit caticuminus.

De scrutinio.

De abrenuntiatione.

[De operibus diaboli.]

[De fide qualiter intellegere debeat.]

De simbolo.

Cur caticuminus exsufflatus (*sic*).

Cur exorcizatur.

Cur accipit caticuminus sal.

De tactu narium et aurium.

Cur pectus unguatur oleo.

Cur scapulae signentur.

Cur pectus et scapulae liniatur (*sic*).

De baptismo [et parvulis et trina mersione].

Cur albis induitur vestimentis.

[De capite chrismate et mystico velamine.]

Cur corpore et sanguine dominico confirmatur.

De constitutione confirmationis.

[De] ut se quisque custodiet post baptisma.

CHART E6

Text 35

De caticizandis rudibus.

[De caticuminis.]

De scrutinio.

De abrenuntiatione.

[De operibus diaboli.]

[De fide qualiter intellegere debeat.]

De symbolo.

Cur caticuminus exsufflatur.

Cur caticuminus accipit sal.

De tactu narium et aurium.

[De unctione pectoris et scapularum.]

De baptismo [et parvulis et trina mersione].

Cur albis induitur vestimentis.

[De capite chrismate et mystico velamine.]

Cur corpore et sanguine dominico confirmatur.

De confirmatione.

[De] ut se quisque custodiet post baptisma.

CHART F1

Hrabanus Maurus (De institutione clericorum, I. xxv–xxx)

XXV.   De baptismatis sacramento
XXVI.   De catechumenis:
           [De competentibus]
           [De parvulis nec renuntiare nec credere possunt].
XXVII.   De catechizandi ordine:
           abrenuntiatio diabolo, operibus et pompis;
           ostenditur ei symbolum et exquiritur si credat in [symbolum];
           exsufflatur;
           signatur in fronte et corde;
           dicuntur orationes ut fiat catechumenus;
           datur ei sal;
           iterum exorcizatur diabolus;
           tanguntur nares et aures cum saliva et dicitur "epheta";
           deinde benedictione sacerdotali munitur;
           ungetur pectus de oleo sanctificato cum invocatione Trinitatis;
           ungetur inter scapulas de eodem oleo.
XXVIII.   De tinctione baptismi et unctione chrismatis:
           consecratus fons;
           trina submersione baptizatur;
           signatur in cerebro a presbytero cum chrismate;
XXIX.   De indumento baptizati et eucharistia:
           traditur Christiano vestis candida;
           tegitur post sacram unctionem caput eius mystico velamine;
           corpore et sanguine dominico confirmatur.
XXX.   De impositione manus episcopalis:
           impositionem manus a summa sacerdote;
           signatur cum chrismate per pontificem in fronte.

CHART F2

Text 45

(margin:) De baptismatis sacramento.

(margin:) De cathecuminis:
    Interrogatur primum si abrenuntiare diabolo et omnibus pompis eius;
    exsufflatur;
    signatur signo crucis;
    datur sal;
    in auribus et naribus tangit de saliva et dicitur "effeta";
    pectus perungitur;
    inter scapulas oleo eodem perungitur;
    parvulorum salus adimpletur per fidem patrinorum.

(margin:) De trina mersione baptismatis et unctione crismate:
    trina mersione baptismatis purificatur;
    crisma super caput.

(margin:) De indumento baptizati et eucharistia:
    traditur Christiano vestis candida;
    candidum etiam velamen suscipit in capite;
    corpore et sanguine confirmatur.

(margin:) De inpositione manus episcopalis et crismatis sacramento:
    signatur in fronte per pontificem.

CHART F3

Text 47

De cathecuminis et baptismi ordine:

Cathecuminus quare dicitur;

Competentes quare dicitur;

Cur signatur;

abrenuntiat diabolo, operibus, pompis;

Cur ei ostenditur symbolum;

Cur exsufflatur;

Cur datur eis sal;

Cur tanguntur ei nares et aures de sputo et dicitur "effeta";

Cur munitur sacerdotali benedictione;

Quare unguetur pectus de oleo;

Cur unguetur inter scapulas;

Baptisma quid est;

Quid est quod baptizandis primo abrenuntiatio proponitur;

[opera et pompae diaboli];

Cur ponuntur cerei in fontem;

Cur insufflatur ipsa aqua;

Pro quid sub trina mersione baptizantur;

A presbytero signatur in cerebro cur;

Quare albis induuntur vestibus;

Cur velamine mystico tegitur caput;

Cur corpore et sanguine dominico . . . confirmatur;

Cur signatur . . . per pontificem in fronte.

CHART G1

Text 7

[De quattuor gradibus baptismi:
    catechumen accipit symbolum et inunguitur;
    competens nomen dederit;
    fidelis sacramento signatur baptismatis;
    christianus crismate ungitur.]

[De catechumeno.]

[De exorcismo? (extirpetur quicquid viciosum est)]

[De sale.]

[De baptismo in nomine trinitatis.]

[De semel aut tertio mersione.]

[De renunciatione diabolo; pompis; conversationibus.]

[De sacramento crismatis.]

[De impositione manus sacerdotis et invocatione spiritus sancti.]

[De corpore et sanguine domini.]

[De pascha et pentecosten, aqua fontis, peccato post baptismum, quattuor sacramentis, baptismo non iterando, et hereticis.]

CHART G2

Text 33 (Maxentius)

[De catecumino sive competente.]

[De sale.]

[De exorcismo et exsufflatione.]

[De scrutinio.]

[De pectore et scapulis? (eiectum exinde spiritum inmundum ex omni parte signatur oleo sanctificato)]

[De abrenuntiatione.]

[De trina mersione.]

[De unctione chrismatis.]

[De albis vestibus (velamine).]

[Ad mensam caelestis perveniunt.]

[De symbolo.]

De corpore et sanguine domini.

CHART G3

Text 49

Pro quid baptizas

Quomodo baptizas:

Trinam facio mersionem;

Oleo et crismate unguo;

Pedes lavo;

Veste candida induo;

Corpus et sanguinem ei trado.

Index

Aachen, 54n, 98, 115, 147, 150, 153

acolyte, 44f., 59, 86, 117, 120

Acts of the Seven Sleepers of Ephesus, 25

Admonitio Generalis of 789, 2, 52n, 67

Admonitio Generalis of 823, 32, 36

Adoptianism, 81n, 106f., 115

Agobard of Lyons, 30, 134, 148

Akeley, T. C., 71n

Albi, Bibl. mun. 38 bis (Al1), 15, 20n, 21n, 24n, 29, 112n, 133, 138

Albi, Bibl. mun. 42 (Al2), 17, 133

Albi, Bibl. mun. 43 (Al3), 15, 20n, 24n, 112n, 133, 138, 144

Alcuin, 4, 6, 18, 29n, 30, 36, 37n, 58, 62n, 70, 80f., 81n, 83f., 90, 106–107, 114, 123, 125, 132, 146, 151

alphabets, 31, 31n

Amalarius, 17, 36, 59–62, 65–67, 83, 88, 110, 118–122, 120n, 126, 131–134, 145, 151

Ambrose of Milan, 75, 109 f., 109n, 124, 127

Ambrosian liturgy, 63n

Amos, Thomas L., 33n, 34n, 36n

Andrieu, Michel, 17, 29, 43, 44n, 45n, 47n, 53n, 54n, 55n, 57n, 59n, 60n, 61n, 63n, 74n, 82n, 96n, 157n, 158n

Angenendt, Arnold, 67n, 96n, 100n, 126n

Angers, Bibl. mun. 277 (An), 20, 29f., 34, 133f., 144

Annotationes de lapidibus et gemmis, 30

anointing of the head, 46, 49f., 58, 64f., 73, 83, 109, 111f., 112n, 113, 126

antiphonary, 14

Apostles' Creed, 14, 26, 45n, 47, 50, 53, 60, 64, 72, 81f.

archdeacon, 20, 35, 36n, 92, 98, 115, 125, 128

Arianism, 105n, 107n

Arno of Salzburg, 25, 29, 31n, 93f., 135; Constitution of, 52n, 67, 158

Athanasian Creed, 14f., 26

Augustine, 1, 6, 28, 70, 80, 94, 116–120, 120n, 121–124

Aurium apertio, 44, 47, 49f., 54f., 60n, 64, 68, 74, 84, 101

Autun, Bibl. mun. 184 (Au), 20n

Baldo, 31n

Baluzius, S., 32n

Bamberg, Staatl. Bibl. Lit. 131 (B2), 17, 29

baptism, definition of, 1, 3, 19; role in the Carolingian world, 2–4; examination on, 6; *ordo* of, 14, 17, 25, 30, 34, 130; sick (*infirmus*) *ordo*, 55, 63n, 82n, 111n, 151f., 156–158; pagan (*paganus*) *ordo*, 50, 55, 63n, 73, 95f., 152, 156–158; baptism formula, 46f., 49f., 49n, 50n, 57n; public, 52n, 67, 68n, 158; "daily," 99; invisible effect of, 91–93; theology of, 126f., 153

baptismal churches, 148

baptismal expositions (instructions), 1, 7–9, 14f., 24–26, 30f., 34f., 37n, 88, 116, 123, 125, 127, 131f., 137, 153f.; as liturgical expositions, 41f.

baptistery, 46

bare feet. *See* shoes, removal of

Bavarian Council (unidentified), 27

Bavarian Law Code, 29

beatific vision (debate over), 28

Beatitudes, 19

INDEX OF SCRIPTURAL QUOTATIONS